What People Are Saying About Bobby and Sherry Burnette and *Love Is Something You Do…*

When I first traveled to Love a Child's headquarters, met Bobby and Sherry Burnette, and saw their outreaches, I immediately saw that they shared our vision of demonstrating the love of God and alleviating human suffering through practical humanitarian aid as they ministered to the poorest of the poor in Haiti. After seven years, we continue to invest in their Jesus Healing Center medical clinic and their widespread food distribution programs. Daily, they allow God's love to shine through them in compassionate acts so that many people may come to know our Savior while receiving nutritious meals, having quality health care, gaining an education, being trained for a vocation, and experiencing hope for the first time in their lives. In *Love Is Something You Do*, you will travel with Bobby and Sherry on the "adventure with the Lord" that led them to the tiny country of Haiti—where the need was the greatest and where the people stole their hearts.

—*David L. Meyer*
CEO, Hand of Hope, Joyce Meyer Ministries

Bobby and Sherry Burnette embody "Love is something you do." It's not just a phrase—it's who they are. Feed My Starving Children has had the privilege of partnering with Love A Child since 1997. I have seen Bobby and Sherry's love in action—feeding tens of thousands of children in Haiti each day. We are honored to work with those whose love for Jesus and the people of Haiti is tenacious.

—*Mark Crea*
President and CEO, Feed My Starving Children

Bobby and Sherry Burnette, founders and directors of Love A Child, Inc., have been a part of the Christian Television Network for more than thirty years. It has been a humbling experience for me to personally visit their mission field. I've watched them bring the light of Jesus, a future, and a hope to citizens of Haiti who have known only poverty and despair. If it is indeed true that "love is something you do," you'll find no finer illustration of this truth than Bobby and Sherry Burnette.

—*Robert D'Andrea*
Founder and president, Christian Television Network (CTN)

In the many years that we have known the founders and directors of Love A Child, Bobby and Sherry Burnette, they have navigated extreme hardships and have endured political unrest, theft, gunfire, government turnover, embargoes, epidemics, and a devastating earthquake. Still, they both continue to befriend the unlovely, the unwanted, the sick, the dying, the hurting, the abandoned, and the needy while building schools and churches; organizing feeding programs, urgent-care centers, and mobile clinics; founding an orphanage; digging wells; constructing a marketplace; establishing agricultural/sustainability programs; building a fire station; installing playgrounds; maintaining a radio station; and sharing whatever they have with so many other ministries in Haiti. They continue to rescue and strengthen the Haitian people—one child, one family, one village at a time. For those who pray, "Lord, make me a fisher of men for You," Bobby and Sherry have demonstrated how to do that: If you show people the love of God by loving them, they will begin to perceive Him. Evie was introduced to missions with Love A Child on a rickety boat ride to a leprosy colony, and we can say that the course of our lives has changed forever by seeing firsthand Bobby and Sherry's "love evangelism."

—*Evie and Mark Ostrander*
Senior pastors, Mission Church, Palm Bay, Florida

I have known Bobby and Sherry Burnette since they were teenagers and dating. Sherry began coming to our church first. She then met Bobby at a gospel tent revival and invited him to the Valentine's Day Banquet at our church. They fell in love...and two years later, I officiated at their wedding. That's how it all got started!

After their many years of evangelistic work in the United States, the Lord stirred Bobby and Sherry's hearts to move to the country of Haiti. They obeyed that call, where God has used them to develop one of the greatest missionary endeavors in that country, called "Love A Child." Through the years, I have seen their integrity and faithfulness to their calling, and we support them 100 percent. They have given their lives to this work of God, which is unique in that they live right there in the orphanage with the children, who look to them as their mother and father. God has worked miracles through Bobby and has brought him back from death's door many times. He is truly a man of great vision and great faith! And without any medical training, God has gifted Sherry to miraculously know how to treat the sick and dying.

Bobby and Sherry still consider me their "spiritual father," and I have found it a privilege and an honor to serve on the executive board of Love A Child for many years—a ministry that touches millions of people and is known all over the world.

—*Pastor Joseph Ronsisvalle*
Rockledge Christian Center, Rockledge, Florida

LOVE
IS SOMETHING
YOU DO®

SHERRY & BOBBY **BURNETTE**

WHITAKER
HOUSE

Unless otherwise indicated, all Scripture quotations are taken from the King James Version of the Holy Bible. Scripture quotations marked (NKJV) are taken from the *New King James Version*, © 1979, 1980, 1982, 1984 by Thomas Nelson, Inc. Used by permission. All rights reserved.

Boldface type in Scripture quotations indicates the author's emphasis.

The authors donate all royalties from this book to Love A Child, Inc., to help meet the needs of children in Haiti.

Love Is Something You Do

Bobby and Sherry Burnette
www.loveachild.com

ISBN: 978-1-62911-560-3
eBook ISBN: 978-1-62911-582-5
Printed in the United States of America
© 2015 by Sherry and Bobby Burnette

Whitaker House
1030 Hunt Valley Circle
New Kensington, PA 15068
www.whitakerhouse.com

Library of Congress Cataloging-in-Publication Data

Burnette, Sherry, 1948-
Love is something you do / Sherry and Bobby Burnette.
    pages cm
Includes bibliographical references.
ISBN 978-1-62911-560-3 (trade pbk. : alk. paper) — ISBN 9781629115825 (ebook)
1. Burnette, Sherry, 1948- 2. Burnette, Bobby, 1947- 3. Missionaries—Haiti—Biography. 4. Church work with children—Haiti. 5. Missions--Haiti. I. Burnette, Bobby, 1947- II. Title.
BV2848.H4A123 2015
362.73'2—dc23
[B]
                                    2015035348

3 4 5 6 7 8 9 10 11 12 ᵾᵾ 23 22 21 20 19 18 17 16

DEDICATION

This book is dedicated with loving thanks to our family, who sacrificed their time "away" from us all those years....

To my mother, Marion Barner (Grandma), who has now gone to be with the Lord. She cared for our two children, Jonathan and Julie, while we traveled and preached the gospel, and stood with us in her prayers.

To our children, Jonathan and Julie, and their children—our grandsons Anthony, Aidan, and Brandon.

To our partners and friends who worked long, hard hours helping us in the ministry; and to our Love A Child office staff, especially Rad and Sandra Hazelip, who run everything for us in the States. Without them, it would be impossible for us to work in Haiti.

Special thanks to Tammie Anderson, who encouraged us to write the book years ago, and who also helps with "Sherry's Journal" and many other things.

Thanks to everyone.... A Haitian Creole proverb says, "You can't eat okra with just one finger." In other words, you need others to help you!

God bless you,
Bobby and Sherry

CONTENTS

FOREWORD

God will sometimes unexpectedly move upon us to give us specific direction about what He wants us to do. That was the case for me about seven years ago when I was staying at a hotel and casually turned on the TV in my room. On the screen were Bobby and Sherry Burnette of Love a Child, Inc. (LAC), whom I had never seen before, showing their work among the poor in Haiti. I was immediately touched by the Spirit, and I found myself on my knees, crying. God clearly spoke to my heart, *You are supposed to support these people.*

As Bobby always says, "Love is something you do!" Our church, Free Chapel, started sponsoring two containers of food (540,000 meals) each month for Haiti's poor and destitute in partnership with Love A Child and Feed My Starving Children. In 2010, a massive earthquake hit Haiti, devastating that already struggling nation. My family and I flew to Haiti to help out; our church, as well as our Kingdom Connection television and Internet partners, supported Bobby and Sherry in facilitating the largest field hospital in the country, which provided medical care and shelter for numerous earthquake victims. My family had the privilege of serving food to survivors alongside LAC staff members. We were also able to pray with some of the recovering patients and visit with Haitian families who were living in temporary tents. God has given us a deep love for the Haitian people, and we have continued to work with LAC to help supply them with food, housing, and sustainability assistance so that they can provide for themselves and live in peace and dignity.

Bobby and Sherry Burnette and their Love A Child ministries are transforming the lives of thousands in Haiti. When the earthquake hit, they had already been ministering in Haiti in various ways for almost forty years, and they had lived there for almost twenty years. Their ongoing work in Haiti is the result of a lifelong commitment to serving God, and this book tells the full, remarkable story of that commitment, of their early lives and ministry, and of how God ultimately brought them to care for children and adults in the poorest country of the world. *Love Is Something You Do* is the fascinating narrative of the Burnettes' journey of faith and compassion—alternately moving, comical, heartbreaking, and inspiring—one that led them from street evangelism in Florida to their current multidimensional work in Haiti, with its spiritual, educational, medical, social, and economic outreaches.

This book is not just the autobiography of two remarkable people; it is filled with stories that demonstrate the extraordinary power of God and His deep desire to seek and to save those who are lost, so that He can give them life and hope. Jesus said, *"Inasmuch as you did it to one of the least of these My brethren, you did it to Me"* (Matthew 25:40 NKJV). Bobby and Sherry are a living demonstration of this proclamation.

Because love is something you do.

—*Jentezen Franklin*
Senior pastor, Free Chapel
New York Times best-selling author

Prologue:

WHEN THE MOUNTAINS MOVED

It began as a typical day in Haiti, the "land of mountains," where my husband, Bobby, and I ministered daily to the needs of the poor, the sick, and the abandoned. There were the normal problems to solve, children to care for, and hungry people to feed. I went to the Caribbean Market that morning to buy food. Then I traveled to the mud-hut village of Le Tant with our medical director, while Bobby stayed at the orphanage with the children. Little did we know that a 7.1-magnitude earthquake was rumbling underground, ready to crush, to kill, and to destroy.

At 4:53 p.m., the earthquake struck. In less than a minute, approximately 316,000 people were killed, 300,000 were injured, and one million were left homeless. In the capital of Port-au-Prince, the presidential palace and government buildings exploded and collapsed. The large concrete buildings, some three stories high, crumbled into piles of concrete and debris. The entire city, including the airport, was devastated. As one missionary said, "It looked like an atomic bomb had exploded." Outlying areas were also severely damaged, and the Caribbean Market was reduced to rubble.

In our many years of rewarding but challenging ministry, we had faced struggles, difficulties, heartaches, threats, and dangers, but we hadn't experienced anything like this. Our lives would never be the same.

PART 1

FAITH, PATIENCE, AND PROMISES

1

THE RAT SHACK:
HOW IT ALL BEGAN

Let me tell you how it all really began. A skinny, young evangelist named Bobby Burnette lay on his bed in a dilapidated old shack in the dark of night. He was hungry, cold, broke—and all alone. Where was the God who had spoken to him in an audible voice when he was just a child? Where was the God of Abraham, Isaac, and Jacob—the One who had told him to "fast and seek the face of God for twenty-one days living just on water," promising that afterward, his ministry would really begin? This shack was the only place he could find to be alone with God, so why didn't the Lord communicate with him? Why didn't He give him a sign—anything?

The December wind whistled through the jagged, broken glass in the windows and the cracks in the walls. Bobby had hung some old quilts over the windows to try to keep the room warm, but it was useless. He lay on the bed, struggling to endure so he could make it all the way through this fast. On the tiny table near his bed, he kept his Bible and a windup alarm clock with bright green hands, which he followed on their circular path during the long nights.

The smell of kerosene and smoke filled the air as the tiny fire flickered in the rusty, old kerosene heater, providing very little heat but just enough light to attract rats and roaches. Bobby would hear the rats as they scurried through the darkness, and he would brace himself. Because the room was so cold, the rats—night after night—would try to crawl into his bed, and he would have to grab the broom that he kept nearby and ward them off.

This night, Bobby felt something scamper across his feet underneath the blanket, and he jumped out of bed to snatch the broom. *How long have I been in this rat shack?* he agonized. *Has it been days—or weeks? I'm so hungry, and the days and nights are so long they're blending together; I've lost all sense of time. I'm so weak I can hardly stand. I can't sleep. My stomach is in constant pain from hunger. And God is a million miles away. I cannot feel His presence. I'm not even sure if He is real…. Maybe I'm losing my mind. Did God really tell me to do this? Did God really tell me to leave my wife and children for twenty-one days and seek His face…?*

It's hard enough to go on a short fast when you have money in the bank, a warm house to come home to at night, the companionship of others who are fasting with you, and the ability to communicate with your brothers and sisters in the Lord, even via a smartphone, an iPad, or a laptop. But what do you do when you're all alone with an invisible God, having no money and virtually no companionship or communication with anyone; when you're fighting the cold, the hunger, and the rats, as well as the lies and deceit of the devil? You have to step outside the realm of your five senses and into a higher realm, a spiritual one, that transcends anything you can see, touch, taste, smell, or hear. You must enter the invisible domain of faith and obedience to God.

From the time Bobby and I first started dating, he had told me about this twenty-one-day fast that the Lord wanted him to go on. Now, nearly four years later, we were married and had two young children, and he was still trying to obey the Lord's instruction. Both Bobby and I believed, as the Bible affirmed, that "obedience is better than sacrifice." *"Hath the* Lord *as great delight in burnt offerings and sacrifices, as in obeying the voice of the* Lord*? Behold, to obey is better than sacrifice, and to hearken than the fat of rams."*[1] In the past, Bobby had been able to fast for five or six days straight, but then he would stop. Later, he would start again, going six or seven days, and then stop. But he had kept trying. In fact, he had fasted so much that his ribs were visible through his skin.

But this time in the rat shack was different. Bobby would have many more days to go on his fast, but somehow it was all part of God's plan and purpose for our lives, which He had ordained before we were even born. To understand the story of that rat-infested shack and why it was so crucial to what God called Bobby and me to do, and to where we are today, we have to go back to our roots and trace the journey that led us to become full-time missionaries in Haiti, the poorest nation in the world, but a place where God is increasingly bringing His hope, His healing, and His new life. As a Haitian Creole proverb says, "You won't know where you're going until you know where you came from."

---

1. 1 Samuel 15:22.

2

"ONE CHANCE IN A THOUSAND"

Risk, adventure, and faith in the guiding hand of God have always been a part of my life. The middle child of five children, I had some major medical complications when I was just five months old and was given "one chance in a thousand" to pull through. My distraught mother prayed this simple prayer: "Lord, if You will heal my baby and save her life, I will dedicate her unto You. I will become a Christian and serve You all the days of my life." God kept His word, and my mother kept hers.

I grew up in New Brighton, Pennsylvania, a blue-collar community where many people worked in the coal mines; there were piles of coal on the hills all around us. Although my mother, Marion Barner, had become a devout Christian after my healing, my father, Samuel Barner, was not a believer. He'd had emotional problems early in life, and he'd become an alcoholic. As the years went by, alcohol often propelled him into fits of anger. He had learned how to use a gun when he was a very young child, and as an adult, he was known for shooting and killing stray dogs and cats. He dug a big hole in the woods in the back of our property, and he used to make one of my brothers watch while he shot a dog or cat and buried it in that hole.

My father did his best to provide for the family, but it was a continual struggle. He had a job in a steel mill for a while, but he didn't like working with anyone of a different race or nationality, and he was soon laid off or fired; I was never told the specific reason why he was let go.

Five Barner Kids on the Cellar Steps

Even during those difficult days of my young childhood, I developed a faith in the Lord that increasingly deepened. My mother had family devotions with all five of us kids every night. She would play the piano, and each one of us would take turns leading the "song service," reading the Bible verse, and so forth.

I remember well the period of time when my father was out of work for over a year. He would not accept welfare of any kind, so there was often no food in the house. My mother would set the table, and then she would get on her knees and pray to God for food. The Lord always answered those prayers. There was never a day when someone didn't knock on our door with fresh beef, a bushel of corn, loaves of bread, watermelon, or something else—always some wonderful item of food for us kids to eat and also to share with other children in our neighborhood who were in the same situation. There would often be five Barner children and additional kids from the neighborhood, sitting on our cellar steps from top to bottom, eating whatever the neighbors had brought us.

Even at Christmastime, when our family had no toys, gifts, or food, my mother still said, "The Lord will provide." The night of Christmas Eve, our little country church sent five carloads of toys, new clothing, food, and shoes to our family.

Despite my family's financial struggles, I have good memories of growing up in western Pennsylvania. I never really knew that we were poor. I just assumed everybody lived like we did, from hand to mouth. And I always knew that God was with me.

The Log in the Woods

My first experience with the Lord occurred when I was about five years old, before I started school. I used to go into the woods to a favorite old log that had fallen across the path, and I would sit there and pray and think about the Lord. One day, while I was sitting there, I felt God's presence. The only way I can describe it is that it was as if a giant "bubble" settled on me and engulfed me. I did not hear an audible voice or see a vision, but the presence of the Holy Spirit came upon me and saturated me. As a result of this experience, I instinctively understood two things: (1) I would someday be on the mission field in a foreign country; (2) I would be involved in a medical outreach. What happened to me that day was profound but not dramatic. When the presence of the Lord lifted, I simply got up from my log and took the short walk back to our house in the country.

I didn't know how God would unfold the plans He'd revealed for my life, but later on, I would discover that they had a lot to do with a certain young man, just a year older than I was, who was growing up in rural Florida under difficult circumstances of his own.

3

"MIRACLE" CHILD

The Old Man and the Young Woman

Seventy-year-old Green Burnette was shocked that he was going to be a father again. This was his third marriage. His first two wives had passed away, and he had already raised two sets of children who were now grown. He had married his current wife, Mittie Bernice Dollar, twelve years earlier, when he was fifty-eight and she was twenty-four. After more than a decade of marriage without children, they hadn't expected to have a family, and Green didn't need another child at this point in his life. He was too old to be bothered raising a baby—even one who, considering Green's age, seemed to be a "miracle" child.

Green and his wife, whose nickname was "Bernie," lived on Main Street in Winter Garden, Florida, in a small, old, "cracker-style" wood house that stood on blocks and had a screened-in front porch. Green grew vegetables and sold them locally to help support the family.

When it came time for Bernie to have her baby, complications set in, and she had to have a C-section. In those days, this was far more dangerous than it is today, but she and the baby came through the delivery safely. At 3:00 p.m. on June 10, 1947, Robert "Bobby" Berry Burnette was born to a seventy-one-year-old father and a thirty-six-year-old mother. Years later, Bobby would use his parents as a sermon illustration whenever he preached his message entitled "Faith and Patience," based on Hebrews 6:12: *"Be… followers of them who through faith and patience inherit the promises."* Bobby would always joke, "My daddy had faith, but my mama had patience. You're never too old!"

Twenty-One Years in Mental Institutions

As patient as Bernie was, the stress of the pregnancy and the delivery—and of being married to a man thirty-five years older than she who didn't want another child—apparently took quite a toll on her emotionally. When Bobby was about two weeks old, Bernie had a nervous breakdown. As they often said back then, "She went crazy." Bernie was sent to Florida State Hospital, a psychiatric facility located in Chattahoochee. Years later, neighbors in the Winter Garden area confided to me that they felt Bernie was "railroaded" into going to the mental hospital. With Green unable to take care of an infant by himself, Bobby was sent to live with his mother's sister, Dorothy, and her husband, Jake, in Orlando. Apparently, Dorothy had always disliked Bernie, and taking over the guardianship of her child was a good chance to get even with her. Bobby believes to this day that "Aunt" Dorothy was not his mother's real sister. She may have been merely a friend or an acquaintance. Tragically, Bernie would remain institutionalized for twenty-one years—until, as we describe in a later chapter, she received a wonderful miracle from God.

Uncle Jake

Dorothy was the only mother Bobby knew growing up. He loved her and called her "Mama," even though she was abusive to him in many ways. To this day, he won't talk about the details. At that time, there were no child protection laws, so Bobby was essentially at the mercy of a cruel woman who always made him feel unwanted, useless, and in the way.

In contrast, Uncle Jake, whom he called "Daddy," was gentle, loving, kind, and tender. He loved Bobby as a son, and Bobby loved him with all his heart. Jake was able to understand his son and communicate with him when no one else could. He would walk with Bobby around their property and tell him, "Someday, this will be your land. I love you, son. This is your land."

Jake had faith in God, and almost every night he would put Bobby on his lap and repeat John 3:16 to him: *"For God so loved the world, that he gave his only begotten Son, that whosoever believeth in him should not perish, but have everlasting life."* Bobby could not speak one word of the Scriptures, but somehow he understood what his daddy was saying. Since Dorothy would not attend church, the times Bobby spent with Jake became his early instruction about God.

Unfortunately, Jake had emphysema. He was often sick, so he was absent during a good portion of Bobby's childhood. As Jake's illness grew worse, he had to go back and forth to Bay Pines Hospital in Tampa, Florida. Bobby would cry every time the family would get in the car and make the drive to Tampa to admit his daddy to the hospital, leaving him and Dorothy to return home alone. To Bobby, it felt as if Jake was being torn from his arms. Eventually, Jake's illness would take his life.

The Toddler in the Sailor Suit

Years later, when Bobby and I started dating, we drove to the small, wood-framed, "ole southern-style" house where he had grown up so I could meet Aunt Dorothy. We came through the back screen door and into the simple kitchen, which was furnished with a small table, four chairs, and a Frigidaire refrigerator, which Bobby always called an "icebox." On the mantle in the tiny living room, I spotted a picture of a cute little toddler with reddish-blond hair, wearing a blue-and-white sailor suit. Later, I asked Bobby if that was a photo of him when he was a child, and his answer surprised me.

"Yes," he said, "that picture was taken of me when I was a toddler, just learning how to walk. I remember the day that picture was taken."

"How can you remember back that far?" I asked him. "I don't know anyone who can remember something from when they were that young. That's unusual."

Bobby replied, "I remember the day that picture was taken because that sailor suit had too much starch in the collar. It was scratching my neck. That was the day I took my first steps. I was walked from the kitchen to the living room, and I fell down a couple of times and got back up." Then, matter-of-factly, he added, "And I remember that day because it was the first time I ever felt the presence of God."

God had made His presence known to Bobby Burnette when Bobby was only fourteen months old. His heavenly Father had His hand on him. Bobby would need that encouragement as he grew older and began to recognize all the problems he faced, including a frustrating disability.

4

A SIX-YEAR-OLD HEARS
THE AUDIBLE VOICE OF GOD

When Bobby was a toddler, it became obvious that he was unable to speak clearly. He could make sounds, but he couldn't say any words that were easily understood. "I don't know what caused the speech problem," Bobby says. "Some people speculated that it was because my father was over seventy when I was born. But no one really knew." As a child, Bobby would get exasperated because he had a hard time communicating with everyone.

Despite—and perhaps because of—this physical limitation, God again made Himself known to Bobby in a miraculous way when he was only six years old. He remembers, "It was a hot summer day in Florida. I was playing outside, and my mother [Dorothy] was not at home. I walked inside the house to my mother's bedroom to get something from the dresser. I don't remember what I went in to get, but I remember that I was by myself. All of a sudden, I heard the audible voice of God.

"I am not saying that I heard God in my heart, or my spirit. His voice was loud, and it didn't come from only one direction; it was everywhere. It came from above, from beneath, and from each side; it came from every direction at the same time, almost like surround sound. It completely filled the whole atmosphere in that room—every atom, every molecule of air, spoke it. It was a strange thing, and it frightened me so that I could not move. But after that experience, if someone had taken me to Russia and tried to brainwash me to believe that there is no God, it would have been impossible! I knew that I heard the audible voice of God that day.

"God told me, 'Bobby, I'm calling you to preach the gospel, because of the heart I have placed within you.' I dropped to my knees because the presence of God was there, and I responded in my heart, *I know it, Lord.*

"I thought, *God said I'm going to be a preacher; well, I'd better learn to talk clear.* I expected to immediately open my mouth and start talking, but I still couldn't speak any words. God's presence left the room, and I grew sad, because the Lord had been right there, and I had believed I would be healed instantly. I had never been able to carry on a conversation with anyone, so I couldn't understand how God in heaven could talk to me, a child, in an audible voice that was so real and call me to preach but leave me unable to speak clearly enough for anyone to understand me. I was in shock, heartbroken, and confused. I knew I had felt the presence of God, but where was my miracle? Why couldn't I talk like everyone else?

"Even though I thought I would eventually be healed, after a while, I became resentful. I would play on my swing set, and when one of the chains of the swing would break because the metal had worn down, I would fall to the ground. Out of frustration—not just because of the broken swing, but because of my pent-up anger over my speech problem—I would strike the ground with my fists, and in my heart, I would curse God."

A Little Boy, a Pencil, and a Piece of Paper

Bobby had few friends at school because the other children couldn't understand what he would try to say. It was as if he was living in a foreign country where he didn't know the language and couldn't communicate with the people. Although he was sent to speech therapy, it barely helped.

Bobby recalls, "When I was a young boy, people would ask me, 'What are you going to be when you grow up?' I always carried around a pencil and a piece of paper with me, so I would take them out and write, 'I'm going to be a preacher.' They'd respond by mocking, 'Say something, preacher; say something.' I'd try to speak, but again only sounds would come out, and they would laugh at me. Some of the kids would say, 'Here comes dummy,' 'Here comes retard,' or 'Here comes crazy boy.' Because of this, I grew bitter against God for a long time. My bitterness may have affected me on the outside; I don't know how I looked to other people, but on the inside I was very frustrated."

To make matters worse, one of Bobby's adult neighbors thought he had the solution to help him talk, but this plan merely added to his disappointment and discouragement. "This neighbor owned a lot of horses and had a big pasture adjoining our property," Bobby remembers. "When I was about twelve, he told me that if I could say the word 'horse' by a certain date, he would give me a horse. I practiced and practiced saying that word, but when the day came and I tried to say 'horse,' I couldn't do it."

The neighbor told Bobby, "You didn't say 'horse' correctly, so you're not going to get a horse. Did you really think you could say the word 'horse' and that I would give you a horse?" He just laughed at the little boy who couldn't say even one word clearly. Bobby never forgot those painful memories, but neither did he forget his experience of hearing God's voice audibly. He just could not understand why he hadn't been given the ability to speak.

The Lady, the Butcher Knife, and the Straightjacket

From time to time, Dorothy and Jake would take Bobby to visit his natural father, Green Burnette. Green would talk to Bobby and then reach into the icebox and bring out some cold grits. He would slice off a portion of the grits and put it on Bobby's plate. Those times are about the best memories Bobby has of his real father.

One day, when Bobby was still very young, he was brought to Green's house, but this time, it was to see his natural mother, who was being released from the mental institution for a short visit. As it turned out, this was the *only* time she was ever released for a visit with her family. When Bernie arrived, she looked at her small son, ran and grabbed a butcher knife from the kitchen, and chased after him to kill him! Bobby ran under the house, which was on blocks, and peered out at the crazy woman who was stabbing the knife into the ground as she wildly crawled after him. Bobby scooted out a different way and ran to hide behind the house.

As he peeked out from the back of the house, he saw a car pull up and policemen get out. They grabbed the woman, holding her as she kicked and screamed, then forced her into a straightjacket and put her in the car. Then the car drove away, with the woman glaring out the window.

All Bobby could think was, *Could that have been my real mother?*

Bernie was taken back to the mental hospital in Chattahoochee, and the iron gates closed behind her once again. Sometimes, even if you're not crazy when you go into a mental institution, you're crazy after you've been there for a while.

Dorothy would often tell Bobby, "You're crazy like your mother! One day, they'll come and put you in a straightjacket and take you away!" Until

Bobby was sixteen, he lived in great fear that one day, he *would* go crazy like his mother, and people would come and put a straightjacket on him, too, and haul him away to the mental institution.

"Your Son Will Never Talk Normally"

When Bobby grew a little older, Dorothy decided to take him to a speech specialist. After the examination, the doctor took Dorothy into another room for a consultation and closed the door. But Bobby could hear the conversation through the wall, and the doctor's words pierced his heart: "Your son will never talk normally as long as he lives on this earth."

After hearing that declaration, his hopes and dreams of ever being able to talk were crushed. All his life, he had been tormented by other children. All his life, other people had thought he was crazy or "slow." Inside, he knew he wasn't either of those things—his mind was sound; he simply couldn't talk clearly.

He thought back to the time when he had heard the voice of God speaking to him, calling him to go and preach the gospel because of the "heart" that He had placed inside him. He was even more confused and angry than before, and he grew to hate the God who had spoken those words of hope and purpose to him. How could God lie to a little boy and still be God?

Tragedy Strikes

Bobby's one comfort in life was his daddy. But Jake grew worse with emphysema and now spent the majority of his days in the hospital. One day, when Bobby was in fifth grade, the principal came to his classroom and took him out into the hall. He can still hear her words: "Bobby, your father, Jake, has died." That was the lowest moment in his life. Not only had he lost the man who had become a father to him, but he had also lost his best friend, the only person who really understood him and encouraged him.

After Jake died, another man moved in with Dorothy, and then both of them mistreated Bobby. This man, who was wealthy, lived there for several years before he died, and he left Dorothy everything. Even so, as Bobby says, "To look at her, you'd never have known she had money. You'd think she was poorer than Job's cat."

In His grace and mercy, God preserved Bobby through all these heartaches until the time when He would send a miracle to him.

5

"I'M NEVER GONNA ACT LIKE THAT BUNCH!"

Miracles often come to us in surprising ways, and this was true for Bobby when God gave him the miracle he had been waiting to receive for so long. Bobby had a good friend named Richard, who was a Christian; he lived in nearby Apopka, Florida, with his cantankerous grandmother. "Grandma" Copeland walked with a cane, had nine cats, and was tight with her money. She loved God with all her heart—but was as mean as a snake! She was an old-fashioned Pentecostal lady, with her hair piled up on her head in a bun. She always wore long-sleeved dresses; she did not believe that women should wear pants, use make-up, or have short hair—anytime, for any reason—and she would flat-out tell people so. She never had a problem speaking her mind. Bobby avoided Grandma Copeland as much as he could. He especially hated two of her cats, which were Siamese and had a mean streak, because whenever he went to visit Richard, they would jump on his back and attack him (to this day, Bobby doesn't like Siamese cats!).

Grandma Copeland attended an Assemblies of God church, which was next door to her house. People called those who went there "Holy Rollers." "They would jump and shout and praise God," Bobby says, "and I thought they were crazy." Sometimes, they would raise their hands in the air and praise God, shout "Amen!" and even speak in "tongues." Bobby would think, *I'm never gonna act like that bunch!* Even Dorothy had warned him, "Don't ever go down to that crazy church; they'll 'put something' on you." Sometimes, at night, Bobby and Richard would sneak over to the church when they had revival meetings—a series of preaching services—and would do things like let the air out of people's tires and throw eggs at the windows.

One weekend in December, when Bobby was sixteen, Richard wanted him to stay overnight, but Grandma Copeland had one condition. "If you want Bobby to spend the night, you boys gotta go to church! They're having revival," she grunted. Bobby thought to himself, *Oh, Lord.* But both boys agreed to the condition. They could sit in the back row, prepared to run in case anyone tried to drag them to the altar.

That night, the more the visiting evangelist preached, the more the power of God fell on the congregation. Many people went to the altar, crying and seeking salvation. Some were filled with the Holy Spirit. In the back of the room, Bobby and Richard kept waiting for the right time to leave, until it became too late to make an "escape." Bobby remembers, "The evangelist's preaching began to affect me. I had kind of left the Lord due to my bitterness and frustration, but when the evangelist gave the altar call, I went up to repent of my sins and receive salvation, just as he'd said."

Bobby knelt down at the altar and began to weep. He prayed out loud as best he could, but as usual, he could merely utter sounds. "They believed in the baptism of the Holy Spirit, with the evidence of speaking in other tongues," he says. "But I couldn't even speak English well. I thought to myself, *Forget this tongues stuff. This isn't for me. I know that for sure.*"

Then the evangelist came by, laid his hand on Bobby's head, and said, "Son, the Lord wants to save you and baptize you in the Holy Spirit." He didn't know Bobby, so he didn't realize that he couldn't speak. Suddenly, God baptized Bobby in the Holy Spirit. His hands went up in the air, and they started to shake. He felt the magnificent power of God, and he found himself "acting like that bunch"!

Bobby recalls, "After I returned to the back row, the evangelist said, 'You, young man, stand up and say something for Jesus. I can tell you got it! Stand up and testify!' I didn't know how I could possibly do that, but something just pulled me up out of my seat." As Bobby stood to his feet with tears in his eyes, he began giving his testimony, speaking clearly!

"I thought, *Wow!* I didn't even finish my testimony; it happened so fast, I jumped over the bench. I may have run around it, but I think I jumped over it. And then I ran out the door. We lived right down the street, and we had a large screen door on the back porch. I almost broke through that door as I ran inside the house, saying, 'Mama, I'm healed! I'm healed! I'm healed!'"

Dorothy knew Bobby had gone to "that church," and she wasn't happy about it. "She told me, 'No, you're not healed.' For as long as I'd known her, she had gone to church only once, and that was for an Easter sunrise service. I said, 'Mama, I'm healed. Look, I can talk.' She said, 'No, let me tell you what happened.' Of course, she hadn't been there, yet she persisted, 'They claim people fall backward in the Spirit, but that crazy preacher came by and laid his hand on your head and pushed you backward—you fell backward, and you hit your head on the church pew, and when you hit your head, it knocked your tongue loose.' I said, 'Mama, it wasn't the church pew that knocked my tongue loose. It was Jesus of Nazareth, the Son of God, who touched me tonight. I got a miracle!'"

That night, Bobby Burnette was saved, filled with Holy Spirit, and healed—all at the same time. The experience was completely overwhelming to him. Something had happened that had changed him from the inside out, and he could never be the same again. While Dorothy may not have accepted what happened, everyone else—including Richard and Grandma Copeland—rejoiced when he was saved and healed that night; they recognized the miracle of his newfound ability to speak. And his speech just got better and better each day.

Thinking back to how it all came about, Bobby says, "I found out that when God tells you something, He will bring His word to pass. He gave me the Scripture of Hebrews 6:12 a long time ago so that I would know that it is through faith and patience that we inherit His promises. Sometimes, when God gives you a promise, it won't happen that day or that month or even that year. But He will bring it to pass. That verse has a special meaning in my life because I was sixteen years old when the Lord saved and healed me. It took ten full years from the promise to the fulfillment, but it happened!"

All-Night Prayer Meetings in an Orange Grove

Right away, Bobby started serving God and preaching the gospel. At the time when Bobby became a Christian, tent revivals were popular, and when he was seventeen, he attended a tent revival meeting where he met another young man named Johnny Mahon. They became best friends, and this strong friendship has continued for nearly fifty years.

Bobby remembers, "We just hit it off. We had both been praising and worshipping God during the service, and afterward he came up to me and shook my hand. Then he asked, 'What would you rather do more than anything in the world?' I said, 'I would rather pray all night.' He said, 'Well, let's go do it!' Johnny's father was in the orange grove business, so we went to an orange grove and prayed all night until daylight under an orange tree. After that, we continued to meet to pray together. And when I say we prayed, I don't mean we sat in a chair and thought about the Lord. We prayed out loud in 'tongues'—the language of the Holy Spirit—for hours and hours.

"Once, we were in the grove praying under an orange tree, intending to pray until morning, when a policeman came out in the middle of the night and shined a light on us. There were some houses nearby, and somebody must have called the police after hearing us praying loudly, calling on God. Johnny tried to talk to the policeman, but the power of the Holy Spirit was upon him so strong that he couldn't do it; he could only continue speaking in tongues! Then I tried to talk to the officer, but the same thing happened. When the policeman found he couldn't communicate with us, he finally exclaimed, 'Oh, good Lord, I give it up. Good-bye.' Then he got into his car and left, and we kept on praying.

"There were other times when we prayed all day. We would often work with Johnny's father in the orange groves starting at seven in the morning, planting trees and grafting buds. But on many mornings, as soon as Johnny and I would step out there, the Spirit of the Lord would hit us, and we would go find a big orange tree to sit under, and we'd start praying. I'm not exaggerating, we would pray until dark without stopping. I don't know how we did it. I doubt I could do it today."

Learning to Walk by Faith

Bobby reflects, "I think back to all those years of praying, and I believe they impacted the work we're doing now. Those prayers made me strong for ministry, 'strong in the Lord, and in the power of his might'[2]—not my might. So many times, we try to be strong in our intellect and our knowledge and our logical ways, but I learned how to be strong in the power of *His* might. I learned that we should do everything that's possible for us to do, and then let God do the impossible.

"At one point, I was in need of money, so I thought I would go pray all night under an orange tree and ask God for a thousand dollars. In those days, that was big money. When I walked back out from underneath the orange grove, it was daylight, and I'll never forget what the Spirit of God spoke to my heart: *Bobby, I'm going to give you ten dollars today.* Ten dollars! I said, 'I was praying for a thousand, Lord.' He replied, *You were asking for a general's*

---

2. Ephesians 6:10.

pay when you're only still a private in My army. Besides, you need only ten dollars a day.

"I had thought that if I could get a thousand dollars, I could do something really big for God. I had all these plans, but God knew what I needed. He wanted to supply my daily bread. And back then, ten dollars supplied all that. He was bringing me on a faith journey, because within three hours, somebody walked up to me out of the blue and said, 'The Lord put upon my heart that I'm supposed to give you ten dollars.' I knew the person, but I hadn't really talked to him in about a week or two, and he didn't know anything about my need. To me, that experience was the same as receiving the one thousand dollars I had asked for, because it greatly increased my faith. And developing my faith was God's intention.

"Later, God would teach me the principle of giving out of my need, which opened up to me an even greater understanding of His provision. However, ever since I received the ten dollars, there have been many times when we've needed money, whether a small amount or a large amount, and it's the most amazing thing how the Holy Spirit speaks to people, putting in their hearts the exact amount we need, and they give it to us. It's the work of the Holy Spirit. Of course, we need to go by logic to a certain extent, but I don't *walk* by logic; I walk by trusting in the Lord and following the Holy Spirit and doing what He says to do. That time in the orange grove was really the beginning of my faith walk."

6

"SOMEBODY NEW IS GOING TO COME INTO YOUR LIFE"

Meanwhile, in Pennsylvania, my mother attended a little congregation called Emmanuel Church, and she made sure all of us kids went to services with her. We would go "no matter what," even during those cold winters. It made no difference whether or not I had boots, or if my socks and shoes had holes in them. There could be no excuse for not going to worship God on Sundays. My father, of course, did not attend with us.

Emmanuel Church's pastor, Ray Kauffman, was a simple man but a great soulwinner. He knew that my dad was out of work and that my family was poor. From time to time, as we were leaving church, he would slip ten dollars into my mother's hand and say, "Go and buy food for the children." Or, he would hand her a large bag of oatmeal or some other type of food in a sack. Sometimes, he would just leave a bag of groceries in our old car when no one was looking.

One time, in the dead of winter, all the tires on our car were bald, but somehow my mother managed to make it to church safely. When the service was over, she was surprised to discover that those old bald tires had been replaced by newer ones. We found out later that the pastor had asked someone to switch our tires for his.

Plaid Shirts, Overalls, and Boots

Pastor Ray would invite my father to come to church but would never push him or condemn him. My father would always evade the invitation by saying, "I would come to church, but I don't have church clothes. I only have plaid shirts, overalls, and work boots." Then, one day, after receiving the same reply, the pastor said, "Sam, if you come to church on Sunday, I promise that you won't be embarrassed or outdressed." My father agreed. He went to church in his plaid shirt, overalls, and work boots, and he was greeted at the door by Pastor Kauffman and his ushers—who were also wearing plaid shirts, overalls, and boots!

My father started attending our little country church every Sunday, and I believe he would eventually have given his heart to the Lord. However, the church's board of deacons decided they wanted someone else to be the pastor, so they fired Pastor Ray. When my father heard about this, he went into a rage and never went back. His drinking became even worse after that.

When I was twelve, my dad couldn't find work, but he had a buddy who had moved to Merritt Island, Florida, and gotten a job fixing televisions. My father joined him, and they started a little television repair business, so my family moved from Pennsylvania to Florida. Because my father's alcoholism always made it difficult for him to hold down a job, I started to work with him part-time in his TV repair shop. In those days, television sets were encased in large, heavy cabinets, and I remember having to help load those huge sets into the truck. Later, my father got a job at the Cape, monitoring televisions and so forth, and he did all right there, but his drinking remained a problem.

In my early teens, I drifted from God somewhat, but by the time I was sixteen, I had come back to God, was filled with the Holy Spirit, and was attending a nearby church. I wasn't dating anyone; I was just in love with Jesus. Then an evangelist visited our church and told me, "Young lady, I want to give you a word from the Lord. You're sixteen. I want you to fast and pray and seek the Lord with all of your heart for thirty days. If you do that, at the end of thirty days, somebody new is going to come into your life, and your life will change from then on." During the time I was fasting and praying, and even afterward, I never thought about a boy coming into my life. I thought it would be an angel of the Lord or something else really *spiritual*. I was so on fire for Jesus that I didn't even think about dating.

7

DISINHERITED

After his conversion to Christ, Bobby was "plumb nuts" about Jesus, and he went to church every time the doors were open—but not without consequences. Although Dorothy had always treated Bobby terribly in the past, she now began to hate him. Her anger hit an all-time high because she could not keep Bobby from going to "that church," which was located just a block from her house.

Dorothy had inherited several bank accounts (each one having a balance of $100,000) from the man she had lived with, and she also owned her house, the land it was on, stocks, and other items of value. Bobby was her only heir, since she didn't have other children. When he'd turned sixteen, becoming of legal age, she'd taken him to each bank and had his name put on the account. But following his conversion, she forced him to make a choice between his commitment to the Lord and his inheritance.

Out on His Own

You'd think Dorothy would have been glad that her son was attending church rather than drinking, doing drugs, or carousing. But she was determined to find a way to stop Bobby from going back there. He remembers, "One night, I was in church, and the service had just started. I sitting in the back, and she came in and dragged me home, telling me, 'You can't go to that church anymore. If you go there, I'm going to kick you out of the house.' Then she locked me in my bedroom. I really wanted to attend that service, so I raised my window, crawled out quietly, and went right back down to the church. Of course, when I came home, she was angry because I had disobeyed her. She said, 'Let me tell you something: The next time you go down there, I'm going to kick you out of the family, and you're going to lose your inheritance.'

"I said, 'Mama, you know I love you and everything, but don't worry about my inheritance. I have an inheritance that's incorruptible; it's unde-filed, and it's reserved for me in heaven.'[3] I went back down to the church that week because there was a revival going on, and when I returned that night, all my clothes and everything else I possessed had been thrown outside. I had an old, black-and-white Metropolitan car, so I packed up my car with my few belongings and went to stay with a friend overnight. The next day, I rented a little shack, and I lived on my own, but I stayed in high school."

Bobby needed money to pay for rent, food, and other necessities, so he got a job at the local A & P grocery store. "This happened at Christmastime in 1962," he remembers. "At home, even though there were many difficulties, we'd always had nice Christmases; but that Christmas, I sat in my shack all alone, with no presents or anything. Yet the Lord spoke to me in my spirit and said, *I will never leave thee nor forsake thee. For lo, I am with you always, even until the end of the world. I am a Friend that sticketh closer than a brother.*[4] All those hardships I faced ended up making me strong in the Lord.

"My mother (Dorothy) took my name off the inheritance, just as she had said she would. After Sherry and I were married, we would visit her every Christmas with the grandchildren. One Christmas, she wasn't at home, and we discovered that she was in the hospital. We went in to see her and to ask if we could help her with anything, such as paying an electric bill, and I'll never forget how the hospital security came in and kicked us out. My mother had always been into fortune-tellers, witchcraft, and Ouija boards; she had ar-ranged that, upon her death, all of her money and land—the land my daddy had said I would someday inherit—and even all her personal items were to be given to a woman who was a gypsy witch. This woman had apparently convinced my mother that she shouldn't even see us, because her whole plan was to get all the money. Security told me I was not allowed back in the hos-pital to see my mother. Later, the only way I knew she had died was because I saw her obituary in the newspaper.

"Jake had saved some gold coins for me ever since I was a little boy. He was very sentimental about them. But the gypsy witch got everything, in-cluding those coins. She even got my mother's papers and our family pic-tures (including the picture of me in the sailor suit), and I'm sure she threw most of them away. But after what happened, I think it's interesting that God

3. See 1 Peter 1:4.
4. See Hebrews 13:5; Matthew 28:20; Proverbs 18:24.

eventually sent Sherry and me to minister in Haiti—the witchcraft capital of the world. Thousands of people who have been bound by witchcraft and voodoo are being won to Christ. I can imagine Satan thinking, *I wish I'd let them have their money so it wouldn't have ended up like this!* But our inheritance in God is infinitely greater than any inheritance we might receive on earth."

A Fishing Buddy

Even though Bobby was living alone in a shack and did not have the influence of a father, God provided a mentor for him. Bobby was now in the twelfth grade at the high school division of Mid Florida Tech. His car wasn't working, so his English teacher, Mr. Brandon, would come by every morning and pick him up for school. "He was a good teacher," Bobby says, "but he had some unusual ways. We both loved fishing, so whenever he was able to get away with taking a day off from school, he would drive me to a 'fishing hole' after he picked me up. We would skip school together! Sometimes, we would fish at Indian River on the east side of Florida. At lunchtime, Mr. Brandon would wade out into the water and pick up mussels from the bottom of the river, then crack them open with a knife and eat them right there. I would sit on shore, eating my sandwich and saying to myself, *I could never do that!*

"Other times, we would fish in various lakes around central Florida. We would basically fish anywhere we could. Then, when we'd go back to school the next day, people would notice that we were sunburned and say, 'We know where you two were yesterday!' I'm not sure how we got away with it.

"Mr. Brandon thought a lot of me, and we were good friends. He always gave me an automatic A on all my homework and an A as my final grade each semester. But the drawback was that, to this day, my English is very bad; my spelling is especially poor, and I wish I'd had better training in it. I'm always asking Sherry how to spell words.

"But everybody needs a fishing buddy, especially if they don't have a father. Mr. Brandon was a good friend, and he became a good father figure to me, teaching me a lot about life."

8

BOBBY BEFORE THE JUDGE

Dorothy was not content merely to disinherit Bobby. She resolved to have him declared insane, just as his biological mother had been. And the heart of her case involved Bobby's very large family Bible.

Bobby explains, "When God first healed me, and I realized I could speak clearly, one of the first things I did was to start selling big family Bibles door-to-door. That type of Bible was very popular then. And everywhere I went, even at school, I would carry my own family Bible with me. I'm not talking about a little New Testament but a *big* family Bible.

"Of course, my mother thought I was going crazy for sure. I would sometimes skip school and head to the woods in order to pray and fast. Other times, I would go into my bedroom, and my mother would hear me in there praying out loud for long periods of time. One day, after I read in the Bible that King David danced before the Lord, I danced before the Lord in my bedroom. I found out later that my mother had looked through the keyhole and seen me.

"A woman starting coming to my high school and calling me out of class to speak to me. I'm sure my mother was behind this, because she was so mad at me for going back to church. I knew my natural mother was in an insane asylum, but what I didn't know at the time was that my grandfather had been committed, too. So, my mother had a psychologist from the state of Florida come out and examine me on several visits, asking me questions about my life.

"I had no idea who this woman was. In those days, the Assemblies of God church was different from the way it is now; they had strict rules about hairstyles, makeup, and other things. Back then, if a woman cut her hair short or wore makeup, it meant she would go to hell. If she wore jewelry, it was a sign of belonging to the 'world.' The woman from the state not only had short hair, but she also wore jewelry and lipstick, so I would tell her she was going to hell and that she ought to get saved. She didn't smile or laugh. She just looked at me as if to say, 'Uh, huh.' When I would talk with her, I always had my big family Bible with me. She asked, 'Do you carry that with you everywhere you go?' I replied, 'Yes, ma'am.'"

One day, after Bobby had been kicked out of the house and was living in the rented shack, his pastor came to him and said he'd learned the wheels were in motion for Bobby to be brought before a judge to determine his mental state. "You'd better get a good lawyer," he said, "because your mother is trying to put you in the insane asylum." The pastor knew that Bobby's real mother had already been institutionalized. Bobby remembers, "I told him, 'I don't need a lawyer. I have a Lawyer; His name is Jesus, and He will be with me that day in the hearing. Don't worry about nothing.'

"I had to go to a competency hearing in Orlando. Just before I went in, someone told me, 'Bobby, don't carry that big Bible in there before that judge. Don't do it.' But that Bible meant everything to me, and I told the person, 'This big Book got me in here, and this big Book is gonna get me out of here!'

"I went into the judge's chambers, and he asked me some questions. My mother Dorothy was present. A sheriff was standing there, also, and I got nervous when I saw he had a gun. I thought, *Am I going to be shot today?* It was a scary thing for a young guy to go before a judge like that and see a sheriff in the room. I had never committed a crime in my life.

"Two of my neighbors came to be witnesses for me. I was surprised to see them there; I didn't know how they had learned about the hearing, but they were able to testify on my behalf because they had known me all my life. They knew about the circumstances of my childhood, about the miracle I had experienced, and about the change that had taken place in me.

"First, my mother testified against me, saying she'd seen me dancing by myself. So, the judge asked me, 'Who were you dancing with?' I said, 'It was Jesus.' And he replied, 'Oh, yeah?' He further asked, 'You carry that big book everywhere you go, you pray all the time, you go pray in orange groves…?' I realized that when he listed them like that, my actions could seem crazy to the judge. The 'evidence' was piling up, and it didn't look good for me.

"The judge kept bringing up the fact that I carried around my big family Bible. He asked me, 'Do you have it with you?' Of course, he could easily see it because it was in plain view. But I picked it up and said, 'Your Honor, it's right here.'

"Then the judge asked one of my neighbors to testify, and she started to come forward, saying, 'Yes, I know him. I know what the Lord has done.' But when she said that, the Spirit of God came upon her, and she started shouting and praising God like an old-time Pentecostal, right in the judge's chambers. That might be hard for many people to believe, but it's what happened. The judge told the sheriff to take her outside the room, because he was unable to ask her any more questions. When I saw that, I thought, *I know they're going to put me in the crazy house today!*

"Next, the judge asked my other neighbor to come as a witness, and she began by saying, 'I know what the Lord has done. He's got a miracle!' But then the Spirit of God hit her, too, and she started speaking in the Holy Spirit and praising God. So the judge told the sheriff, 'Take this woman out of here.' My mother spoke up then and said, 'Judge, didn't I tell you?' I thought to myself, *They've been talking together. I bet they're going to put me away.*

"Finally, the judge said, 'Mr. Robert Berry Burnette, please stand up in front of me.' He looked at me very sternly, but he also looked like he was in shock after everything that had happened in his chambers. He paused for about a minute or so, which felt like an eternity to me standing there before him. I thought the sheriff was about to cart me away to the mental institution in Chattahoochee. But the judge finally said, 'Mr. Robert Berry Burnette, I can say one thing: I just wish this world had what you've got. Case dismissed.'

"I walked out of there a free man, praising God and carrying my big family Bible."

9

BOY MEETS GIRL

Over on the east coast of Florida, in Merritt Island, I had now reached the age of seventeen. One night, I traveled with my mother to Orlando to attend a big gospel tent meeting featuring a lady evangelist by the name of Bea Medlin. I happened to be wearing a pink sweater that night. Eighteen-year-old Bobby was also in attendance, and at the end of the meeting, he went up front for prayer. Afterward, he turned around and glanced over the congregation, and he saw a girl in a pink sweater near the back of the tent.

Bobby remembers, "The Spirit of the Lord spoke to me as clear as day, saying, *She has a pure heart, and you're going to marry her. She will be your help-mate.* I didn't know her; I'd never talked with her or even seen her before. I'd always thought I would be like the apostle Paul and never get married. But I went right back there and introduced myself, saying, 'I'm Bobby Burnette, and the Lord showed me you have a pure heart.' I didn't tell her the rest!"

We immediately liked each other, and that night, I invited Bobby to attend a Valentine's banquet at our church. Everybody had to invite someone, and I didn't know anybody else to ask. Even though Bobby and I lived about sixty miles apart, he drove out and took me to the banquet. Afterward, we went back to my house and were sitting in his car, talking, when he asked me to marry him. "Although this was only our first date," Bobby says, "we knew each other in the Spirit. It was just right."

When I looked at Bobby, I recognized that he was the answer to the fast that I had gone on the previous year. He was the "someone new." So, when he asked me to marry him, I said yes with no hesitation. I related what the evangelist had said to me, and then I told him, "You're the one, and I'm going to marry you."

Bobby says, "Right after that, I went in and asked her father for his blessing, I did it the proper way they did things then. But even after I had asked her to marry me, I would try the Spirit, asking, 'Is this really the Lord's will?' And He confirmed that it was."

For two years, we dated long-distance. Even though Bobby's Metropolitan car was broken down, he wanted to see me so much that he would still travel daily all the way to my house. Bobby says, "Every day after school, I would hitchhike over to see Sherry. I would sleep on the couch at her family's house that night, and the next morning, before daylight, I would get up and hitchhike back to school. I had it bad!

"Every day, Sherry would write me a love letter, and I would read it and reread it, going over certain parts again and trying to read between the lines. But the Spirit of the Lord spoke to me very strongly one day when I was reading one of Sherry's letters. He said, *Bobby, I want you to read My Bible more than you read her love letters.* I was so enthused about her love letters, but the Lord wanted me to stay enthused about His Word and to read His Word every day with the same passion. He let me know that His Word is His love letter to us."

Quitting High School

In the spring of 1966, in the midst of the Vietnam War, Bobby and I were both getting ready to graduate from high school. But then something unexpected happened. Bobby was making excellent grades (of course, Mr. Brandon always gave him an A!), but about three months before graduation, the Spirit of God told him to quit school. The dean called him into his office, and he acted shocked, saying, "What in the world are you doing?" Bobby answered, "The Lord's Spirit told me to quit school." Of course, the dean didn't understand that, and he said, "No, don't do that. You only have three months to go." Although Bobby could understand his point of view, he knew he had to follow God's leading.

Bobby obeyed God and quit school, so he did not graduate with the rest of his class. Meanwhile, I graduated and went to work at Southern Bell Telephone in Cocoa, Florida, close to home. Bobby then received another specific direction from the Lord: "During the summer, the Spirit of the Lord told me to go *back* to school when it began again in September. So, I went back to repeat my senior year. (Of course, I had Mr. Brandon as my English teacher again. The delay just meant another year of fishing!)

"I made good grades once more—but then I was drafted for Vietnam. At that time, everyone was going to Vietnam, and I really wanted to join them and fight for my country. There's something in young men that makes them want to go and fight; they all want to be soldiers. I knew I was going to be a preacher, but I wanted to be a soldier, too. Well, I had to tell the draft board that I was still in high school. They said, 'No, you graduated last year.' I replied, 'I was supposed to, but I didn't. I dropped out of school, but I went back, and I am in twelfth grade.'

"Because I was still in high school, I could not be drafted. I believe this was God's way of protecting me. His plans for my life didn't include my going to Vietnam, even though I would have gone in a heartbeat. Since then, no matter what things look like, and no matter how strange God's instructions seem to be, I try to do what the Holy Spirit tells me to do."

10

A BRAND-NEW LIFE AND AN UNEXPECTED MIRACLE

On August 18, 1967, Bobby and I were married. Our wedding was tiny because we didn't have much money—in fact, my wedding dress came from the Salvation Army, and we had bologna sandwiches at our reception! But it was a nice wedding, and we were so excited to finally be married and embark on a brand-new life and ministry together. Bobby had been able to earn forty dollars by digging up orange trees and selling them for a dollar a tree on the day before our wedding. The only money we had in addition to that forty dollars was a gift of a hundred dollars from my brother Robert. We were so thankful for that! The years ahead would be a mixture of ministering together while trying to keep afloat financially.

Bernie's Mind Is Miraculously Healed

Bobby's birth mother, Bernie, had been committed to the mental institution in Chattahoochee, Florida, but later on she was transferred to an asylum in Milledgeville, Georgia. By 1968, she had been institutionalized for more than twenty years, and everyone assumed that she would remain in a psychiatric facility for the rest of her life. But God had other plans, and they began to unfold about a year after we were married.

Bobby explains, "There was a woman named Theresa who, like almost everyone else, did not know my real mother and assumed that Dorothy was my biological mother. One summer night, Theresa was at a prayer meeting we attended, and she began to prophesy to me under the Spirit of God. In the prophecy, the Lord said, 'I am the Lord thy God of all flesh, is there anything too hard for Me? I have seen thy mother locked up in the insane asylum, but before this year is over, I will touch her mind and heal her, and she will be made whole.' Afterward, Theresa came to me, somewhat in shock, and said, 'Oh, Bobby, what did I say? I know your mother. She's not in the insane asylum.' I said, 'Theresa, my real mom has been in an insane asylum for twenty-one years.'"

About three months later, Bobby received a letter from the asylum in Georgia, saying, "Your mother is well. Please come up and sign the release papers." Bobby's prayer buddy, Johnny Mahon, had a brand-new pickup truck, so the two of them drove together to the asylum in Georgia, and Bobby signed the papers for his mother's release, accepting responsibility for her for a full year so that she could come live with us. At that time, I was pregnant with our first child, Jonathan. "I remember sitting with her in the den at the institution," Bobby says, "and I asked her, 'Mama, how did God heal you?' She replied, 'You know, this man named Oral Roberts would be preaching every Sunday on our black-and-white TV set, and we would be sitting around here looking at him. One day, he said, "If you have a problem, if you even have a mental problem, just come and lay your hand on the television set, and when I say 'in the name of Jesus of Nazareth, be thou made whole,' you will be made whole."' My mother had gone up and touched the TV set, just as Oral Roberts had said to do. She told me that when he said the name of Jesus, 'something snapped. My mind came back. I looked outside, and I'd never seen the sky look so blue. Things looked different. It was as if all these years, I was in a dark cloud, like a helmet was sitting on my head. I can't explain it. All of a sudden, everything came loose.'"

Bernie's mind had been instantly healed, and she was soon able to find employment. Looking at her, nobody would ever have known she'd been in an insane asylum. Bobby says, "She actually had more wisdom and sense than I did."

All in God's Plan

Soon after his mother was healed, Bobby was drafted again. He remembers, "I underwent the physical and everything. But I asked them what I should do about my mother because I'd just gotten her out of the institution and was responsible for her. They told me, 'Well, you can't go in.' Again, I was kind of disappointed. But it was all in God's plan. I wanted to go to Vietnam, but God wanted me in His army instead."

Sadly—and only God knows the reason why—Bernie died of cancer on June 24, 1969. She left us her little, wood-framed, Florida "cracker-style" house, which was up on blocks, and we lived there for a while. We knew her as a loving, kind, humble woman, with a sweet, childlike spirit. Freckles dotted her face, and she always pulled her reddish-brown hair back in a bun. She wore simple cotton dresses with small flowers on them, and flat shoes. When she was happy, she always said, "Hot dawwg," with a Georgia-Alabama drawl. And she taught me how to make the best fried squash and onions.

11

TAKING IT TO THE STREETS

Bobby and I were passionate about reaching people for Jesus, so early in our marriage, we went to see our pastor, Joseph Ronsisvalle, of Rockledge Christian Center in Rockledge, Florida, to tell him about our ministry plans. Bobby told Pastor Joe that he wanted to go out and preach all over the world—that he was going to be a big evangelist. Wisely, Pastor Joe calmly replied, "Bobby, if you really want to be a preacher, first get a soapbox and go out there and preach to the poor people on the streets right here." He also tried to get Bobby to go to a Bible college first, but Bobby told him, "I don't have time for that—I'm in a hurry."

Pastor Joe definitely had his hands full with us! One day, he was in his living room, and he heard a loud squeaking sound coming from about a block away. He went to investigate, and he saw that Bobby and I had taken his advice. Bobby was preaching on the street corner using a soapbox as a platform and a microphone that was sending out quite a lot of feedback!

A Soapbox, a Microphone,
and Funeral Chairs

Because Bobby and I wanted to be in ministry full-time, doing street evangelism and holding street meetings, we decided to sell our house and buy a truck that would be able to transport all the equipment and supplies we needed. We went to Cocoa, which was near to where my parents lived, and held meetings in African-American neighborhoods where everyone lived close together in very poor communities.

We would find a small empty lot, often by the side of the road. Then we would set up a four-foot by eight-foot wooden platform, two small floodlights, and about a hundred chairs, borrowed from a local funeral home. Bobby would ask one of the black sisters if he could run an extension cord from his small PA system through her window into an outlet in her home, so that he could use it to preach. We didn't have the capacity to play any music, so I would sing into the microphone, and then people would begin to come out of their houses to see what was going on. Bobby had read the Scripture in the Bible that says to go out to the "highways and byways" and urge people to come in to God's kingdom, and that is what we did. As a result, a lot of alcoholics and prostitutes came to our meetings, and people were saved, healed, and delivered. We started on Willard Street in Cocoa, and from there we went out conducting meetings all over the state of Florida over a period of three or four years.

Street preaching had its challenges—physical, financial, emotional, and spiritual. Since these were open-air meetings, the weather was always a factor, but Bobby was persistent. When it rained, he would just stand there and preach, even when nobody came to the meeting. Sometimes, people would sit inside their cars and roll down their windows to listen to him, but he would have to keep preaching in the rain.

When we were doing street preaching, we had no other means of support than the offerings we received, and sometimes they would be only $2.75 or even just seventy-five cents a night. We had a hard time raising enough money to buy food or to put gas in the car. Every day was a struggle. One way we survived was by asking people to bring us some canned goods or other food to the meetings, and that really helped.

The "Illustrated Sermon"

When you do street evangelism, anything can happen. Once, a meeting really backfired on us. Bobby explains, "Early in our ministry, Sherry and I and Johnny Mahon held an open-air street meeting in a poor, African-American section of town in Apopka, Florida, which is in the central part of the state. That time, I borrowed a lot of chairs, so I had about two hundred chairs set up, with an aisle down the middle. We were flat broke, as usual, and we had come to our last service in that town. I wanted to give a big altar call for people to come to Christ. We thought that a 'resurrection service' would touch a lot of people. I would tell them about the resurrection of the dead and how we're all going to stand before God one day and be judged. And I would tell them how Jesus is the Resurrection and the Life and how He raised His friend Lazarus from the dead. I thought that would go over really well. I was also concerned about our finances, so I told Johnny, 'We have to get enough of an offering tonight for gas money so we can afford to go on to the next town. We have to have a crowd tonight.'

"To attract people to the meeting, we went around with a bullhorn that day, saying, 'Tonight, we're going to have an illustrated sermon about Lazarus, and Jesus raising the dead,' and we gave the address where the meeting would be held. I didn't realize it at the time, but most of the people didn't really understand what 'illustrated' meant.

"We got Johnny's brother, Pokie, who looked like a hippie and had long blond hair, to play Lazarus. He wasn't a Christian, but he agreed to help us out and take part in the sermon. Of course, we didn't have a tomb, like in the Bible story of Lazarus, so we decided to use a simple coffin. Pokie put on a suit and got inside the coffin—a white, homemade box—in the back of our big white truck, which served as a backdrop to the preaching platform. Johnny and I would both preach, but before that, I would ask for six people to volunteer as 'pallbearers.' I would say, 'Let's bring the body out and lay him in the front here, and let's have a viewing of the body.' We would place the coffin on blocks in front of the congregation. After this, Pokie was supposed to listen for my cue. When I said the words, 'Jesus said in a loud voice, "Lazarus, come forth!"' he was to open the lid and come out, praising the Lord, illustrating the resurrection of the dead.

"Things didn't go quite as we'd planned. We had closed the lid to the coffin, which was inside the truck, before bringing it down in front of the people, and we must have closed it a little too tight. We should have just left the lid open, because Pokie lay inside that coffin for about an hour! But when we went to open the lid again for the 'viewing,' I saw how tight it was, and I thought, *Oh no, is he getting any air?* We finally got the lid off, and I thought Pokie would crack a smile or look up at me or something—but he was totally still. I turned to Johnny and said in a low voice, 'He may be dead!' We didn't know what to do, so we just continued with the service. We invited people to come by and look at the 'body.' All I could do was hope that the illustration wasn't as real as it looked.

"There were some drunks in the front row drinking whisky from bottles, and other listeners scattered throughout the other rows. But then, more people started driving in. Because this was an evening meeting, their car lights shined on the platform. They'd never seen a coffin outside at night, and this white coffin all lit up looked really eerie. Word spread, and everybody started driving over and parking their cars. There were now about three hundred people gathered, and everybody was looking at the body in the coffin.

"Pokie still didn't smile or move an inch, and I thought, *Oh, man!* We decided to start preaching because there were so many people there. We had a 'preaching tag team,' where I would preach for five minutes and then Johnny would preach for five minutes, and then I would take over again and preach for five more minutes, and so on. After we did that for a while, I gave the cue, saying, 'Jesus said in a loud voice, "Lazarus, come forth!"'

"I had hoped 'Lazarus' would come out with his hands raised up, praising the Lord. But when I said those words, Pokie suddenly kicked the lid to the coffin completely off the box, sending it flying up into the air and scaring the living daylights out of me! The next thing I knew, he came *crawling* out of that coffin. First he swung one leg out. Then he swung the other one. And when he finally stood up, the whole coffin fell off the blocks and tumbled toward the audience. Some of the half-drunk guys in the front row shouted, 'Holy Jesus!' Others yelled, 'Holy Sh--!'

"Then Pokie came off the platform and started moving down the middle aisle between the chairs, with his hands straight up in the air and his long blond hair blowing in the wind. He was shaking and saying, 'Aah, aah, aah!' Many people screamed, and some of them yelled, 'The dead man's alive!' Everyone took off, knocking over chairs, diving under cars, leaping over cars, dashing across the street, running into nearby buildings, and crying out for mercy.

"In the end, there wasn't one person left to give an altar call to. We didn't even get to take an offering. About ten minutes later, some of the young guys came back to beat up Johnny and me after they'd had a chance to think about what had happened and got really mad about the service. I told Johnny, 'We have got to get out of here!' We ended up borrowing some money for gas from Pokie and quickly left town. We had no more illustrated sermons after that!"

"I Know What I'm Doing, Lord"

Bobby and I certainly had a lot of lessons to learn early in our ministry, including how to listen to the Lord's leading. Another time, Bobby bought a new GMC pickup truck on credit. We went to preach at a church one evening, and Bobby wanted to take an offering that night to go toward one of our first missionary trips to Jamaica. However, the members of this church didn't have much money, and Bobby didn't want them to see the truck and think we had loads of money and didn't need the offering, so he told me that we'd better park the truck at the back of the church.

Bobby remembers, "The plan was to preach, greet everyone, and then get in the truck to drive out the back way. So, after we preached, we got in the truck and were ready to leave when the Spirit of God spoke to me as clear as day, *Bobby, go out the front way, and not the back way.* But I had already decided what I would do, so instead, I pressed the accelerator to go out the back way. Once more, the Spirit of the Lord said, *Bobby, go out the front way, and not the back way.* I said, 'I know what I'm doing, Lord!' and continued to leave the back way. All of a sudden, the truck felt like it was in midair, and then it landed hard on the front bumper; we were completely vertical. What I hadn't seen in the dark was that there was a six-foot ditch in our path that somebody had dug to put in pipes.

"Fortunately, Sherry and I were both all right. But everybody who'd attended the meeting was still hanging around talking, and they heard the crash. They came running over to us, saying, 'Are you okay down there, Pastor?' They had to help us pull the truck out. I knew then that I really should have listened to the Spirit of God and gone out the front way, and not the back way! Sometimes, when the Holy Spirit tries to tell us something important, we just get in the way."

12

"THE JUST SHALL WALK BY FAITH"

In October 1969, our son, Jonathan, was born; and just over a year later in November, our daughter, Julie, was born. We were staying in a small rented trailer in Cocoa, Florida, not far from my parents' house, and we had very little money. In fact, when Jonathan was a baby, we couldn't afford to go to a pediatrician, so I wasn't able to take him for regular checkups to see if he was growing properly. Instead, I would take him to the post office, where a friendly worker would weigh him for me on the postal scale! But God knew our situation, and He always took good care of our children!

After Julie was born, Bobby decided he was ready to finally complete that twenty-one-day fast that God had called him to do. At the beginning of this book, I explained that when Bobby and I first started dating, he told me that God had instructed him to go on a long fast, and after he had done that, his ministry would really begin. The whole time we were dating, and even after we got married, Bobby made many attempts to finish that long fast. He even tried fasting in the orange groves, where he had done so much praying, but the fast didn't last long.

At one point, while we were still dating, Bobby rented a tiny trailer that unfortunately was right next door to the Merritt Island Volunteer Fire Department. Every Sunday, the fire department would cook fried chicken to sell, and while Bobby was fasting, he could smell the aroma as it drifted over to his trailer. If that wasn't bad enough, the firemen blasted out announcements on their bullhorn, calling out, "Bawk, bawk, cluck, cluck. Come and git yer fried chicken, right here!" Well, that was it; Bobby was so hungry for chicken that he broke his fast. He had just enough money in his pocket to pay for a meal, so he decided that he would start his fast again "tomorrow," and he bought some fried chicken with French fries and biscuits.

I went to see Bobby at his trailer but found it empty, and my heart sank when I realized that he had broken his fast again. I knew he would be on his way home, walking along the four-lane highway to hitchhike back to Orlando. I don't know what got into me, but I started running down that highway, sobbing and chasing after him, with cars whizzing past me. I really thought Bobby had "backslidden," or disobeyed God. When I finally caught up with him, he told me that he had fasted for several days, but that he was weak and hungry and would start again tomorrow.

Bobby had such great faith in God, and he had always been so sure he needed to do this fast. I have met many people in my life who have said that God told them something, but it soon became clear that was not the case. However, Bobby knows the voice of God, and when he tells me, "God told me this," or "God told me that," I know I can believe it. And, from the beginning, "he knew that he knew" that God had instructed him to go on a long fast.

But Bobby and I were now married and had started a family, and he was still trying to complete that fast. I truly wanted to be supportive and to continue to stand behind him as he struggled to obey God, but frankly, after all the starts and stops, I just wanted him to get it over with so we could have some relief! Working in ministry was not easy for us, and I thought that God would perhaps raise us up a little financially after the fast. I was never too proud to buy what I needed from Goodwill or the Salvation Army, but being able to have a new dress once in a while sounded good to me. We knew that if Bobby could just finish the fast, the glory of God would come down and touch him, and all our worries would be over. We would have no more financial problems, and we would have the worldwide ministry that we had always dreamed of.

So, I was encouraged in December 1970 when Bobby told me he was finally ready to complete the fast. All we needed was a place for him to be alone to fast and seek God for three weeks. We obviously didn't have the funds to get a hotel room for him, so we drove up and down the streets of Merritt Island and Cocoa looking for somewhere for him to stay—without success.

Then a friend of ours in the ministry who had a number of local rental properties, and who knew about Bobby's desire to fast, approached Bobby with an offer. "It's not the best," he said, "but I have a rental shack in Cocoa that you can use rent-free to go on your long fast and seek the Lord. It would the perfect place for you." He put the key in Bobby's hand, and we were excited that he now had a private place where he could pray. We didn't know that he would be tested before he even started the fast.

A Tempting Offer

Bobby remembers, "At that time, I was preaching, but I was also working with Johnny Mahon in the orange grove. We would graft trees and also try to sell them to make a living. The day before I went on the fast, a man came by and offered me a big contract worth a lot of money—more than I could have dreamed of back then—if I would plant the orange trees he purchased. He was very serious about hiring me. By that time, our GMC truck had been repossessed, so we were driving an old junk car. This man told me he would lend me a brand-new truck to drive while I was fulfilling the contract.

"I had a decision to make. Should I go for the money, or should I go forward with the fast I had planned? Taking the contract would have made life a lot easier for us, but I thought, *Well, I've been trying to fast for years, and I haven't been able to do the twenty-one days, but I'm going to do it now.* Besides, the Spirit of the Lord was on me so strong that I had to do that fast; I had to do what God had told me to do. So, I declined the offer. The man said, 'I don't understand, but okay, I'm going to go give the contract to somebody else.'

"Sometimes, you have to say no to money or to other seemingly good things in order to obey God. Whatever you are meant to do in life, you have to start off by doing what God tells you to do, because Satan will always present another option or another plan to get you off track from what God has called you to. It happens to people every day."

I fully supported Bobby in his decision to decline that offer because I knew it was the right thing to do. Many things can come along and distract us from God's will for us. But as the Bible says, *"To obey is better than sacrifice."*[5] In other words, the Lord wants us to do what He says to do, when He says it.

Something like a Scene in a Horror Movie

Bobby and I drove with the children to our friend's property, which was located in the poor section of town. Bobby says, "Our last turn brought us onto a dirt road, where we saw the house number on a small wooden shack that looked like it should have been condemned. There were broken-down old cars in the front yard, and the weeds had grown tall. All around were other flophouses in need of repair.

"It was wintertime, and even though we were in Florida, it was cold out. When we unlocked the door to the shack, pushed it open, and went inside,

---

5. 1 Samuel 15:22.

we thought we'd entered a scene from a horror movie. The wooden slats creaked underneath our feet. There were no curtains on the windows and no panes of glass in them. We had brought some quilts and old sheets with us, so we hung them over the window frames. These didn't do much to keep the wind from coming it, but at least there was an old kerosene heater in the living room that had a little fuel in it.

"Everything was dark and dingy looking. We flipped on the light switch, and amazingly, the lights came on. How long the electricity would last, we didn't know, but I wasn't too worried about it because I'd brought my flashlight with me. The shack had an old sofa, a small table with wooden chairs, a bed, and a nightstand. There was also a bathroom and a small kitchen.

"I sat down on one of the chairs and told Sherry, 'Honey, I am going to stay here and fast and pray, and this time, I really mean it. I know I have told you many times before that I was going on this fast, and I always broke it. But this time, I can feel it. I know I can do this. I want you to come by and check on me every day and make sure I am still alive. I know that God is going to speak to me and show me some very spiritual things. I might see a vision of Jesus. Maybe He will tell me mysteries of the kingdom of God, or give me the power to lay hands on the sick so they will be healed. Or maybe He will send us out into all the world to preach the gospel. I am not sure what the Lord will do or what He will reveal to me—*but this is it.*'"

I hated to leave Bobby there. As I went out the door, the look on his face seemed to say, "How am I ever going to make it with no food for twenty-one days, when all hell comes against me?" Seeing that shack had been depressing enough, but I had to drive away by myself with two hungry babies in the car and absolutely no money for diapers or anything else. Tears welled up in my eyes and then spilled down my face. Many people who knew us thought we were "losers" in the ministry. They thought that Bobby was crazy for going off on this long fast…and they thought I was crazy, too. But I had hope that the next day when I returned, I would find out that Bobby had seen a vision or heard a word from Jesus!

From Bad to Worse

The first night of Bobby's fast wasn't anything like he'd imagined. He remembers, "Besides my Bible, I'd brought along a book about fasting by an evangelist who had gone on a forty-day fast and written down what he'd experienced, which he said everybody who went on a long fast would experience, too. I was sure it would help me to keep going for twenty-one days without food.

"In the evening, I began to read the book by the tiny light glowing from the kerosene heater—which I hoped had enough kerosene to last through that cold night. Then I began to get excited as I read, 'After the first three days of your fast, you will lose all your desire for food. You will not be hungry.' I was already hungry at the start of the fast, so having my appetite taken away sounded great to me.

"After this, I climbed into the lumpy little bed to go to sleep, but I was shaking from cold and hunger. It was very dark, and I could hardly see the tiny flame from the kerosene heater. All of a sudden, I heard scratching noises. I thought maybe a thief was trying to break in. Maybe someone was coming through the window, which was covered only with a quilt. My heart started pounding when I realized the noises were coming from *inside*. Whoever it was, they were already here.

"All of a sudden, I felt something in the bed with me, moving up and down inside the sheet. I thought maybe it was a demonic spirit. I screamed and jumped out of bed, and I started frantically feeling around for my flashlight in the dark. When I switched it on, I saw a huge rat running across the bed! But there wasn't just one big rat; there were many of them! I grabbed the broom and started beating on the rats to kill them. I didn't know how I could stay another night in this rat shack."

Dead Rats in the Corner

The next day, I drove our clunker over to the shack, anxious to know if Bobby had seen any visions, had any dreams, or heard the voice of God. When I came through the door, I was horrified to see a pile of dead rats in the corner of the room. Bobby told me about his harrowing night and his hunger, but he was still hopeful. He told me that, according to his book, his hunger would leave him in two or three days—and it would be easy from then on. I thought, *Right*.

The next two days came and went. When I visited Bobby, I saw that he was getting a little discouraged. He told me, "I feel weak, and my knees are shaking. I have been vomiting every day, and I can't sleep at night. I keep looking over at that old wind-up clock and staring at the hands. Time passes so slowly when you're hungry." I felt really bad for him, but he bravely said, "That's okay. I'm still hungry, but the book says that by the seventh day, I will feel just like Superman." But, on the seventh day, instead of feeling like Superman, Bobby was so weak he could hardly stand.

Meanwhile, I went to visit my parents, and my father was really upset with Bobby. He told me that he could not understand why any man would leave his family and go "seek the Lord" rather than get a job. I tried explaining, but it didn't do any good. My dad had never liked the fact that I had married a preacher (especially one who ministered to black people), but now the preacher had turned into a crazy man who shut himself up inside a rat shack with no food for twenty-one days so he could hear from the Lord. Thank God my mother believed in us. She had told Bobby, "If God told you to fast and pray for twenty-one days, you'd better do it."

I continued to visit Bobby briefly every day. He was extremely weak and looked very thin. Bobby remembers, "I was having trouble standing for any length of time. On the thirteenth day, I told Sherry, 'So far, I have felt hungry, weak, dizzy, and about to die. But, according to this book, I should start seeing visions.'

"That night, I was killing rats and freezing half to death. I was really hungry, and I started vomiting. The smell of that thick kerosene smoke was probably enough to make anyone sick, even if they weren't fasting. All evening, I had been staring at those green hands on my alarm clock as the time plodded on…9:00 p.m., 10:00 p.m., 11:00 p.m., 12:00 midnight. Then, a little after one o'clock in the morning on the fourteenth day, I looked up and saw a vision! It was like looking at a television set! I saw chicken, frying in a pan! I saw cornbread, dripping with butter, and black-eyed peas! The vision was so real, I could actually smell the fried chicken! I thought I was going to see Jesus or an angel, but instead I saw chicken frying in a pan!

"When Sherry came by the next day, I told her about my vision. She went over and picked up the book written by the evangelist, but I grabbed it out of her hands and threw it against the wall. I told her, 'Take that book and throw it in the trash. That man has never fasted a day in his life! He just wrote that crazy book to make money.'"

I threw the book into the trash can—and Bobby continued his fast. But the hunger pains, the sickness, the cold, and the huge rats weren't the worst thing he experienced. The worst part of it was that God wasn't saying anything to him; He seemed to be a million miles away. The presence of God was nowhere to be found, and it was as if Bobby was praying against a brick wall. The situation was almost unbearable. We were so broke, and here Bobby was trying to believe in a God who told him to fast for twenty-one days, drinking only water, and that God was going to reveal something to him that would be the "key" to our future ministry.

In spite of everything, Bobby stuck it out, spending the full twenty-one days in that rundown rat shack, drinking nothing but water as he fasted, prayed, and sought God. On the twentieth day, Bobby said to me, "Sherry, whatever you do, be here tomorrow at ten in the morning with orange juice. *And don't be late!*" Poor Bobby—the next day, I had car trouble, so I was very late…while he paced back and forth, waiting. When I finally arrived, he got in the car with his few belongings, and we went to our little rental house, where I fixed him some crab cakes.

That was the last time we saw the rat shack. Finally, Bobby had been able to obey God.

Crushed Expectations

We had been ready to receive the blessings of God, but now we were in shock. Bobby had been trying to go on this long fast ever since we were first dating. Now, after he had finally done it, there was nothing to show for all his suffering. "I was so discouraged," Bobby remembers. "After all that time of fasting, I thought I would have seen an angel or Jesus Christ or a great light from heaven or something else supernatural, but nothing happened. I hadn't heard from God, and I hadn't felt His presence. In fact, I had felt closer to God *before* I fasted."

There had been no visions or dreams. There had been no supernatural manifestations. There had been no angel sent from God with a special message for Bobby and Sherry Burnette. We couldn't understand it. What was God doing?

Walking by Faith, and Not by Sight

And then…the breakthrough came. Bobby explains, "That night, I told Sherry I wanted to go and spend time with the Lord in the other bedroom. I could feel the presence of God so close to me. In the middle of the night, I was sitting in our rocking chair, and all of a sudden the presence of God and His glory filled the room, and the Lord spoke to me, saying, *The just shall walk by faith, and not by sight.*[6] *Son, I wanted to show you that you are not walk-*

---

6. See, for example, Hebrews 10:38; 2 Corinthians 5:7.

ing by what you can see or feel or touch or taste. You are walking by faith, and this is your KEY to the ministry. Ever since that night, Sherry and I have walked by faith—believing more in the invisible spiritual realm of God than in the visible physical world. Hebrews 11:27 says, 'For he [Moses] *endured, as seeing him who is invisible.*'"

The rat shack taught us that even when we can't feel God or see Him, even when we're suffering, He's still there, working to fulfill His purposes. Knowing that truth takes faith, and the Lord knew we needed to stretch our faith. He knew that the things we were called to do would have to be accomplished by faith, or they would never be accomplished at all—they would never become a reality. The twenty-one-day fast may not have changed everything overnight, like we expected, but it was the kickoff point. It was the foundation for everything that followed. It taught us to "walk by faith, and not by sight."

13

CHICKENS, COBRAS, HEADHUNTERS—AND DYING CHILDREN

In the early 1970s, we were still doing street meetings, but our ministry was making a transition as we began to go on missions trips to other nations. We traveled to places like Jamaica, the Bahamas, and Haiti, taking the children with us before they were old enough to go to school. Bobby went by himself to additional countries like Honduras, India, the Philippines, Trinidad, Venezuela, Costa Rica, Mexico, and others, because we couldn't afford for all of us to go. We went on more and more missions trips throughout the decades of the seventies and eighties, and Bobby also continued to preach at meetings and crusades in America.

Going on these missions trips was our adventure with the Lord. We never had the money to go on any of them until about the day before we were to leave. If we had the money in place two days beforehand, we considered it a real miracle. One time, we went to the airport by faith, because we didn't have money to buy tickets, and someone walked up and gave us the money for everything. God was teaching us how to live by faith; and as we obeyed Him, the funds came in.

Roosting Chickens in Jamaica

Our very first missions trip was to Jamaica in 1971. Bobby recalls, "A fellow American by the name of Jesse Slabe invited us to join him on a trip to preach with the four Blair brothers, including Gilbert, who lived and ministered in Jamaica. I'll never forget how we rode in that old car of Gilbert's. He lived in a valley in the middle of the mountains, and he zipped around those mountain roads like a native Jamaican—and they drive *fast*. It was my first trip, and I was scared to death; I wanted to get out of the car so bad. I thought, *I don't know if I can take this kind of life.*

"We stayed at a house in Mile Gully, Jamaica. I normally loved eggs for breakfast, and the morning after we arrived, I woke up and saw that they had cooked me eggs. Those eggs looked like they had been sitting on the plate for quite a while, but that wasn't the real problem. Standing on my plate with his feet right on top of those eggs was a *chicken*. I yelled, 'Get outta here!' and the chicken flew out through the window. Then I said, 'Gilbert! Keep the chickens outta here, man!' I guess he'd just gotten used to them walking all over the place, inside and out.

"But when we preached that night at his church, many people came to the Lord. Even though there was no language barrier to overcome, since Jamaicans speak English, I found that preaching in the churches in Jamaica was different from preaching on the streets in Florida. With the street evangelism, most of the people we ministered to did not have any background in church and were not used to preachers. But the Jamaicans were familiar with church, and they were very responsive to altar calls."

Open-air Preaching in India's Rainy Season

Several years later, in 1974, Bobby felt that the Lord wanted him to go to India to minister during the month of October. An Indian man by the name of Pastor Chacko helped to set up a week of open-air meetings. "I was trying to expand our ministry and have larger meetings to reach more people," Bobby says. "Pastor Chacko had lined up a location way in the interior of the country for people who lived in the jungles. But when I arrived in India, the rain was coming down in sheets, with no end in sight. I started doing some reading about the country and asking people about the weather, and they said, 'Oh, this is the rainy season. And when it rains in India, it *rains.*'

"I was confused because I had felt like the Lord wanted me to come to India to preach during this particular month. I paced the floor of my small hotel room, asking God, "Why would You send me here in the rainy season to have an open-air crusade?" The Holy Spirit spoke to me strongly, saying, *Bobby, it won't rain everywhere.* That sounded simple enough, but I didn't know what He meant by it. The next day, we started driving to the place where the meetings would be held, which was roughly forty-five minutes away from our hotel. The rain was pouring down until we were about fifteen minutes from the meeting site. Then, for no apparent reason, it stopped. I realized then what the Lord had been saying to me.

"Before we reached the site, the car made a quick stop, and I got out to stretch my legs. Immediately, I found myself face-to-face with a cobra that stared at me with his head up, as if ready to strike. I had almost walked right on top of him! I thought, *Holy smokes, I didn't know that kind of snake was out here!* I was scared out of my wits, and I got right back into the car.

"Then, for the entire week of meetings, it rained cat and dogs all over the area except for our particular location, which was always completely dry. The first night, I told the people, 'The Lord said it will not rain any night that I am here. But when I am through, it will rain.' The lack of rain made the crowds increase as the week went on, because they knew God had done something special for them. There were probably thousands of people in attendance. They could not get over the fact that there was no rain. It was a divine, supernatural miracle.

"I had intended to stay at the same hotel the whole time I was in India. It cost only about a dollar a day in American money—but there was a good reason for that! It was the nastiest place I had ever seen in my life. I don't think they had cleaned the floor in two years. The Indians who stayed there had a habit of spitting a lot, so the floor was solid spit. There was also spit and blood on the walls. The commode was broken and hadn't been cleaned, and there were flies everywhere. Even my bed had blood and slime on it. But I had no money to go to a different hotel. I tried to sleep, but the stench was so bad that I thought, *I can't take this smell; these fumes will kill me.* All of a sudden, God took away the foul odor, and it actually started to smell like roses in that room.

"After we started to hold the meetings, I told my companions, 'Let's just stay out here in the bush where there's no rain.' That way, we avoided the difficult trek back and forth through the sea of mud every day. Normally, the ground at the site would have been flooded, but we were able to stay there in a little hut on dry ground. That was infinitely better than that disgusting hotel—despite the fact that there were cobras all around us. The guys who were with us said, 'Watch out for the cobras.' After having seen one close up, I told them, 'Don't worry about that. I'm watching out!'

"On the last night of the meeting, I finished preaching and gave the altar call. As soon as the altar call was finished, rain immediately started to pour down. The people recognized that as an additional sign from God. The Lord demonstrated His power and love to the people of India in a way that was very meaningful to them."

Surrounded by Headhunters in the Philippines

In 1979, Bobby traveled to the Philippians for a month while I stayed in the States to work in the little ministry office we had established in Cocoa, Florida. For the first leg of the trip, Bobby planned to fly to Los Angeles to meet a man named Andrew Rasmussen, who was the head of the Independent Assemblies of God. They were to stay two nights in a hotel in Los Angeles— kindly paid for by Andrew. Then, they would fly to the Philippines together. Bobby had his plane ticket from Florida to Los Angeles, but he had no money for the rest of the trip. He had booked the same flight to the Philippines that Andrew was taking, but he hadn't paid for it yet. The day arrived when he was to leave for Los Angeles, and he still didn't have the funds. However, he flew to Los Angeles anyway with only twenty dollars in his pocket, but with the faith that if God wanted him to go, He would provide the money.

After Bobby's plane left that day, a woman by the name of Angela Sorrels walked into our office and said to me, "The Lord told me that you had a need, and He told me to give you this money." She opened her pocketbook and dumped out a pile of cash onto my desk. It was *three thousand dollars*.

That was really big money in those days, and I was overwhelmed. Even though I could hardly talk because I was crying so hard, I called Bobby in Los Angeles and told him how God had provided for us. Bobby remembers, "I could not believe the phone call I got from Sherry. She wired me enough money for my ticket to the Philippines and for expenses. Traveling there wasn't as costly as it is today, so there was a lot of money left over. That meant Sherry had enough money for herself and the children to live on while I was away. God supplied everything we needed."

As it turned out, getting the funds to travel to the Philippines was one thing. Surviving the trip was a different story. Bobby says, "We went out to the Lesonne Islands to preach, which was a headhunter region. You had to get permission from the different headhunter tribes in order to go through their territories, or they would kill you. Thankfully, Andrew Rasmussen's organization had gotten all those permissions before we arrived. But Andrew didn't go with me because he was an older gentleman and the trip would have been too rugged for him. He told me, 'You're a young man; go take care of this.'

"I rode out there on a mule, accompanied by several Filipino guides. Along the way, I saw human heads hanging from the huts. This was a status symbol—the more heads you had, the bigger man you were. When I saw those heads, I thought, *What are we doing out here? These people will cut off your head!* I was the only white guy among the Filipinos, and I was afraid that the headhunters would want a white head to add to their collection!

"At the location of the meeting, there was a huge church made out of brush that some of the Filipino believers had built. I knew one of the workers who had helped to construct the pulpit, and when I went inside the building, I was horrified to see the head of that poor man lying on top of the pulpit, his eyes looking up at me. They had cut off his head as a sign for me to stay away. I was terrified, and I prayed, *Forget this! God, the first thing I'm going to do is get out of here.* Immediately, I went out and jumped back on my mule, but the animal wouldn't move. I got a stick and beat him, saying, 'Go!' But he still wouldn't budge.

"The Filipinos were scared, too. It was their friend who had been beheaded. Desperate, I told them, 'Lead me out of here. Get me out of here. Let's go!' But my mule wasn't going anywhere. Then the Spirit of God spoke to me as clear as day, saying, *Get off that mule and go back in there! I have somebody I want you to meet.* So, I got off my mule and went back inside. Who should show up but about a dozen of the main headhunters, who quickly surrounded me. I was standing right near the pulpit where the head still lay, flies all over it. These headhunters were carrying bows and arrows and big knives, like machetes. One of the Filipino men translated for me, and the first thing the headhunters told me was that each arrow had a poisoned tip.

"The Spirit of God said to me, *Don't be afraid. Preach to them.* He wanted me to *preach? Now?* But I acted like I wasn't afraid any longer, and I stood there and preached to them the story of Jesus and salvation—and most of those headhunters came to Christ that day. We had good meetings there, with a church service every night. You have to do things like that when you're young because when you grow older, you wouldn't do it for a million dollars!"

After Bobby concluded those meetings, a church was built on that site, which became a witness for Christ in headhunter territory. The early church leader Tertullian wrote, "The blood of martyrs is the seed of the Church." It seems that the life of that faithful Filipino believer who was beheaded was a seed for the gospel of Jesus Christ in that region.

Mobile Clinic in La Gonave Island, Haiti

One of the villages we worked in often during our early years as missionaries was La Gonave Island, off the coast of Haiti. While Bobby was busy conducting some evangelistic crusades in the States, I decided to start bringing in mobile clinic teams to minister there. I was drawn to La Gonave Island because I had always heard that there were many lepers there, and I wanted to touch them, as Jesus had, and give them some hope.

When we conducted these mobile clinics, our teams had to bring in everything we would need for a full week. After arriving in Haiti's capital, Port-au-Prince, we would usually travel a couple of hours to the town of Montrious and stay at a hotel there. Then we would travel all the rest of the way to the island on small boats filled with Haitian boatmen, our volunteers, our luggage—including our medical supplies, our sleeping bags, and our food—and anyone or anything else the captain let on board.

I always dreaded that ride across the water to the island, which took three and half hours. I didn't really like riding on any boat, but I was especially nervous about these vessels. They weren't nice new motorboats with cabins for shelter; they were old, recently glued and duct-taped, overloaded, ugly wooden boats, with motors that often malfunctioned and sails that desperately needed mending. They were the same kind of boats that many Haitians were using to try to escape their country and find a better life in the United States. Their boats were in such bad shape that hundreds of them never even survived the journey. Knowing this, I would squawk at the captain about being careful not to overload our boats, but he always found room for "one more"—not just one more person, but one more chicken, one more goat, one more cow....

Not only was it nerve-wracking to ride on the boats, but just getting on and off them was a challenge—and often embarrassing for the ladies. I had warned the women not to wear skirts but instead to wear culottes or split-leg pants. Because there were no docks, a Haitian boatman would come up behind you, squat down, and put his head between your legs, quickly lifting you up onto his shoulders and carrying you through waist-high water out to the waiting boat. The boatmen didn't mean anything improper by this; they just assumed it was easier to carry women on their shoulders, and this was their practice. (Men had it a bit easier; they were usually just toted on the backs of the boatmen.) After you were carried to the boat, someone on board would pull you by the arms as you staggered into—or were dumped into—the boat. For all this, the Haitians would charge a dollar a "ride."

A Tiny Haitian and a Big Green Skirt

One time, it happened that a female member of our team was rather stout. Not only that, but instead of wearing culottes or something similar, she had decided to wear a long, green flared skirt. As everyone else was being "grabbed up" by the Haitian boatmen (all of whom weighed about 95 pounds), I noticed two of the boatmen in a big discussion. They were trying to figure out (1) who could carry this woman, and (2) how much they would charge.

In a few moments, one of the stronger guys came over to me and held up two fingers. He wanted double the price. I reached into my pocket to pull out the money, and the next thing I knew, that tiny, muscular, sweaty, barefooted guy came up behind our volunteer and lifted her up. His feet sank down into the sand, and he wobbled and grunted, but he managed to actually stand up, hoisting her onto his shoulders as she kicked and screamed.

Then her skirt fell down over his face, and he wrapped his hands around her knees. She had nothing to hold on to but his head. Slowly, he made his way to the boat, sinking down with each step. All you could see from the back was part of a Haitian man and a lot of green skirt.

When he finally arrived, the guys inside the boat reached down for her, pulling on her arms, while the boatman in the water pushed her up. She was almost there when she slipped and fell into the water! The pushing and pulling began all over again, but it was even more difficult, since they were dealing with a wet body. There was lots of Haitian conversation going on, and some of it was about "too little money for too much *blan* [foreigner]." Finally, after a big shove, our volunteer landed on the wooden boat, soaking wet but happy she had made it.

The Boy Who Ate Mud

All our trips to La Gonave Island were for the purpose of bringing our mobile clinic to Haitians who otherwise would never have access to medical care. During each trip, many wonderful volunteers—nurses, dentists, and other workers—ministered to the needs of hundreds, even saving lives. But there was one incident at La Gonave that has been very hard for me to talk about because the memory of it always brings me to tears.

I had frequently heard about the Haitian children being so hungry that they would eat "mud cookies," or dirt, but I had never actually seen it myself until I went on one of our mobile clinic trips. (Consuming dirt makes children susceptible to dangerous bacteria and parasites, and it caused many deaths among malnourished and starving children.) The trip was difficult from the start. The team was getting ready to depart for Montrious, the area where the boats leave from, when I became very sick, so the team had to go on without me. I really thought that I had malaria, and I crashed in my bed in our small motel room.

In a day or two, a visiting missionary nurse came to my aid with some chloroquine, and soon I was much better and able to make the trip to join the others. After a hot, three-and-a-half-hour boat ride, we sighted the shoreline. In the distance, I could see one of our volunteer team nurses frantically waving her arms at me.

After I was hurried to shore, the nurse, with tears in her eyes, said to me, "Sherry, come quickly! A little boy is dying. We can't do anything to save him."

"What's wrong with him?" I asked. I thought we could send him by boat to the hospital on the other side of the island.

"He's been eating mud," she said.

I was shocked. I hurried up the pig path that led to the village, and I could hear screams and an unearthly cry as I came nearer. Then, under a tree, I saw a mother sitting with her dead son in her arms. His name was Joseph. He looked about eight years old, and his face, hands, feet, and stomach were horribly swollen. Then I noticed brown dirt around his mouth. The men of the village were trying to pry the child's body from the arms of his mother, who clutched him even tighter to her breast.

A Mother's Story

The woman was rocking her son back and forth, back and forth, crying and wailing (as most Haitians do when there is a death). She kept saying, "I told him not to eat mud…. I told him not to eat mud." I could hardly speak. I didn't know what to do.

The local minister, Pastor Chesnel, came to interpret for me, and I learned the whole, heartbreaking story from the grieving mother. Each day, the boy's father would leave their mud hut to try to gather sticks to make charcoal to sell so he could buy food for the family. The mother would leave, also, to try to find plastic bottles to sell or to search through the garbage dump for anything else that could be taken to the market and sold.

Then the mother had discovered that when she was away, Joseph had started to eat the dirt from the floor of their hut because he was so hungry. Time and again, she had warned him, spanked him, and threatened him not to eat mud. To compound the tragedy, what little food she had been feeding him—flour and water, a little rice, a handful of cornmeal—was not only not enough but was the wrong kind of food to give a starving child.

As I listened to her story, I just stood there crying...still not knowing what to say. Finally, the men of the village pulled the child from his mother's arms and carried him to the porch of the pastor's small house, his mother still rocking back and forth, crying and screaming.

A Piece of Rope, a Dirty Sheet, and a Few Boards

We followed the group of men and watched as they laid the child on the dirt floor of the pastor's hut. A few men left and quickly returned with some thin rope or twine, which they used to tie Joseph's feet together. Then they did the same with his hands. With another piece of the rope, they measured him, then left. A few minutes later, someone came in with a dirty sheet and wrapped the boy's body in it.

In just a short time, we heard hammering in the distance. They were already building a small coffin for Joseph. Death was apparently so common to these village people that it was practically an everyday event. The Haitian pastor came to me and said, "Madame Sherry, you are the leader of the group. You need to go and say something to encourage or comfort the mother."

Who, me? I thought. *I have never had a child die, much less from eating mud because he was starving. What could I possibly say to this to mother?* But I went with the pastor to visit Joseph's mother and to put some money in her hand to pay for the funeral. Even those few pieces of wood for the coffin would cost money she did not have.

Then I hugged her, and I began to cry. I really tried to think of some words of comfort, but I found myself sobbing so much that I could hardly speak. I was embarrassed that I was the one who was supposed to be an encouragement to her when I had nothing adequate to say. I just kept telling her that I loved her, even though I didn't know her, and that I was so sorry and wished I had known Joseph sooner. I would have made sure that he was never hungry.

Through the interpreter, she said, "I know your heart is sad. Thank you for coming. Thank you for caring. Now, you must feed other hungry children so that they will never suffer as my son Joseph did."

Our team was staying at Pastor Chesnel's church and school, sleeping on the floor, and the next morning, I woke up early and heard a Haitian man singing nearby. I looked out the window and saw the man carrying a coffin on his shoulder. I asked someone what he was singing, because it didn't sound like any of the songs I had heard before. I was told that the man was making up the song as he went, and he was singing, "My son will never be hungry again…he is in heaven."

Even now, I can close my eyes and see that little boy with dirt around his mouth. I can see the men tying his feet together, and his body being wrapped in a sheet. I can see the face of his mother and hear his father singing as he carried that coffin on his shoulders.

14

DRIVING AND FLYING
BY FAITH

During the 1970s, while Bobby and I were learning to trust God to fund our missions trips, we still faced many financial challenges at home, and we needed additional lessons on the ways in which God provides and how we should respond to His provision. Because we had so little money, we always drove old, beat-up cars. In the late seventies, we were praying hard for a decent vehicle. Then someone we knew told us the Lord wanted him to give us a car. We were very excited until the man came by one day and dropped off a beat-up old Nash. If you've never heard of a Nash automobile, it's because they stopped manufacturing them in 1957—that meant the vehicle we were given was at least twenty years old.

That car smoked so badly that when we would stop at a red light, the people in the cars next to us would roll up their windows to keep out the smoke! Not only that, but the car had so many dents and dings that it was, as Bobby and I like to say, "pure dog ugly." Driving around in that car was truly embarrassing. Bobby said to me, "I've been telling everybody God was going to give us a car, but we can't let anybody see this car. We're parking it behind the office." When we had the GMC pickup, we'd wanted to hide it because it looked too good. Now, we wanted to hide this car because it looked so bad!

We had the Nash car for about a year. One day, we had a visit from a friend named Pat Cool, a pastor who helped support himself and his ministry by selling water softeners. He told us, "God wants me to give you my gold Lincoln Continental." God moved us from an old Nash to a beautiful, gold Lincoln! It wasn't a new car; it was about four or five years old, but it was immaculate and had all the latest features. The seat moved up and down electronically, and the windows and door locks were automatic. We'd never owned anything like it.

Unfortunately, we did not have that car for very long. If Bobby had a bad habit, it was overgenerosity—he had even tried to give away our first house!—and he gave our Lincoln to a very poor family who didn't have a car. After that, we believed God would immediately give us another car; we thought that now He might move us up big time. Yet it seemed that God had provided that car not only for *us* but also for our *ministry*. Apparently, even though we had given the car to a family in need, we had given it away presumptuously. As a result, for a long time, we had no automobile at all. We had to hitchhike to our meetings or ride the Greyhound bus. It was as if God was telling us, "Well, I just provided you with a car, but you gave it away. Why should I give you another one?"

Unfortunately, our next vehicle was another junk car that was going to pieces and smoked badly, just like the Nash. One day, we were traveling with our children on Interstate 4 in Florida to preach a revival in Plant City, which was over a hundred miles away from where we lived. Suddenly, our car engine died and started smoking so terribly we thought it was on fire! Bobby and I and our two children had to hitchhike the rest of the way to Plant City for the revival and then find a ride home.

Eventually, we achieved more balance in our finances and learned to trust the Lord to provide what we needed in order to best serve Him in ministry. This process took a while, perhaps because one of those needs turned out to be an airplane.

"You're Gonna Learn to Fly a What?"

Bobby knew God wanted us to continue traveling to places like Jamaica, Haiti, and the Bahamas to preach the gospel, conduct medical clinics, and minister to the people in other ways, and he thought it would be easier if we had our own plane to fly to the islands. We always had to haul a lot of supplies on these trips, and there are some things you just can't bring with you on a commercial flight. Additionally, he thought it would be a lot more convenient for us and our teams to come and go when we needed to. So, one day, Bobby told me, "The Lord's speaking to my heart; I'm going to learn to fly an airplane." I was in shock. My exact words to him were, "You're gonna learn to fly a *what*? Bobby, you can't even drive good!"

But Bobby started taking flying lessons in 1979, and we still have his logbook in which the instructor detailed his "progress." Bobby remembers, "At the end of that year, I flunked my first flying test. It broke my heart. The instructor said, 'I'm telling you the truth, Bobby. The more you fly, the worse you get!' Well, the fact was, flying an airplane scared me.

"In January 1980, I took additional lessons, and I finally passed the test. Only forty hours of flying are required before you can take a flight test, but it took me a lot longer. And even after passing my test, I was still full of anxiety when I flew. I told myself, *I have to overcome this fear.* It took me a hundred hours, but I finally got over my fear of flying."

"Mr. Faith"

Bobby flew trips within the United States until he got more experience and could move up to a larger plane that we could take overseas. Our first plane was a Cessna 150, which is a small, two-seater, single engine aircraft. One of Bobby's first solo flights was just a brief trip within Florida—but it was especially memorable. Bobby says, "About a week after I got my license to fly, I drove to Rockledge Airport, which was near our ministry office in Cocoa. I was getting ready to fly to Gainesville to deliver some books.

"While I was at the airport, a guy came into our ministry office who I always called 'Mr. Faith.' This was at the height of the positive confession 'faith movement.' With many people who were in that movement, you could never say anything that seemed like a negative statement, such as 'I don't feel well.' And this man was 'Mr. Faith' all the way. When he came to visit, he would always preach at me, saying, 'Bobby, you need more faith; you need more faith.'

"Of course, Sherry and I certainly believed in living by faith, but I have to say, this man drove us crazy. He would correct almost anything we said, and we cringed when we saw him coming to see us. That day, he came into the office, asking, 'Where's Bobby?' Sherry told him, 'Well, he's at Rockledge Airport, about to take off.' Mr. Faith said, 'You think I could go with him?' She said, 'Yeah, if you hurry, you can go with him!' (Anything to get him out of the office!)

"Sherry called the airport to let me know he was coming, so I waited for him. It was a very windy day, and the crosswind was strong. With Cessnas, you can get a lot of turbulence, and at that point in my flying experience, I really shouldn't have taken off because it wasn't safe. When you first get your pilot's license, you really don't know how to fly—believe me, you're still learning. I was naive, and I didn't realize that strong wind would be too much for my level of skill.

"But along came Mr. Faith, saying, 'Oh, praise God, praise Jesus.' He climbed on board and asked if he could go with me. I told him I was going to Gainesville and then flying right back again. He repeated, 'Oh, praise God, praise Jesus.' He was very holy, full of faith. I started to take off, but my little Cessna was like a kite in that wind; it took everything I had to keep that aircraft in the air. Having just passed my test the week before, I was still scared to death to fly under any conditions. Mr. Faith looked at me and saw my fear.

"I had climbed about a thousand feet when we hit an air pocket, and the plane suddenly dropped about two hundred feet. I almost had a heart attack. Then I heard Mr. Faith say, 'Bobby, I didn't know you were a pilot all these years. How long have you had your license, brother?' I said, 'Mr. Faith, I just got my license.' He said, 'Oh, my God.'

"As we flew along, the bad weather continued, and I struggled with the updrafts and downdrafts; I was just trying to keep the plane as steady as I could. Mr. Faith was holding on the small handle next to him, and his hand was turning purple. He asked, 'Bobby, Bobby, do you think we're going to make it?' I answered, 'Mr. Faith, I don't know.' That really scared him. All of a sudden, he started crying and praying out loud. I was surprised; I hadn't meant that we were about to crash right then! I was just talking as I tried to fly that plane.

"I knew Mr. Faith had a wife and family, but all of a sudden, he started confessing his sins out loud—including the fact that he'd been having an adulterous affair! He was saying, 'Oh, God, please forgive me for my sins. Oh, my God, you know all about my girlfriend on the side, but God, I'm sorry.' I couldn't believe it. I looked over at Mr. Faith, crying and asking God to forgive him for having an affair. Well, I have to admit that, even under those circumstances, I was enjoying the situation after all the rebukes he had given me for not having enough faith! Then he stopped confessing. But I said to him, 'Oh, Brother, don't stop. Tell God *everything*.' I was even more surprised when he started asking God to forgive him for having an affair with a *second* woman. You don't usually get to hear the confessions of someone who thinks he's about to die!

"Finally, we got to the airport in Gainesville, but as I was descending to land, the air traffic controller suddenly said, 'Pull up, pull up, pull up!' I pulled up, and the controller told me, "Wrong runway!" Being a new pilot, I was still uncertain about which runways the controllers were talking about when they gave out the numbers. In this case, there were three runways that crisscrossed, and it was a little confusing. After I pulled the plane up, I came around and tried to find the right runway, but I must have started toward the wrong one again because the controller shouted, 'Pull up, pull up! How long have you had your license?' I said, 'I just got it.' He replied, 'I believe it.'

"Mr. Faith was still crying, and he said, 'Oh, Bobby, Bobby. You have to get me down. Please, Jesus.' The controller instructed me, 'Follow the airplane in front of you; he will lead you down.' The plane I was supposed to follow flew into the clouds, so I flew into the clouds, too. Well, to fly in clouds, you need to be IFR-rated, which means instrument flight rules, and I was only VFR-rated, meaning visual flight rules. It's a wonder I didn't crash right there, because when you fly in clouds, you really have to know how to fly. Thankfully, we came out of the clouds in about two minutes.

"I don't know what happened when we were in those clouds, but when the plane popped out of them again, I didn't see either the other airplane or the airport anywhere. I asked Mr. Faith, 'Do you see the airport?' He said, 'No! Oh, my God, no!' I called the control tower and said, 'Can you give me a vector, a heading?' After the controller gave me the vector, I pulled the plane around, spotted the airport, and came in on the right runway this time. But when we landed, the Cessna really bounced up and down as it taxied to a stop. Mr. Faith was hanging on for dear life, but we finally made it.

"I quickly delivered the books I had transported and was ready to head back to Cocoa, so I called, 'Let's go, Mr. Faith.' He was over at a telephone booth, so I asked, 'Who're you calling?' He said, 'I'm calling Greyhound! I'm going back by Greyhound bus.' I told him, 'I thought you had all kinds of faith.' He replied, 'I ain't got that much! I'm never going to fly again.'"

Bobby and I always chuckle over this incident. We learned that even though many people can talk faith and look very holy, the real question is whether they can walk out that faith and maintain good character in their lives. But this story has an unusual ending. Strangely, "Mr. Faith" died about two weeks after that trip, at only forty years old. Just before he died, he had told Bobby, "I'm going to live for a long time, because God's with me; the Bible says that I have long life." The next day, he was riding in his car with his son, who was driving, and his son ran a stop sign. Another car hit them on the passenger side, and he was instantly killed. He had never expected to die that day. It could be that God used that airplane trip to urge him to straighten out his life because he didn't have long to live.

Night Vision

Of course, having faith is never a license to be reckless, and I thank God for protecting us in those early days as we struggled to make do with the equipment we had. After Bobby gained more experience flying, he moved up to a Cessna 172 and then to an old, twin-engine Aztec, number 5658Y (5658 Yankee). He had to pass another flying test to be licensed to fly the Aztec, and this time, he performed excellently.

One day, Bob D'Andrea, owner of Christian Television Network (CTN), based in Clearwater, Florida, asked Bobby, "Can you fly us back and forth between the Clearwater station, where we're holding a telethon, and our station in Cocoa?" We knew Bob well because our TV program aired on his network (and still does today), and we had become good friends with him.

Bobby agreed to transport Bob during the telethon, and on one of the flights, he had to land at the small airport at Merritt Island after dark. Bobby remembers, "There was no control tower at that airport, and there were no lights on the runway. My landing light had burned out, but I hadn't been able to replace it because I didn't have any money. Bob was in the front seat next to me, and he asked, 'How can we land? Everything's totally dark.' I said, 'Bob, just take this flashlight and stick your hand out the window as far as you can, and shine the light and try to find the runway, would you?' (Sherry had to do the same thing many times!) As we were landing, I told Bob, 'Don't lose that runway; shine that light so that I can see! Hold that light still!' To, this day, Bob ribs me about that landing, because he had to hold the flashlight all the way down. But we landed all right."

Having the Aztec opened the way for Bobby to pilot us back and forth on many of our missions trips, as he had hoped. By that time, we were frequently traveling to Haiti, and not long after we got the Aztec, we planned a missions trip there. When we were ready to leave, we got into the plane with Bobby's copilot, David, and three other people who would be ministering with us. I'm sure it inspired a lot of confidence in our fellow travelers when David started reading the airplane manual out loud to Bobby, reviewing the instructions on how to fly the plane! But our visitors would soon have even more reason for misgivings about the trip.

Bobby relates, "After we took off, we flew to Fort Lauderdale to get gas. When we were ready to leave again, we could not get the airplane cranked no matter how hard we tried. The battery kept going dead on us, so we were about to have the battery charged. Then, an experienced pilot came by and said, 'Look, boys, you forgot to turn on these two magneto switches. If you turn those switches on, your motor will crank.'

"Well, that problem was solved, so we took off again, but soon we were in the middle of a tricky situation. When I'd bought the plane, the owner hadn't told me that the gas tanks didn't work correctly. One tank would burn fuel normally, but the other tank wouldn't, so after a while, the weight wouldn't be evenly distributed. As we flew, the plane became so lopsided that we had to land and switch tanks. We had to keep adjusting because of the fuel, but we finally made it."

Tail Numbers in Magic Marker

The Aztec was an older plane, and somebody had promised us that if we stripped the paint and painted it white with a primer, they would give us a free paint job. So, we stripped it and used a cheap primer on it. But the person who had promised to do the paint job didn't follow through, and we didn't have any money to buy paint ourselves, so we had to leave it like it was. After that, Bobby and David decided to fly to Honduras. They had to write the tail numbers on the plane in magic marker!

Bobby remembers, "We flew to Honduras and Haiti many times with the plane in that condition, and *every* time we returned to Florida, a DEA jet would come up behind us and follow us home. When we landed, the agents would check over the plane and ask, 'What are you doing, hiding your identification?' I would tell them, 'Believe me, if we were drug smugglers making that kind of money, don't you think we would have bought a better plane than this? Please.'"

Another time, my friend Becky and I were flying out of Haiti after a missionary trip, with Dave piloting the Aztec. We were at the beginning of the flight, so the plane was full of fuel. Just after we took off from the Port-au-Prince airport, we lost an engine. Poor Becky asked me, "Sherry, is it normal to have oil shooting out of the left engine?" Dave had to turn around and make an emergency landing. Then the Haitian mechanics took the airplane apart and laid out all the pieces on the runway, but they couldn't put it back together again. Becky and I had to fly home by commercial airline. It took three months for us to get the Aztec back together so it could be flown again. As Bobby summed up the situation, "It was a mess."

Our missionary trips always seemed to give us one adventure or another! But we always went back because we saw the great needs of the people. We wanted to tell them about the love of God and to demonstrate that love by feeding people and conducting our medical clinics in the remote areas, as well as building churches, schools, and orphanages. We were responding to God's question in Isaiah 6:8, *"I heard the voice of the Lord, saying, Whom shall I send, and who will go for us? Then said I, Here am I; send me."*

15

TENT MINISTRY IS NOT FOR COWARDS

In 1980, a retired postmaster built a church in Rockledge, Florida, which was not far from our ministry office in Cocoa. This man wasn't called to be a pastor, but he had a kind heart, and he wanted to start a congregation there. However, after only a year, attendance had dwindled to about twelve people, and the man asked Bobby if he wanted to buy the church and the property. We didn't have the money, but the Lord sent somebody to give us enough for the down payment. The postmaster financed the loan himself, and we paid him a certain amount each month toward the principal.

That's how, in 1981, we began to pastor Harvest Temple church on Eyster Street in Rockledge. The church did very well; attendance grew so that the church was soon packed out. At the same time, we were producing our own radio program, and we were still going back and forth to Haiti on the Aztec to do missions work there. Even so, we made a point never to miss a Sunday service at Harvest Temple.

A Big Foot and a Little Shoe

After we had been at the church for two years, I had an unusual dream. I had never before had a dream containing a message from God, but I knew this dream was from the Lord. In my dream, Bobby was sitting on the edge of our bed, leaning over to put his shoes on. Even though his foot was much larger than his shoe, he was still trying to cram his foot inside it. I woke up and thought, *Wow, that was really weird; what did that mean?* All of a sudden, the Lord spoke in my heart, *You're trying to cram a ministry of preaching the gospel to another country into a ministry that is much smaller, and that's why it won't fit.*

Bobby and I knew we had to make a change. We told our congregation that although we loved them, we needed to follow what God had told us to do and get back to doing more evangelism and missions work. Our time at Harvest Temple had come to an end, and we turned the church over to somebody else.

Learning to Be "Tough"

After we left Harvest Temple, we continued to go on missions trips to Jamaica and Haiti, and Bobby also went to preach in Costa Rica, Guyana, and South America. In the late 1980s, Bobby started to hold gospel tent crusades as Bobby Burnette Ministries in various cities around the United States. We did tent meetings for several years, beginning small but using increasingly larger tents as we expanded the ministry.

Bobby loved doing the gospel crusades, but managing a tent ministry was not easy. He explains, "You have to drive to all these cities hauling a heavy tent, constantly putting it up and taking it down, arranging to hold the meetings and publicizing them. You also have to deal with bad weather and storms. Evil spirits come against your ministry, and you have to learn to fight back against them. We didn't realize it at the time, but during this period in our lives, God was teaching us how to be tough and to overcome obstacles. The Lord was preparing us for full-time ministry in Haiti, where we would have to be strong just to survive, as well as to do what God had called us to do."

The Circus Versus the Gospel Tent

Bobby continues, "One of the places we went to was Augusta, Georgia. I asked a minister friend of mine named Rev. Jim Whittington to come and minister with us there. A local man had lent us the use of his land to hold our camp meetings, but two or three days before our meetings were supposed to end, a circus came to town and started setting up right near us. They hammered away, making a racket, even when we were trying to hold our meetings. The man who had let us use his land must have leased it to the circus to use after we were finished, and I guess he'd allowed them to come in early. And some of those circus people were as mean as snakes!

"On the last night, as I was preaching, the circus people were out there working when a tough-looking circus guy walked into our tent, sat in the back row, and started to give me smart-alecky looks. Once in a while, he would make an obscene gesture in my direction. We had a fellow named Riley Ferguson who worked with us in the tent meetings; he helped with the music during the service, and he also handled the setting up and taking down of the tent. Riley loved Jesus, and although he was a small man, he was tough—you didn't mess around with him.

"After the circus guy started to cause trouble, Riley came over to me and told me to instruct everybody to close their eyes, raise their hands, and praise the Lord. I did that as Riley went to the edge of the tent where the man was sitting. Then, while everyone else was fully occupied praising God, Riley knocked the guy on the ground with one blow!

"The man got up and went to tell the other circus guys, and then more of them started coming in, looking for a fight. By that time, the service was almost over. Riley later told me that the circus guy had said to him, 'Well, I've never been to a church where they just beat the hell out of you!' But the circus people didn't cause us any more trouble. I think they liked us because they found out we were just as tough as they were.

"In other cities, too, there were some tough people, like motorcycle gang members, who would come off the road to sit in on our meetings, looking to cause trouble. After that incident in Augusta, whenever I spotted trouble, I would tell the congregation, 'Now close your eyes, raise your hands, and praise the Lord,' and that was the sign for Riley to do something about it.

"One time, during a gospel tent meeting in Cocoa, some witches came in and stood at each corner of the tent as if they were putting curses on us. When it was time for the offering, they picked up dirt and threw it into the offering plate. I walked up to them and said, 'That dirt can't hurt the offering because it is blessed by God. If you want to throw some more dirt, go ahead and throw it.' We just couldn't let that kind of thing bother us."

The Everglades Drug Dealer

During this time, God let Bobby and me know, by some unusual means, that He was with us. We were using a tent that was about sixty by eighty feet, but Bobby felt like the Lord wanted us to expand to a larger one. He remembers, "We were in Ocala, Florida, along Highway 200, conducting meetings. One night, when we had a lot of preachers on the platform, I got up and told the people, 'You know, we're going to expand and get a bigger tent, and after we buy it, we're going to come right back here and set it up to show you what you invested your money in.' Everybody clapped, and then I told them what

God had shown me: 'One person is supposed to buy the tent, the tractor trailer truck, and everything that goes with it. God is going to put a figure in your heart of what to give.'

"I waited for a minute, and then a woman came walking up. I didn't know her, but I knew she had driven a brand-new Mercedes Benz to the meeting that night. She had a check in her hand for a hundred thousand dollars. As I looked at her, the Spirit of the Lord said, *She is not the one. Tell her that I will bless her as if she had given it, but she can keep the money and sit down.* So I said, 'Thank you, ma'am, but you're not the one.' You could hear a pin drop in that tent, especially among the preachers on the platform, because I had declined a large donation.

"I hadn't mentioned a specific amount of money that was needed. I hadn't said that I needed a hundred thousand dollars because I didn't need that much to buy the new tent and truck. But after I waited another minute, a second woman got up and came to me with a check for a hundred thousand dollars. Again, the Spirit of God told me, *She's not the one. Tell her I will bless her as if she had given the money, but she can keep it.* So, I told the woman that she could sit back down with the money. Again, the whole place was silent. The preachers on the platform that night were in awe. Nobody could believe it. And if I hadn't been in the Spirit, I wouldn't have believed it, either. When you're in the Spirit, you don't go by what you see or by what you feel; you go by faith in what God is telling you. So I continued to wait.

"Then a third woman stood up and said, 'I will bring you cash in a big shoebox tomorrow night.' This woman didn't look wealthy; in fact, she looked rather ordinary. But the Lord confirmed that she was the right one, so I said, 'Everybody, she is the woman.' I didn't know how much money she had in the shoebox; she didn't tell me.

"The next night, she came back with a large, square shoebox. I opened up that box in front of everyone, and it was full of hundred-dollar bills. After the meeting, I asked her, 'Where did you get that money?' She said, 'My husband's a drug dealer.' I said to myself, *Oh, my goodness.* Then I asked her, 'Well, where is he?' I wanted to know if he was around anywhere, wanting his money back! She said, 'He's in prison.' I thought, *Thank God.*

"Then she told me that before they had moved to Ocala, they had lived in the tiny community of Everglades City, Florida. In the 1970s and 1980s, Everglades City was famous for drug smuggling. The fishermen there had formerly run honest businesses, but then the government passed so many laws on fishermen that they couldn't comply with them, and they were all put out of business. This woman's husband was one of those fishermen.

"There was high demand for marijuana during those days, and drug smugglers started to go to the out-of-work fishermen and say, 'You have all these boats; why don't you haul marijuana for us?' So, almost every fisherman in Everglades City started transporting drugs. I still occasionally preach in Everglades City, and the old-timers tell me there used to be houses that had entire bedrooms filled with money. People had closets filled to the ceiling with hundred-dollar bills. What the fishermen did was definitely wrong, but most of them weren't hardened criminals. They got caught up in the smuggling when they lost their businesses and couldn't feed their families.

"At about that time, many other people in Florida became involved in smuggling, too; Miami was built on drug money. In fact, many times, I was offered fifty thousand dollars in cash to use my Aztec plane to bring back marijuana. I would tell them, 'You're crazy. I'd never do that.' Once, when I flew to the Bahamas, there were bales of marijuana right out on the runway; people were sorting it out and loading it on planes to fly it to America. And the police were right there, doing nothing about it, because they had been paid off.

"The DEA eventually arrested all of the fishermen in Everglades City in a sting operation and put them in prison. Because they were mainly a bunch of old fishermen, they served only about three or four years total. The authorities had confiscated all the drug money they could find, but this woman's husband had managed to hide some of the money, putting it in shoeboxes. After the woman gave me one of those big shoeboxes, she said, 'He has a lot more money under the bed.' I think he wanted his wife to use what she needed while he was in prison but to save most of it for when he got out. But with that money, I bought a new tent that was two hundred sixty feet long and ninety feet wide. I also bought a tractor and trailer to haul the tent and all the equipment.

"Somebody might ask, 'Why did you take money from the devil? That was drug money hidden under a bed.' Well, I say that the devil had it for long enough."

A Sudden Storm

In 1990, we took our tent to Fayetteville, North Carolina, to conduct meetings. By that time, Riley no longer worked with us, and we'd hired a man named Pops, an old circus man, to handle the tent. He knew how to properly set up a tent, and he kept it beautifully. Bobby remembers, "I had done a lot of advertising in Fayetteville for a special service. The day of the service, the skies were blue, the weather was perfect, and the tent looked great. I even told Pops, 'I've never seen the tent look so tight and so good.'

"But then the Spirit of God spoke to me, saying, *Go back and tell Pops to tell everybody there will be no service tonight.* I quickly went back and said, 'Pops, the Lord said no service tonight. Don't let anybody under this tent.' Pops said, *'What?'* I didn't understand why the Lord had told me to cancel the meeting, especially since I had spent that money on advertising. But I went by faith in what the Spirit of God had said, not by sight or logic—not by the blue sky or by the expectation of a large crowd.

"I went to eat dinner at a restaurant that evening, and the weather was as clear as ever. At about eight o'clock, I returned to the area where the tent was, and suddenly, from one moment to the next, our tent was no longer standing; it had been torn to pieces. Part of it was lying across some electrical wires. The organ and the chairs had been flung into the street. It was as if a strong wind had suddenly come out of the blue sky, hit the tent—and nothing else—and then left. To this day, nobody knows what it was.

"Pops had stayed with the tent, and he was in it when the storm hit. Earlier, he had told anybody who came by, 'Don't go inside; you can't go inside.' If a crowd had been inside when the storm came, somebody would probably have been killed, but the Lord protected them. Pops had to go to the hospital to be checked out, but fortunately, he escaped with minor bruises."

Bobby had loved that tent so much that he probably would have kept on doing tent ministry indefinitely. Before the storm, he had been planning to purchase an even bigger tent than the one we were using. Losing the tent was heartbreaking for us, and it seemed at first as if the devil had won a victory. However, we later came to understand that God had used this situation to "burn our bridges" behind us so that we couldn't turn back to what we had been doing but would have to move on to the next step in His plan for our lives.

16

VALLEY OF DECISION

After our tent was demolished, Bobby and I didn't really know what our next step should be. We decided to attend a tent revival being held at the fairgrounds in Orlando. I remember that I was sitting on an aisle seat, earnestly seeking the Lord's direction. I kept praying, *God, what do You want us to do? What do You want us to do?* Then the evangelist walked over to me and said, "Ma'am, stand up. The Lord has a word for you. You and your husband are in the valley of decision. You're trying to decide where to go, what to do, and you don't know. You are about to make a decision, and when you make this decision, God is going to bless you, and you will be happier than you've ever been in your life."

Bobby and I believe that when you're in the valley of decision, God won't move on your behalf until you make a choice and take some action. Even if it's the wrong decision, He'll get you back on the right path. But you can't just sit there; you have to step out in faith. And when you do, God will bless you.

The decision the evangelist was talking about was the decision to uproot ourselves and move to Haiti so we could minister there full-time. Looking back on how we got there, we can see that God had been progressively leading us in that direction for twenty years.

The Haitian Children Steal Our Hearts

As I wrote earlier, we traveled to Haiti for the first time in 1971, shortly after we went on our first mission trips to Jamaica. Bobby remembers, "We'd been going to Jamaica at Christmastime to feed the poor living in the mountains, and someone said to me, 'Bobby, you ought to go to Haiti, because they're even poorer there.' I told Sherry I would go down there first and check it out. I didn't know any Haitian pastors or anyone else in Haiti. I flew down with a friend of mine, Rev. Paul Keck, not realizing that the country was in the middle of the Mardi Gras carnival. At that time, I had never even heard of Mardi Gras. There's already a lot of voodoo in Haiti, but during Mardi Gras, voodoo is king.

"That first trip was just a short one, only about three days. We spent our time there just meeting people and getting to know the country a little. It was distressing to see all the poverty and desperation there, but what stole my heart about the country was the children. I told Sherry, 'Once you see the children of Haiti, you'll fall in love with Haiti.' When Sherry came the next time, she felt the same way. The children are what stirred us about Haiti."

"If God Is so Good, Why Is My Baby so Hungry?"

Haiti and its children became like a magnet for us. For many years, Bobby and I would travel back and forth there, using any chance we had to help in any way we could. We found ourselves spending more and more time in Haiti, and less and less time in the States. We even started a daily radio program on a small station, WWBC, in Cocoa so we could tell people stories about Haiti and our outreach there. After Bobby got his pilot's license and was flying the Aztec to Haiti, I would do live interviews with him on our program via telephone about his experiences there and what was going on in the country.

At first, our whole focus in Haiti was on preaching the gospel—evangelizing and winning souls to Christ. We had never done humanitarian work before, except for building a soup kitchen in Jamaica and constructing a school and a church in the mountains of Haiti, but these were small things. We didn't have any concept of organizing feeding programs, conducting medical clinics, running an orphanage, or developing sustainability projects, like we are doing today. We would go to Haiti solely to preach, seeking to attract big crowds to hear the gospel.

However, two incidents that occurred early in our trips to Haiti changed our entire perspective and ministry there. Bobby remembers, "I saw a little Haitian girl in the streets, crying in the rain. She had her head down and her hand outstretched, and she was trying to sell some candy. I asked someone who could speak Creole to find out why she was crying. The interpreter explained that the girl said she had to sell the candy because she needed to buy some food or milk for her baby brother, but she had been there all day and hadn't been able to do it. That tore at my heart."

The second incident was when Bobby and I were just about to complete a series of open-air crusades in a place called Carrefour. At one of the meetings, there were many people in attendance, and we were up there telling them through an interpreter how good God is and how He can do this and how He can do that. When we finished speaking, a lady at the back of the crowd (she must have been standing on top of something so she could be seen) held her baby up in the air. The infant had red hair and a big, barrel chest—signs of malnutrition and starvation—and his arms were dangling at his sides. The woman screamed something in Creole, and our interpreter translated for us, "The woman said, 'If God is so good, why is my baby so hungry?'"

That was the turning point for us. That's when we really started to think about how we could do more to show God's love to people. You have to preach the truth of the gospel, but living out the gospel of the kingdom includes caring for people's physical needs. There is a Creole proverb that says, "A hungry person can't hear." It can also be translated, "An empty sack can't stand." How could the people hear and receive the gospel of salvation when they were hungry and weak and just trying to stay alive?

Bobby and I continued to minister in many countries, but we found that our hearts and minds were always compelled toward Haiti. From 1971 to 1991, we made about four hundred trips there, preaching the gospel and ministering to people's physical needs. In 1985, we established Love A Child, Inc., to focus on working to reduce poverty in Haiti's poorest areas, which we call the "regions beyond."

Transformation Under a Coconut Tree

I had actually wanted to move to Haiti for years, even since we first started traveling there. One time, I had suggested to Bobby, "Honey, let's move to Haiti." His response was, "Sherry, are you crazy? People are getting into boats and risking their lives to leave Haiti illegally. They're trying to get out, and you want to go in? If you want to be a missionary, pick a country, but mark my words, I will never move to Haiti." I didn't ask him about it again, but I continued to pray about it.

Bobby had gotten burned out doing missions work in Haiti, so he didn't travel there much between 1986 and 1991, but I kept going there to conduct medical clinics and to do other missions projects, with Bobby's blessing. However, even though he was not in favor of the idea of moving there, we actually started to give it some serious thought. We'd gone on hundreds of missions trips, but *living* in another country, especially a third-world country, would be entirely different.

Shortly after the tent meeting in Orlando where the evangelist gave me the word from the Lord, I put together a mission team to go to Haiti to minister for a week. Bobby remembers, "I had not gone to Haiti for a while, because some people there had lied to me in order to get money, and I didn't want to go back. But Sherry just kept on going there, and she wanted me to go along with her and the rest of the team on this trip. I was scheduled to be in Georgia preaching in a crusade just before that, and at first I told her, 'I'm not going to go.' But when the meetings ended, I said I would come. I brought along two or three people who'd worked with me at the crusade, and we met Sherry and the team in Haiti. The first night I was there, I was restless. I kept telling Sherry, 'I have to get back to Florida to our office; there's a lot of work to do, and I'm behind in it. I've got to go. I've got to get out of here.' I planned to fly out the next day.

"The team was going to travel on the back of a flatbed truck about twelve hours into the interior of the country. Who wants to do that? But Sherry talked me into staying instead of flying home. So, the next day, I was on the back of that truck, bouncing up and down on the rocky path. (There weren't any paved roads on our route.) There was no shade from the sun on that flatbed, and it was *hot*. I prayed, *If I ever get out of here, Lord, I'm never going to come back.*

"When we finally arrived, I climbed off the truck. Sherry was talking to the rest of the team, and I went to sit by myself under a coconut tree. As I was sitting there, the Spirit of the Lord spoke to me, *Bobby, you and Sherry are supposed to move to Haiti in forty-five days.* Immediately, I went and told Sherry what God had said."

When Bobby told me that God wanted us to move to Haiti right away, I couldn't believe it. I still wanted to move there, but I also wanted a chance to organize the move and get everything together. Forty-five days was a *little* quick! But suddenly, Bobby couldn't wait to move to Haiti. He remembers, "Before, I wouldn't have moved there for a million dollars," but when the Lord gave me that word in the Spirit, He changed my heart at the same time. He changed my mind; He changed my attitude; He changed my whole perspective; He changed everything. Before, because I had been burned out from working among Haitians, I didn't even want to be around them any longer. But suddenly a great, overwhelming love for the people came into my heart."

The God of "More Than Enough"

There was only one problem—we couldn't afford the move. We had lost our tent and all our ministry equipment at a time when most ministries were still feeling the fallout from the scandals involving televangelists Jimmy Swaggart and Jim Bakker. Donations to most ministries, including ours, had slowed dramatically, and our mail had dropped to practically nothing. Many days, no mail came in at all, and we were on the verge of bankruptcy.

But then something very interesting happened. After we began to tell people that we were going to move to Haiti, the donations suddenly increased. We wrote an appeal letter to our ministry partners, and funds began to come in. Previously, after we had sent out one of our appeal letters, we would receive about a hundred dollars total. This time, not only did many of our partners send money, but they also started telling others about our plans to live and minister in Haiti; the word spread, and many other people made donations. We also told our radio listeners about our move, and they gave generously, also.

Bobby was especially concerned that we obtain a proper vehicle to use in Haiti. He says, "I knew many missionaries in Haiti, and their cars would always be breaking down, so I prayed, 'Lord, I don't want that. When we move to Haiti, please God, I need a vehicle that's not going to break down.' I didn't want my car to have mechanical trouble in the middle of voodoo country!"

God answered that prayer in a wonderful and unexpected way. Bobby remembers, "There was a man in the hospital named Harry Whitaker who was dying. He would listen to us regularly on the radio and give us money, though in smaller amounts, like most people gave. He would call in and ask for prayer, so we knew about his situation. One day, I went to visit him in the hospital to pray for him because he was very sick. After the prayer, he said, 'Bobby, I'm glad you came by here, because the Lord told me to tell you something. I want you to go to the Isuzu dealer down the street here and pick out any Isuzu you want, and I will give you a check for it.' We went down and picked out a brand-new Isuzu Trooper, and he wrote the check for it. Although this man had been dying, he was totally well again just two days later."

God provided everything we needed to move to Haiti, including the funds for us to have the Isuzu shipped there. We arrived on July 1, 1991, as full-time missionaries. It was the beginning of our greatest blessings—and our biggest challenges yet.

Sherry,
at age 7

Bobby, at age 6,
when he heard
the audible voice
of God.

Bobby's birth certificate, with the ages of his parents.

Uncle Jake

Pastor Joe

They Practice What They Preach

By LESLIE ELLIS

TODAY'S WOMAN

KEEPING UP
- Auto repairs: Things your mother never told you. Page 4.
- Working Woman: Page 5.

YOU
- Are your insurance needs clear? Page 4.
- Stay-at-home mother spreads out doing working moms. Page 5.

Sherry Burnette
She's one-of-a-kind missionary to Haiti

Haiti orphans get local help

Pastor Bobby Burnett tried to pack a ton of clothes and aspirin for his trip to Haiti, but it wouldn't all fit. The stalled plane at Rockledge Air Park could only hold about two-thirds of the $16,000 in donated clothes, food and toys to be airlifted today to 2,000 orphans in Haiti. Other charity missions are planned by the program sponsors, a Rockledge church and Cocoa mission. Story, 2B.

PASTOR BOBBY BURNETT, PILOT KEN YOUNG LOAD PLANE FOR HAITI MISSION TRIP
...not all the $16,000 in only donated clothes, toys, food and drugs would fit for this charity trip

Local church airlifts charity to Haiti

By LEAH METCALF

PART 2

"LAND OF MOUNTAINS"

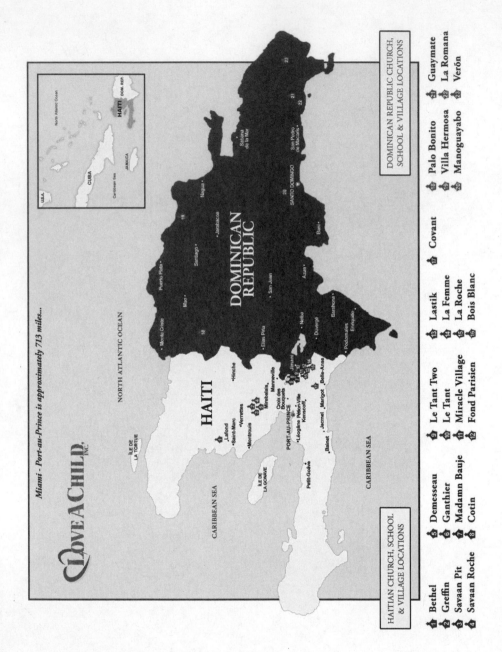

17

"LOVE YOUR NEIGHBOR"

"Beyond the mountains, more mountains."
—Haitian Creole proverb

In the parable of the good Samaritan,[7] Jesus taught us to "love our neighbor"—not just with words but with actions, because *love is something you do.* To Bobby and me, the small Caribbean nation of Haiti, which is only an hour and forty minutes by plane from Miami, was our neighbor. God had called us to love and serve this neighbor, whose people—especially the children— were in distress. No longer would we just live "next door" and come for regular visits, but we would live among them and experience life alongside them, suffering when they suffered and rejoicing when they rejoiced.

Sometimes, people in the States ask us, "Why don't you feed the poor here instead of in Haiti?" For Bobby and me, that's an easy question to answer. Jesus said, "Go ye into all the world, and preach the gospel."[8] When we went to Haiti to preach the gospel, we found men, women, and children who were starving and sick, so we fed them and reached out to them with medicine and other assistance in the love of God, just as the Good Samaritan did in Jesus' parable.

Why Haiti? If, just one time, you could hold a dying child in your arms and look into his or her eyes, you would know the answer to that question. We are here rescuing one child at a time, one person at a time...just one more. That's what makes life worth living.

---

7. See Luke 10:25–37.
8. Mark 16:15.

Land of Mountains

Bobby and I want to introduce you to our adopted home. Haiti is about the size of the state of Maryland and has a population of ten million people, who share roughly one third of the island of Hispaniola with the nation of the Dominican Republic. These two countries have very distinct cultures—Haiti was influenced by French colonialism, while the Dominican Republic was influenced by Spanish colonialism.

Christopher Columbus landed on the island in 1492, and at that time, the Arawak Indian tribe called the *Taíno*, meaning "men of the good," were living there. *Haiti* comes from a Taíno word meaning "land of mountains." The Spanish quickly occupied the island and named it La Isla Española, or "The Spanish Island," and the name was later shortened to Hispaniola. The Spanish exploited the gold mines and made slaves out of the Taíno. Slowly, these gentle people were wiped out, either by massacre, ill-treatment, or disease. Before the Spanish arrived, there were reportedly over three million Taíno. Fifty years later, most of them were gone. To create a new labor force, the Spanish imported black slaves from Africa, treating them just as cruelly as they worked the mines.

Later, the Spanish left the island to go to South America, and in 1625, the first French adventurers landed in the northern part of Haiti on the island of Tortuga, renaming it St. Dominique. When it was a French colony, Haiti was so wealthy that it was known as "the pearl of the Antilles" (today the term "pearl of the Caribbean" is often used). The French brought in thousands of slaves from the Ivory Coast of Africa, and these slaves brought their voodoo beliefs with them. The French subjected their slaves to the same kind of abuse that the Spanish had inflicted on theirs. At that time, the population of Haiti was divided into three main groups—the whites, the slaves, and the mulattoes. (A great number of the mulattoes were children of slave women who had been raped by the colonists.)

Slowly, the slaves began to organize a rebellion. They met secretly, and during their voodoo ceremonies, they plotted how to overthrow and kill their masters. On August 14, 1791, a voodoo priest named Boukman led a rebellion against the slave owners that eventually resulted in the founding, in 1804, of the Republic of Haiti—the first black independent country.

Even though the people won their freedom, in the more than two hundred years since the founding of the republic, Haiti has had a volatile history of political unrest, corruption, racial tensions, and economic crises. From 1957 to 1971, Francois Duvalier, known as "Papa Doc," ruled the country. A former physician, he was obsessed with voodoo, and he created the notorious *Tonton Macoutes*, a large paramilitary force that carried out his threats and killings. When he died, his son, Jean-Claude Duvalier, called "Baby Doc," succeeded him. He ruled according to his own brand of excess and brutality until he was overthrown in 1986. In the years following, there has been a pattern of political turbulence that, combined with natural disasters, social tumult, and economic instability, continues to wreak havoc on the lives of the people.

The "Silent Crisis"

Until the 1960s, Haiti's main export was coffee. When world coffee prices fell so low that Haiti could not compete in the marketplace, Haitians were forced to find something else to grow in order to feed and support their families, and they began cultivating corn, peanuts, and bananas. But it wasn't long before someone came along who taught Haitian farmers how to use trees to create charcoal, and charcoal production became the most popular means of livelihood. Hardly anyone considered the consequences of harvesting trees without replacing them. A lack of trees has led not only to the collapse of the charcoal industry, but also to scarce water and food. "In the last five decades, more than 90 percent of [Haiti's] tree cover has been lost....The resulting erosion has destroyed an estimated two-thirds of the country's fertile farmland since 1940, while its population has quadrupled."[9]

Since there isn't adequate soil on which to plant crops, or water to enable them to grow, many owners of small farms are abandoning their land. The production of crops is shrinking even more, leading to a further reduction in the food supply. (The staple diet of Haiti has always been rice, but now it cannot even grow enough rice to sustain its own people—it has to be imported from Miami.) A large portion of the population is retreating to the capital city, Port-au-Prince. But conditions are extremely crowded in the city, and people have to find whatever jobs and housing they can find; many people are even paying to share one of the limited number of beds, sleeping in shifts.

9. Tim Collie, "Haiti: 'The World Doesn't Have Any Idea How Bad This Situation Is Getting,'" *Sun-Sentinel*, December 7, 2003, http://articles.sun-sentinel.com/2003-12-07/news/sfl-haiti1dec07_1_haiti-floods-silent-emergency.

The United Nations has referred to Haiti as a "silent crisis."[10] The soil erosion runoff has killed off mangroves, coral reefs, and marine life close to the shore. To bring in a good catch, fishermen now have to go out far from the coast, but the majority of them cannot afford boats that are safe enough to do this. Additionally, floodwaters "rush down the mountains like an avalanche...Rivers and lakes are dying, and tons of mounting garbage and contaminants are breeding disease."[11]

There are some very wealthy people in Haiti who live in magnificent homes—most of which are better than the houses many Americans live in—and send their children to elite schools. But they are only about 5 percent of the population, and Haiti is the poorest nation in the Western Hemisphere and one of the poorest countries in the world. The World Bank reports that "more than 6 million out of 10.4 million (59%) Haitians live under the national poverty line of $2.44 [US] per day and over 2.5 million (24%) live under the national extreme poverty line of 1.24 [US] dollar per day.[12] The unemployment rate is very high, and the younger blacks in Haiti are especially frustrated by the lack of jobs, so many of them resort to stealing, drug dealing, kidnapping, and other gang activities.

Most of the people lack even simple medical care for diseases and injuries, many of which would be easily treatable. More children are sick than well in Haiti, and malnutrition rates are high. Some parents sell one or more of their children into slavery so they can afford to feed the rest of the family. Hungry children eat tree bark, weeds, clay, small rocks, charcoal, and even goat feces, and homeless children scavenge for food alongside dogs and other animals. Twenty percent of children die at birth, and many of them die before their fifth birthday.

Astounding Resilience

Most of Haiti's poor are hardworking people whose main goal in life is just to survive each day. They live a very simple life. The father of the family usually builds the home, or *kay pay*, himself using mud and sticks. Afterward, the women help to plaster the walls with mud. If no husband or father is present in the home, the women either have to build the *kay pay* for themselves or find somewhere else for shelter.

10. http://www.un.org/press/en/2003/sag150.doc.htm.
11. Collie, "Haiti: The World Doesn't Have Any Idea."
12. http://www.worldbank.org/en/country/haiti/overview.

In rural areas, the men spend their days gardening, pushing heavy carts, carrying loads, or trying to catch a few fish. Some of the families are able to own animals like chickens, goats, or cows. Trades are passed from father to son, such as making fishing nets or sewing garments, and both men and women in Haiti develop sewing skills. Whenever they have free time, the men talk with the other men of the village, play with their children, or have a game of dominoes.

Some of the women compare themselves to "donkeys" or "pack mules" because of the work they need to do to keep themselves and their families going. Besides the many tasks involved in taking care of their families, they carry heavy loads on their heads to the market. Wherever they are able to find a source of water, they use it as a chance to wash clothes, take a bath, or catch up on neighborhood gossip with other women who have gathered there.

Every day, these poor families face the task of finding clean water and carrying it home in buckets. Many of the children help out by walking long distances to get the water from a riverbed or from a public well. They carry their heavy buckets home on their heads, often needing to make several trips back and forth to collect enough water for the day. When they aren't doing chores, Haitian children from poor families make games or toys out of anything they can find, such as sticks, discarded plastic water bottles, or even the rusty rim of an old bicycle tire. Their opportunities for education are extremely limited, if they exist at all.

But the Haitian people continually amaze Bobby and me with their resilience and their ingenuity when facing difficulties. We don't know where they find the reserves to stay alive and keep going. They are also remarkably philosophical about life, having a proverb for any situation they may find themselves in. But they constantly worry about how to find food for themselves and their children, and they live according to many superstitions. Many mountain people believe that a mother and her newborn child should stay inside their mud hut for weeks. While a new mother is permitted to bathe in a tub of water and leaves, the baby isn't given a bath for about a month. Furthermore, parents will not name their baby until months after the birth, because they don't know how long the child will live. The Haitian people are gripped by many other fears, as well, driven by the voodooism that is so prevalent throughout the country.

When we moved to Haiti—this land of mountains, adventure, political turbulence, poverty, voodoo, and precious people—we knew that the needs, as well as our calling to help meet them, were infinitely greater than we could handle. But we also knew, as the Haitian Creole proverb goes, "God says, 'Do your part, and I'll do Mine.'"

18

COUP D'ÉTAT

"The constitution is paper, bayonets are steel."
—Haitian Creole proverb

When Bobby and I moved to Haiti on July 1, 1991, we found a two-story cement block house to rent in the mountainous area of Mt. Noire. In order to get to our house by car, it was necessary to have four-wheel drive, and we especially appreciated that gift of an Isuzu Trooper! From our home, we could see the city of Port-au-Prince, especially when it was lit up at night. We thought we had rented a furnished house, but when we arrived, we found out that the owner had taken most of the furniture with him when he left. Since furniture is always very expensive in Haiti, we weren't able to replace much of it. The house had a long, winding cement staircase that went up to the second floor where the bedroom was; the stairs had no railing, and we didn't feel safe on them until the landlord eventually put up a handrail. But the house was comfortable, especially because it was cool up in the mountains and gave us some relief from the heat. Another feature was that there was a big wall around the house with a large, solid gate, which we could lock at night for security.

Then, barely three months after we arrived, when we were just starting to settle in, Haiti was seized by a coup d'état. On September 29, President Jean-Bertrand Aristide, the country's first democratically elected leader, was thrown out, replaced by a military regime. Bobby remembers, "There was no law and order, and we thought we might be killed at any time. At night, there was shooting and screaming. We were so grateful for that wall and gate at our house, because they saved us during the coup. People would get shot at night—sometimes right in front of our gate. We'd hear gunfire all around us, and we'd get scared, thinking a stray bullet was going to come through our window and hit us. During the night, we'd often jump out of bed and fall flat on the floor for fear of flying bullets. Thankfully, they never did come through our windows or walls.

"Daily life was also hazardous. Once, I was driving past a store in the town of Petionville, near Port-au-Prince, and the Lord said to me, *Go forward, go fast.* I accelerated, and just after I cleared the store, a bomb exploded, blowing up the building. Another time, Sherry was with me, and we were on our way to a large pharmacy in Port-au-Prince that made its own medicines. We wanted to buy some medicine for Sherry to use for people who came to our house seeking free medical treatment. We had almost arrived at the pharmacy—the building was right in front of us—when the Spirit of the Lord told me, *Turn right—right now.* I immediately turned right, and Sherry said, 'What are you doing? There's the pharmacy.' After we got about half a block down the street, the whole pharmacy blew up. We would have been right in the middle of the blast. The Lord spared our lives once again.

"A while later, I was driving by myself when a man just started shooting in my direction with a 9-mm gun. None of the bullets hit my car, and there were other cars behind me, so I kept going. But when I drove past the man, he fired again; I was so close to him that I saw the flame come out of his pistol as the bullet left. I was terrified; I could have been shot in the head, but the bullet didn't hit me.

"One day, Sherry and I heard an announcement on the radio telling people that if they saw any white people in the area where we lived, they were to kill them! We were about the only white people in our area, but thankfully, nobody tried to kill us. We had been kind to the Haitian people, and they knew we were there to help.

"Some Haitians who were opposed to the regime would often set up roadblocks made of piles of burning tires. They'd wear their red voodoo *mouchouas,* or scarves, tied around their foreheads, and they'd be armed with machetes and knives. Using those barricades, they kept anyone from passing through; it was very hard for people to go anywhere, and it hindered Sherry and me from getting out to minister to people. Even worse, Haitians would sometimes use flaming tires as a form of execution. They would pile up tires and then put somebody inside them and set the tires on fire, burning the person alive. They called it 'necklacing.'"

Desperate Times

In response to the coup d'état, the United States government initiated sanctions against the regime, followed by a trade embargo, which affected the whole country. Eventually, the UN authorized international sanctions against Haiti. The sanctions and embargo lasted for three years, and goods and services quickly became scarce. Bobby remembers, "I would have to take our Isuzu and sit in long gasoline lines where the row of cars would extend for miles along the side on the road. I would sleep off and on in the car as I inched my way to the gas station. When I finally got there, I would find myself in the middle of a swirl of hundreds of cars, trucks, and motorcycles coming from every direction, trying to get to one little pump for gas. All the Haitian drivers would be yelling and fighting with each other, cutting in line, or bribing the gas station attendant to get special treatment. It was a nightmare."

Because of the gas crisis, some Haitians would smuggle in gas by boat from the Dominican Republic and then sell it for a high price on the black market. Other Haitians would make money by selling imitation gas. They would combine a small portion of gas with avocado, and it would look just like gasoline inside the clear plastic gallon containers they sold on the streets. However, they would have to keep shaking the jugs to keep the mixture from settling at the bottom and giving away their scam. If anyone used this "gasoline" in a vehicle, it would ruin their engine, so Bobby and I would always beware of any sellers who were constantly shaking their containers!

Soon, all the gas stations in Haiti closed because the gas reserves ran out and nothing could be shipped in commercially. The nation's banks began to close, and almost all the businesses suffered; many stores could no longer operate. We had only recently established Love A Child as a resident humanitarian organization in Haiti, but amazingly, God gave us favor with the Haitian government throughout the embargo. They gave us permission to pick up a monthly gas allotment; we could get two drums of diesel fuel and a drum of gasoline from a US government ship that came in to aid humanitarian workers. But gas became so rare among the people that sometimes our vehicle would be the only one on the road as we traveled to do ministry work or pick up supplies. To protect our limited gasoline reserves, we had to keep our drums of fuel in a pen with a Rottweiler dog to prevent it from being stolen!

Bobby and I were also amazed that the Haitian government permitted us to have a small amount of money wired in, while most other organizations weren't allowed to do this. We couldn't bring in much money, and we soon found ourselves in severe financial need, but we wouldn't have survived or been able to carry on our ministry at all without that small amount of funds.

The money we arranged to have wired in came from the donations that people made to us through our radio program, which aired on a station in Clearwater, Florida. We had one staff member for Love A Child in America who worked in our one-room office in Naples, Florida. She ran the ministry for us in the States, collecting our mail and helping to coordinate the radio show.

Despite the chaos around us, we never missed doing a single radio program. We had a Walmart cassette tape recorder that we used to record our programs, and normally we would send the tapes back to the radio station in Florida by air, via FedEx or DHL. But because of the embargo, there were no planes coming from or going to the United States. So, we would have to go to the telephone company building in Petionville, which had phone booths inside. Then, we would have to stand in long lines and watch the clock so that we could get a phone booth about five minutes before we were to call in the broadcast "live from Haiti." It was a fifteen-minute program, and we had keep the door to the phone booth shut to muffle the outside noise; as a result, it would become unbearably hot in there. Meanwhile, many exasperated people would be pounding their fists on the transparent plastic door to our booth, wanting their turn to make a call! We did this every morning, Monday through Friday, throughout the embargo. We had many listeners in America who wanted to hear news about what God was doing in Haiti, especially since not much information was getting out.

Additionally, all during the years of the embargo, we had virtually no electricity, and we lived mainly by candlelight. Often, Bobby and I would have to go somewhere early in the morning before the sun was up. I always wanted to look my best, so I figured out how to put on my makeup by candlelight while balancing a flashlight between my chin and my shoulder. It worked well until one morning when I got too close to the candle and almost caught my hair on fire! We did have a small generator, so once a week I would have the luxury of firing up the generator after I had washed my hair so I could run an electrical cord upstairs to use my blow-dryer.

Once in a while, we were able to buy some propane that was brought in from the Dominican Republic, but most of our cooking was done over charcoal. Due to the embargo, there wasn't much food available from the few stores that did remain open, and most of it was smuggled in from Jamaica. But we were able to buy beans and rice locally from street vendors, so we ate a lot of beans and rice in those days!

Every night, we would sit on our patio by candlelight and listen to the Voice of America broadcast on our battery-operated radio. It was the only program we could get, and it allowed us to keep informed a little bit about what was happening in the rest of the world—and sometimes even in Haiti.

The Cost of Taking Up the Cross

It was nerve-racking to live through the coup and the embargo, but God told us, *Just keep on working here. Keep on going for Me.* So, even though the crisis continued from year to year, we stayed and kept up our ministry work as best we could. In the midst of all this, Bobby and I were trying to cope with the normal adjustments that come with moving away from the familiarity of home and living in a new country. Even though we had previously gone on many missions trips to Haiti, we were still absorbing the language and the culture, and we had a large learning curve. Just learning how to navigate a vehicle up and down steep Mt. Noire and other mountainous regions in Haiti was often a life-and-death experience!

But there was something even more difficult than adjusting to the differences in culture and environment. Although I had wanted to move to Haiti and had no doubts about it even afterward, it was very hard for me to move away from my mother, our two grown children, and our close friends—and even the security of living in the United States—so I struggled with feelings of regret and loss.

Those feelings didn't go away after the first few months or even the first year. All through the years, we have continued to miss being around our children, Jonathan and Julie—and later, our grandchildren. We would return to America periodically, but only after having been absent for many birthday celebrations, special get-togethers, Thanksgivings, and Christmases. As my mother aged, whenever we came back to the States for a visit, she would say, "I wish I could keep you here." That would tear at my heart. But my mother knew that our calling to Haiti was in our hearts and on our shoulders. We would be able to visit her for only a few days at a time because of our ongoing responsibilities in Haiti, and when we left, she would stand on the porch and wave good-bye to us as we drove away. I would look back at her through the rearview mirror and wonder, *Will I ever see her again?*

No one knows the number of times I have walked the floor at our home in Haiti with tears running down my face, feeling guilty because we missed our grandchild's birthday or because we couldn't be with our daughter who was sick or because I could envision my mother standing at the door watching us leave, or I was imagining her sitting at home, longing for the next time we would come back to visit her. Jesus said, *"If any man will come after me, let him deny himself, and **take up his cross daily**, and follow me."*[13] Bobby and I have been missionaries for almost twenty-five years now, and I believe the greatest sacrifices missionaries make are those that require them to be separated from their family members.

Separation is one of the costs of the cross, but we are so thankful that both of our children have always told us, "Put God first." They have always let us know that they are proud of us. And even though the sacrifices were great, they were constantly willing to let us obey the Lord before anything else. And God has always taken care of our children, our grandchildren, and all our loved ones.

In the end, our first priority was to be where our heavenly Father had sent us. No matter how strong the pull toward family and home, once we "put our hands to the plough" and made the decision to move to Haiti, we have never looked back.[14]

---

13. Luke 9:23.
14. See Luke 9:62.

19

MILK FOR THE CHILDREN

"What the ant has, she gives to her babies."
—Haitian Creole proverb

When we first arrived in Haiti, we struggled with having enough money just to eat and stay alive in a country where things were in a desperate state politically, socially, and economically. (As Bobby likes to say, "We were as poor as Job's cat!") But God wanted to expand our outlook and broaden our faith.

Bobby explains, "One day, while we were driving down the road, Sherry and I were talking about how God seemed to be blessing everyone but us. We felt that good things—namely, money—hardly ever came our way. (We didn't even have the funds to buy a new door for our orphanage refrigerator, which had rusted and fallen off a year earlier. The caregivers at the orphanage were using an ice chest for the perishable food and the refrigerator shelves as a pantry!) But we were about to be reminded of a great truth—one that applies to any believer: If God has called you to something, don't give up. No matter how hard it is, keep on going, because He's got a blessing for you!

"That day, the Spirit of the Lord told me, *Go buy a bag of powdered milk for fifty dollars, and give it to all the children in your neighborhood.* Fifty dollars was a lot of money for us, and it took about a month to save it up. After we finally had the full amount, Satan whispered to me, *You'd better keep that fifty dollars. Don't spend it on powdered milk.* I ignored him and bought a large sack of powdered milk and gave it out to the children, and they just loved it! All Haitians seem to love powdered milk, and it's actually very expensive there now. But the children would be so hungry that, many times, they wouldn't even wait to mix the powdered milk with water but would start eating it raw!"

Divine Provision Broke Loose

Bobby continues, "After we gave away that first bag of milk, it was as if divine provision broke loose in heaven. Almost immediately, somebody in America got in touch with us by telephone and said, 'I'm supposed to buy you a whole container of powdered milk and pay to transport it there.' So, they sent a large container of powdered milk, and we gave that away to the children, too. Then two more people sent big containers of powdered milk, paying for it themselves. Following this, money came in from somewhere in Europe for additional powdered milk. The more powdered milk we received, the more we gave away, and the more we gave away, the more powdered milk we got back from God. We got so much milk that it actually became too much for us to handle, and I finally had to say, 'Stop!'

"But giving away that fifty-dollar bag of powdered milk didn't just multiply into many containers of powdered milk. It also broke open other heavenly provision, providing us with more opportunities to feed the poor. Once, somebody shipped us a forty-foot container of salted fish—forty thousand pounds of it—to give out. When it arrived, the government of Haiti told us, 'We need this fish for our army.' They wanted to pay us three dollars a pound for it, which would have made us a lot of money, but we wouldn't do it. They fought us over that fish, but we won, and we gave the fish out to the poor. We believe that if we had sold the fish and kept the money, God would not have blessed Love A Child and made it what it is today."

Taking in Our First Orphans

Some years before we moved to Haiti, we'd started a church and a small Christian school in the village of Petit Desdunes, Haiti, which the people called "Babylon" because it was so wild (we'll let you know the reason for that later!). The schoolteacher in that village told me about a widowed mother of four who was dying, and whose children were starving, and he asked me to deliver some medicine to her. I'm not a nurse, but I'd organized teams for the mobile clinics we'd taken into Haiti, and I was treating people for minor medical needs at our house in Mt. Noire, so I was determined to do anything I could to help this woman. When I went to see her, she was lying on the floor of her tiny mud hut, which was probably no bigger than most bathrooms in America. I gave her every antibiotic I could think of, and I prayed for her.

My heart sank when the medicine didn't help, and I didn't know what else to do. I went back a couple of days later and knelt beside this dying woman whose four children were slowly wasting away, the oldest of which was probably eleven and the youngest of which was four. She pulled me toward her and said, in Creole, "When I die, I want you to promise me you're going to take care of my children."

What else do you say to a woman on the verge of death who makes such a request? You answer, "Yes, of course I'm going to take care of them." She died about a week later, and when I heard the news, I went to Bobby and said, "Honey, we are going to take in those four children from Babylon whose mother just died."

Bobby got kind of upset about that plan...well, actually, he got mad! He told me, "Sherry, we have two children who are grown and gone! We waited all this time until they were grown up so we could work together even more for the Lord. Now you want to take in four children to raise? Are you out of your mind?"

He went on, "I was raised by a woman who never loved me—and I could feel it. If we take in these children and raise them but don't treat them like they are our own kids, they will know it. And I don't know if I could ever love them like we love our own children. We have to love them like they are our flesh and blood, and I don't know if I have that kind of love."

There wasn't really anything more I could say at that point. But when we went back to Babylon to see about making some kind of arrangements for them, the whole village was standing there with the children, waiting for us. The two youngest were really bad off. The four-year-old girl weighed about sixteen pounds and had the telltale red hair of malnutrition and starvation. The villagers told us emphatically, "You said you were going to take them. If you don't, they're going to die, and it will be your fault." I had been thinking of trying to give the local pastor money so that he could care for the children, but now they were telling us that we had to take the children home with us.

We put the children in our Isuzu Trooper and headed back, not knowing what we were going to do with them. It would be too cold for them in the mountains where we lived. Haitians get cold in temperatures that most Americans would consider very warm. Our house was about four hours from the children's village, and there was a big difference in temperature between the two areas. We lived high enough in the mountains that clouds would pass through our windows, and many days, we would wear sweaters in the house. The children could develop pneumonia, especially with their fragile health.

Bobby and I knew a Haitian pastor in a warmer area who had free space on the top floor of his church, so we rented a room there and hired a woman to look after the children until we could figure out more permanent arrangements. They needed a lot of care because their health was so bad. The doctor told us it would be a waste of time to keep the younger girls because they were going to die anyway, and we would be stuck with their funeral costs. But we refused to give up on them, and we nursed them back to life.

Well, it's amazing how love can grow! When you offer someone love in obedience to the Lord, He gives you more love. And that was God's plan for our lives with these orphaned children. He filled Bobby and me with a tremendous love for them that has only gotten stronger and stronger through the years.

The names of the two older children were Liberty and Sheline, and the younger ones were Julianne and Jonise. Because we were still learning the Haitian culture and language and weren't able to communicate well with the children, we didn't find out until later that all of them—but Julianne in particular—were afraid that we would *eat* them, because they had heard rumors that if a white person got a Haitian alone, they would eat them alive. The adults from the children's village knew us, because we had built the church and the school there, so they didn't believe that myth, but the children did. Imagine losing first your father and then your mother, only to be taken away from your village by strangers that you thought might eat you at any moment?

After a little while, one of the people who worked at our house in Mt. Noire found us a house to rent, and we moved the children and their caregiver there. A short time later, we took in four more children whose mother had died. Then we took in two more children, followed by more children, and our first orphanage was born. And we've continued to care for precious orphaned, abandoned, handicapped, and former *Restavek* slave children in Haiti ever since.

20

ALL IN A DAY'S WORK!

"The crab that walks too far falls into the pot."
—Haitian Creole proverb

There are parts of Haiti that are absolutely beautiful, especially in areas where the wealthy live. The sunlit mountain peaks and well-kept valleys with attractive homes remind me of photos you'd see in *National Geographic* magazine. But the everyday world of missions work in Haiti isn't like that—it is one of mud-and-stick huts where mosquitoes, roaches, rats, bats, tarantulas, and snakes are all around; it is also one in which people's superstitions cause them to seal themselves in their huts out of fear; and it is one in which you have to battle steep mountain passes and rocky, muddy terrain just to get to your destination.

Roaches, Rats, and "Lougarous"

In the early days of our missions trips to Haiti, when Bobby and I would travel to various villages with our medical teams, we would often stay in churches, schools, or other cement block buildings; but when there were no buildings available, we would stay in mud huts. (We still do this today whenever we go out to the provinces or up on the mountains in Haiti to do our medical clinics or other projects.)

When we stayed in the mud huts, there would sometimes be so many roaches crawling around that the walls looked like they were moving. But I was more concerned about the rats, and I always slept with my hand on my flashlight—a practice I continue to this day. I wanted to be able to shine my flashlight to at least *see* where the rats were and to let them see me, hoping they would go away, but most of them didn't! Bobby and I soon got used to the fact that there were rats *inside* the huts (a reminder of Bobby's rat shack experience in Florida!). Besides, we were always so tired at night after doing the mobile clinics that, most times, we would immediately fall into a deep sleep until morning—oblivious to the roaches, the rats, and everything else.

One of my good friends and "partners in crime" in Haiti is Donna Bryce, who serves on Love A Child's board of directors. Bobby and I first met Donna and her husband, Eldon, when we both lived in Mt. Noire. When we learned that the Bryces had been in Haiti since 1983 and that through their Feed a Child ministry they conducted mobile clinics similar to the ones we were doing, Donna and I started swapping stories of our various clinic adventures.

I told her that during the early days, when Bobby had to be in the States to do an evangelistic crusade, I would hold mobile clinics with my friend Sandy Stafford, who was a nurse. Sandy and I had to pack our own food, which we kept in our suitcases along with our medicines. Each night, the rats would come in and get into anything they could, and the noises would begin—tearing, crunching, chewing, and clicking as they ran up and down the walls. I would usually shine my flashlight, see the rats, and say, "Sandy, it's just rats. They only sound loud, like they're chewing into a microphone. Just go to sleep, and they will eat and leave!"

When I told Donna how I'd said to Sandy, "It's just rats," she told me a story about a time when she and a friend were staying in a mud hut while they conducted a clinic. In the middle of the night, Donna's friend woke her up and said, "Something's biting my feet!" Donna was used to dealing with various insects on those trips, so she drowsily said, "Oh, it's just mosquitoes. Give them a squirt of bug spray and go back to sleep."

In the morning, when Donna's friend woke up and pulled back her sheet, she saw that her toes were bloody. It wasn't any mosquito—a rat had been biting her! Donna said she always felt bad about telling her friend to just squirt some bug spray and go back to sleep!

My other "partner in crime" is my good friend Evie Ostrander. She and her husband, Mark, are the senior pastors of Mission Church in Palm Bay, Florida, and they are also on Love A Child's board of directors. Evie often accompanied me on our mobile clinics and still does to this day. But the first time Evie and some others from their church came on one of our medical clinic trips, we went to La Gonave Island—the same place we had to travel three hours by boat to get to, after being hoisted into a vessel by a Haitian boatman! Since Evie was new to Haiti, Mark felt that his beloved wife should carry a knife with her on the trip, just in case something should happen.

All of us women on the team slept on the floor of a local church in our sleeping bags. One night, Evie was sleeping next to a member of her church named Judy who had her hair in a bun with a hairnet pulled over it. Some rats made their way into the church and started crawling around. Rats usually like to climb up to the wooden rafters of these church buildings and scurry back and forth as they scavenge for food and materials for their nests. That night, one of the rats was making its way across the top of an old wooden rafter when it lost its footing and fell down—right onto Judy's hairnet! Judy screamed, Evie woke up and instinctively grabbed for her knife, and the rat got tangled in Judy's hairnet. There was a lot more screaming in the dark as Judy tried to get the rat out of her hair, wriggle out of her sleeping bag, and avoid getting sliced by a wildly waving knife, all at the same time. Finally, we got the flashlights on, and thankfully everyone was fine—except for the rat.

The real creatures out in the field are bad enough, but the imaginary ones can make life pretty uncomfortable, too. The Haitians are afraid of a mythical creature called a *lougarou*—part werewolf, part bird—flying inside their hut at night and killing them, carrying off their baby and murdering it, or causing some other type of great harm. The Haitians like to sleep in hot temperatures anyway, but to guard against lougarous, they close up every wooden window tightly, stuff old rags into every crack, cover every opening, and keep the door closed, even if it's 110 degrees inside!

The first time Sandy and I had to spend the night inside a mud hut in the village of Babylon, we experienced this practice firsthand. Every gap in the hut had been sealed, so there was virtually no ventilation, and it was extremely hot inside, making it almost impossible to sleep. If we opened our door to let in some cool air, someone would inevitably come along and shut it to protect us from lougarous! Likewise, whenever Bobby and I would stay overnight in one of the bedrooms of the rented house we used for our orphan home, the Haitian caregivers would close every window and door at night; the air would be stifling, so that we would be dripping with sweat by morning. To this day, almost every home in Haiti is completely shut up at night for fear that the family will be attacked by a lougarou.

Even most Haitian Christians have a hard time shaking off this superstition. One time, mischievous Bobby decided he would play a practical joke on the Haitian director of our orphanage. He remembers, "The man who ran our first orphanage loved God and taught the Scriptures well; he could quote one Scripture after another. But he still believed in lougarous. Many Haitians believe that certain people can turn into this creature and that some animals—such as dogs, cats, or birds—are in fact lougarous in disguise, and you have to watch out for them. One Thanksgiving, Sherry and I thought we would have a traditional American meal of turkey with all the fixings. Turkeys are not plentiful in Haiti, but I found a place where they were selling them, and I was able to buy a large, live turkey. Our orphanage director had never seen a turkey before, so I decided to tease him, telling him that if he heard the bird making an unusual noise in its throat, he'd better run for his life, because that meant it was a lougarou. I put the turkey in the yard, knowing that it was going to gobble; and when it did, that poor guy just ran. He wanted to move all the kids out of the orphanage, and he refused to eat that turkey at our Thanksgiving meal!"

Many radio stations in Haiti broadcast stories about lougarous. In fact, on some of the Christian stations, people give testimonies about how the Lord "delivered them" from lougarous. (Well, it's almost got us believing in lougarous!)

Mountains, Mules, and Mud

Bobby and I had many opportunities to deal with roaches, rats, and other critters, as well as the people's fears of imaginary creatures and of voodooism, because we were continually traveling deep into the remote areas of Haiti's mountains. We would build churches and Christian schools in various places in the interior of the country—like Greffin, Savaan Pit, Savaan Rock, Covant, Demesseau, and many others—just as we do today. Journeying to these remote regions or getting around once you arrived there was a challenge at best, and the trips could be hazardous. Often, walking or traveling by mule or donkey was the only way to get to an area.

Mules are excellent animals for traveling on narrow mountain paths because they can safely put one hoof in front of the other, never slipping. Of course, that doesn't mean that riding on them is fail-safe! Most of the saddles used in Haiti were designed for animals that are bred in the United States or elsewhere, but the mules in Haiti are skinnier, so the saddles don't fit them well. Besides that, many Haitians don't treat their animals well, so their mules are not gentle. Whenever a mule is carrying a load and thinks that load is shifting, it will either stop in its tracks—or kick. And if you're on its back and it feels the load shifting, it will want to throw you off. Just to saddle these animals, the Haitians will pull one of their legs up and tie it, thinking that they won't be able to kick if they have the use of only three of their legs. But Bobby and I are witnesses that they can stand on two of their legs, with one leg tied up, and kick with the fourth one. They seem to be built to kick sideways, backwards—any way!

Bobby and I have had many mishaps while riding mules and donkeys. One time, I was thrown off a donkey toward the edge of a mountain, but the Haitians who were with us grabbed me and caught me, saving my life. Another time, Bobby fell off a mule and landed on a pile of rocks, and we thought he'd been severely injured. He remembers, "I didn't realize that my saddle was dry-rotted, and as I was going up the mountain, the straps broke, and I fell backwards off that mule right onto my head. I had actually woken up that morning with a bad headache, but strangely, when I got up and shook myself, my headache was gone, and I felt great!"

Often, we'd travel to such distances that we would need to take our four-wheel-drive truck or some other vehicle. Because of the rugged terrain or the poor condition of our truck—or both—we were always breaking down in the middle of nowhere or getting stuck in the mud. One time, when Bobby wasn't with me, I was driving the truck with a Haitian interpreter in the general area of Savaan Pit, which is far up in the mountains. Unfortunately, the tires on our truck were bald to begin with, and I got a flat, so I began to back the truck down the mountain. Suddenly, the wheels started sliding, and the back wheels went right off the side of the mountain, so the truck was just dangling there. I was so scared that I dug my fingernails into my hands until they were almost bleeding. I hardly dared to breathe because I felt like if I moved even a little bit, the truck would go over the side. We would be killed, and our families might never know what happened to us.

I urged our interpreter, "Don't get out; don't move. We've just got to figure out what we're going to do." I started praying, but before I could think of anything to do, I felt something behind us pushing us. My back tires felt like they had grip, so I put my foot on the gas, and then something suddenly gave us a push, and I started to drive back up the mountain path. I turned my head to see who had helped to push us out, because I wanted to thank them and give them a tip, but there was nobody in sight. We really felt that God's angels had pushed us back onto the mountain road to safety.

A similar thing happened to Bobby and our friend Mark Ostrander. They were driving in the Isuzu from the villages of Greffin and Savaan Pit.

The rest of the team had already gone ahead farther up the hill on foot and was waiting for them under a tarp by the side of the road. Bobby remembers, "It was dark, and it was pouring down rain, which is very dangerous on those narrow dirt roads on the mountains. Everything turns to mud, and it has a consistency just like butter that you can sink right down into. When we went around a corner, the Isuzu suddenly started to slide sideways, and the car was heading off the cliff—driver's side first. There were no guardrails, and the drop was five thousand feet, straight down. I yelled, 'Mark, open the door, and get out *now*!' I was thinking that I could slide over and follow him out the passenger side before the car went off the cliff. Mark hurried out and immediately slid in the mud toward the back of the car, as the vehicle kept moving toward the edge of the cliff.

"Just as the car got to the edge, a group of about thirty Haitian men suddenly appeared out of nowhere. When it rains in Haiti, nobody goes outside, because Haitians easily catch cold; they could get very sick and even die. But that day, even though it was pouring down rain, all these men appeared, surrounded the Isuzu, pushed it up and forward about thirty feet to get me out of danger, and then disappeared. Mark slogged his way up the muddy road, jumped in the car, looked at me, and said, 'Did you see that?' Stunned, I answered, 'Yes.' We sat in silence for a minute, and then we both said, at the same time, 'Angels!'"

Another time, the truck carrying Bobby and me, the Ostranders, and the rest of our team was stuck in the middle of nowhere in the mountains. We had taken an old truck that didn't have four-wheel drive, and we thought we would have to walk all the way back down out of the mountains to get home. Suddenly, a land cruiser pulled up, and out jumped two guys wearing black jackets and gold chains and carrying shotguns. They came walking up to us, looking like killers, and we were petrified!

Then one of them said, "Looks like you're going to need some help." It turned out that they were actually rich business owners, and they had just been out shooting birds! They didn't say anything else to us; they simply walked back to their cruiser and got out the biggest chain I'd ever seen. Then they hooked our old truck onto their brand-new cruiser and pulled us several miles down the mountain, all the way to where the land was flat. After we thanked them, they just drove off. It was as if God sent the mostly unlikely people to help us. Who would tie our junky truck to their brand-new cruiser and drag us over rough terrain for several miles to a safe spot? Nobody but someone God would send.

Haitian Ingenuity

It took a while for Bobby and me to get adjusted to living and traveling in the mountains, but the Haitians are used to it, and they have an amazing ability to work around difficult situations. One time, I had to go far up in the mountains to the village of Savaan Pit, and Bobby wasn't with me. I was using our four-wheel-drive truck, and I took an interpreter with me, but I should have known better than to go because, again, the tires on our truck were bad. To get to Savaan Pit, you first have to drive across a wide stream that's formed from water coming down off the mountain and flowing into the valley. After that, you have to have enough momentum to start climbing up the mountain slope. Once you start, you can't stop at all, or you won't make it; you have to zigzag up the steep mountain passages until you reach the top.

That day, after successfully crossing the river, I began to take the first hairpin turn when I got a flat tire, and I had to back down to the foot of the mountain. I didn't have a spare tire, but my Haitian interpreter had an alternative plan. After he removed the flat tire, he placed a flat piece of stick into the hole. Then he took a plastic cup, lit it, and melted the plastic over the hole. I had never seen anyone repair a tire that way before. I happened to have with me a small pump for a bicycle tire, so he used that to pump the tire back up again. We started out once more and made it through that first curve and then all the way to Savaan Pit. Unfortunately, the ride back wasn't as smooth—it took us hours to get home. My tires kept blowing out, one after another, and I had a total of *nine* flat tires that day. But my interpreter calmly kept repairing them the same way he had the first one.

Another time, Bobby and I went with Mark and Evie Ostrander in our large truck to the mountain church in Greffin, which was situated near a slope at the top of the mountain. We wanted to tape our television program there, reporting on what God was doing in people's lives in the area. Bobby was driving, and as he got close to the church, the truck started to slide down the dirt slope on its left wheels, causing the truck to tilt. We all jumped out on the right side. We tried to push the truck back up again, but it kept slowly sliding down the side of the mountain. We just could not figure out any way to get the truck back up again.

Finally, Bobby said, "Well, we have to go in and tape our TV program." Then the pastor of the church came out with an old piece of rope and said, "We can get it out for you." Bobby told him, "Pastor, thank you, but you don't have a truck, and you don't understand how they work. This is bigger than you are." He replied, "Okay."

We went inside and recorded our TV program as quickly as we could because we knew we'd have to deal with the truck situation afterward. We didn't know it, but as soon as we had gone inside, the pastor had told the Haitians to "do their own thing"! By the time we finished the program and went outside again, our truck was parked right in front of the church, waiting for us! We couldn't believe it.

While we had been stumped, the Haitians had known exactly what to do. Beside each tire on the right-hand side, opposite the slope, they had dug a trench. Then they'd taken the rope and tied one side of it around the right door handles, and the other side around the trunk of a palm tree. Several of the Haitians had jumped up and down on top of the bumper, and every time they did, the people holding the rope would shimmy the truck to try to scoot the right wheels in those slots. They had worked and worked at it until they'd finally gotten them in. When the two tires landed in the places where they'd dug, all the tires were on an even plane, and someone just got in the car and drove it over to the church.

The Haitians have rescued Bobby and me from some other seemingly impossible situations. Bobby says, "The Haitians can figure out ways of doing things that most other people never could. One day, when we were in Babylon, it was so muddy that people were slipping and sliding everywhere. Our truck got stuck in the mud up to the axels, and I thought, *We're never going to get out of here*. Other big trucks tried to pull us out, but it didn't work. It was so bad that many of the people who tried to help us got stuck, too.

"Then these Haitian guys without any shirts on came up to us and said, 'We're professional mud people. We'll get you out—for a little bit of money.' I told them, 'If you can get us out, I can say that I've seen it all, because it's impossible.' Then we watched them go to work using their hands and pieces of wood as they dug in the mud and made ditches. The next thing I knew, they'd gotten the truck out."

The Haitians have a word called *degaje*, which refers to getting yourself out of a bad situation. If someone needs money or anything else, they'll tell him, "Oh, go degaje," meaning, "Go figure it out," or "Go get yourself out of the situation." And they go and do it!

It's all in a day's work in the remarkable land of Haiti.

21

VOODOO VERSUS THE POWER OF JESUS' BLOOD

"If you want to catch a wild horse, find a tight corral."
—Haitian Creole proverb

Until we moved to Haiti, Bobby and I never really understood the evil side of the spiritual world. We still don't fully understand it, but we know a lot more about it now than when we first arrived. Haitians are very superstitious because voodoo is an integral part of their culture. The witch doctors and others who practice voodoo wield a lot of power, using their positions of influence and their fear tactics to extort money from people. The Haitians are terrified of the witch doctors because they fear having a spell cast on them that would bring them bad fortune, sickness, or even death. At its essence, voodooism is one of the evil methods Satan uses to steal, kill, and destroy the people of this world.[15]

When Haitians become Christians, they love God, but as we mentioned earlier, they often have a hard time getting over their voodoo superstitions, just like the director of our first orphanage did. They don't participate in voodoo practices themselves, but they're still afraid of the witch doctors and anyone else who uses voodoo. And most of them believe that if a person dies, it's because someone practiced voodoo on them. We try to show them that they don't need to be afraid of the witch doctors or of voodoo in general but to trust in Jesus Christ and the power of His blood to protect them from all evil.

---

15. See John 10:10.

Through the years, voodoo people have attempted to put spells on Bobby and me, and they still try to do this all the time. Recently, I was driving through the gate of our ministry compound to do some errands when, right outside the entrance, I saw something that looked like a car battery. I got out and looked at it and saw that it was actually a miniature coffin. It had been set on fire, so smoke was coming from it, but there was a light drizzle of rain that day so the fire hadn't gotten very big; inside were a piece of a cow's leg, eggshells, and some red strings—which are often used in voodoo ceremonies. I saw some Haitians standing nearby, staring at the coffin, but nobody would come near it. Haitians won't ever cross over something like that or even go around it.

This voodoo box was more of an annoyance to me than anything else. It was right in my path, and I wanted to get on with my plans for the day. But I also wanted to demonstrate to the Haitians that they had nothing to fear, so I said, "Oh my goodness, another stupid voodoo thing." I kicked it with my foot to put the fire out, and then I reached down and picked up the cow's leg and threw it into a nearby ditch. Casually, I said, "Oh, voodoo string? Isn't that just scary!" I picked up the string and tossed it aside. Then I said, "You're going to try to frighten me with a tiny coffin?" and I threw the box to the side, too. All the Haitians just stared at me as if they were thinking, *I can't believe she actually touched it!*

Drums on the Mountain

The practice of voodoo was still pretty new to Bobby and me when we first moved to Haiti, so we decided to record an actual voodoo ceremony one night. Bobby explains, "I woke Sherry up at about one o'clock because I heard a voodoo service going on down at the base of the mountain on the opposite side. We could hear the voodoo drums beating because the sound carried so well. I told her, 'Let's take our tape recorder and go down there. This would make a really good radio show. Wouldn't it be interesting for people to hear all those voodoo drums and all that stuff? I could describe it for them like a news correspondent.'

"The moon was out, so it was bright enough to see the path ahead of us; but we had to be real careful walking around because someone might see us and try to harm us, so we moved along very quietly. It would take about twenty minutes for us to wind our way to the bottom of the mountain, so we began taping the program as we went. I started out with something like, 'Yeah, brothers and sisters, it's the middle of the night, and we're walking down the mountain to a voodoo ceremony'—you could clearly hear the voo-doo drums in the background!

"On our way, we stopped by the home of our friends Donna and Eldon Bryce and asked if they wanted to come with us to tape the voodoo service. They said, 'No, not tonight...it's a little rainy for us—ha!' Of course, we didn't blame them one bit for not wanting to come, but somehow that didn't stop us! Sherry and I continued on, and when we got to the site of the voo-doo service, we hid behind a row of bushes. We saw three human skulls on a table, and the Haitians were in a frenzy, doing all kinds of dances. They killed a goat and were drinking blood and doing all these other things, and I was talking really low into our tape recorder, telling the listeners all about it.

"All of sudden, the witch doctor saw us and started coming toward us. For a few seconds, I kept on recording, saying, 'Uh-oh, here's the witch doctor, coming at us with a machete! We'll be back. Bye.' Then Sherry and I took off running all the way back up the mountain to our house, scared out of our wits. The witch doctor never did follow us; I guess he was too busy with the voodoo service. But we decided to send in the tape ending with my last comment about the witch doctor coming after us. We just let the people hang in suspense until the next program!"

Demonic "Snakes"

Although we enjoyed doing that radio program (in between being petri-fied), we knew voodooism was serious business. Whenever we minister the gospel in Haiti, we fight against evil spirits that want to keep the message of Jesus Christ from reaching people. Bobby remembers one of our early en-counters with a demonic manifestation. "The very first church we built was in Wysek," he says. "I was doing a series of meetings there, and each night, for three nights, when I would stand up to preach, three Haitian men who were sitting in the back would fall down on their stomachs with their arms at their backs and their legs straight, and then they would literally slither like snakes up to the platform. I don't know how they did it; I'd never seen anything like it before, and it spooked me. Of course, all of us Christians would immedi-ately go over to them and start to pray for deliverance for the men.

"This would always happen at the very beginning of the meeting, so I never got to preach. The Christians would be praying out loud and trying to cast out the demons, and eventually my voice would go hoarse. Finally, we would grow tired and stop praying, and the men would just get up and walk away normally, as if nothing had happened.

"Satan's whole purpose for that manifestation was to take the focus off the Word of God and put all the focus on him. He can't stand to have any attention put on Jesus. But before the fourth meeting, the Lord taught me the meaning of the Scripture, '*Whatsoever ye shall bind on earth shall be bound in heaven: and whatsoever ye shall loose on earth shall be loosed in heaven.*'[16] God told me, *Bind that spirit tonight, even before you get to the service.* I bound the evil spirit, and that evening nothing happened; those men just sat in their seats. So, I told everybody, 'Tonight, I bound the spirit of those guys sitting back there. And now I bind that spirit again. I'm preaching the Word of God, and these men cannot crawl on this ground tonight.' And they didn't. We had bound the evil spirit, and we had loosed, or released, the Spirit of God to work. The Holy Spirit came down in a mighty way, and many people came to Christ. Then I prayed for those three men, and the demons that had possessed them cried out and left them. God set them free completely!

"So, to minister in Haiti, we had to learn the power of binding and loosing. We would bind the evil spirits and loose the Spirit of God before we arrived at a church, so the devil was already tied up and couldn't disrupt our meetings. We also learned that it's better to take demon-possessed people outside of a meeting to minister to them, rather than trying to cast out the demons in the middle of a service. This allows the Holy Spirit to continue to move among the people. But we had to learn that the hard way."

The Witch Doctor Who Fell into His Own Ditch

Another time, we held a series of open-air gospel meetings in Carrefour, with several thousand people in attendance. This was the same place where the woman had screamed at us, "If God is so good, why is my baby so hungry?" On the final night of meetings, Bobby was directly confronted by demonic forces. "I had just stood up to preach," he remembers, "when a witch doctor that everyone was terrified of came up and told me, 'You're not going to preach tonight. If you do, I'm going to put a spell on you like I did the other man.'

"Everyone at the meeting knew that the witch doctor had put a spell on a man who was a Jehovah's Witness. Jehovah's Witnesses don't believe in the

---

16. Matthew 18:18.

power of the blood of Jesus, so the man hadn't prayed for Jesus' protection. Soon, the man's whole body, including his arms and his legs, had become deformed. The witch doctor warned me, 'In three days, when you wake up, your arms and your legs will be twisted out of shape, and you'll look like a monster.' Then he threw some white powder on the platform. Everybody in Haiti is really scared of that white powder, because it means death. I told the witch doctor, 'We're covered by the blood of Jesus Christ, and you cannot touch us.' He replied, 'I'll show you. I curse your God.'

"I preached anyway, standing right on top of that powder; and everybody stared at me. But we thanked God because many people came to Christ that night. Three days later, we were scheduled to return to Carrefour to do a follow-up with the people who had been converted. On the third morning—the time when the curse was supposed to take effect—I woke up at daybreak. Being human, although I knew the Lord would protect me, the first thing I did was to look at myself closely in the mirror, and I was relieved that everything looked normal! Sherry and I then got into our Isuzu Trooper and drove over to Carrefour. When we arrived, people stared at us again; they couldn't believe that Bobby looked fine, having no deformities.

"Then the wife of the witch doctor came to us and said, 'Come to my hut!' So, the first thing we did was to follow her to go see the witch doctor. When she opened the door to their small hut, we saw the witch doctor lying on the floor. We were shocked to see that his arms and his legs were deformed, and that his whole body was twisted out of shape. Later, we remembered the Bible verse that says if your enemy digs a ditch for you, he himself will fall into it.[17]

"The witch doctor's wife pleaded with me, 'Pray for him; pray for him.' I wanted to pray for him, but I couldn't do it because God wouldn't allow me to. To this day, I don't know why; God hasn't told me very often not to pray for someone. But the Bible does say, 'Lay hands suddenly on no man, neither be partaker of other men's sins.'[18] The witch doctor may somehow have crossed over a line. So, while I normally would have started praying out loud for him, I had to turn around and walk away. The people of the village had already been shaken up when they'd seen that Sherry and I were okay, but when the witch doctor received the very curse he'd tried to put on us, everyone started

---

17. See Psalm 7:15.
18. 1 Timothy 5:22.

talking about it. Many people in that village and in that area came to know Christ after they heard what happened."

The witch doctor died shortly afterward. There is a Haitian proverb that says, "When a Haitian lies down at night, fear lies down beside him." That witch doctor had been terrorizing the people in his area for years, but this situation showed them how the power of God protects us when we love Him and are covered by the blood of Jesus.

"Ghostly" Visitation

Although we've had many experiences with the evil spiritual world during our time in Haiti, one of the earliest manifestations of demonic activity that Bobby and I dealt with was in our own home in Mt. Noire. Bobby remembers, "The house we were living in was originally built by our landlord for his wife; many people have told us she was the most beautiful woman in Haiti. When she died, her husband moved out of the house, and he later rented it to us. This man told me that his wife had been killed in a car accident, and I felt bad for him.

"We liked the house, but strange things began to happen there soon after we moved in. If we plugged in the coffeepot and then went upstairs, we would find the cord unplugged when we came down again. And Sherry would notice that things in the kitchen had been moved around from the way she had left them. She would ask me, 'Have you been in the kitchen? Did you move this? Did you do that?' I told her I hadn't moved anything around.

"During our first three years in Haiti when the embargo was going on, Sherry and I were always together at our house at night. But after the embargo was lifted and we could travel, Sherry would sometimes go to America for a week or so at a time to check on things at our office or to help her mother if she was sick. And whenever she would leave, things would *really* get strange at our house! The first night I was home alone, something woke me up. When I opened my eyes, I saw a woman in a nightgown standing by my bed, looking down at me. I could see her form, but I could also kind of see through her. She had long, coal-black hair, light skin, and long fingernails painted red. Seeing her scared me so bad that I said, 'Jesus! The blood of Jesus!' and she vanished.

"The next night, it must have been about two or three in the morning when I heard somebody coming down the hallway, making a flopping sound as they walked, as if they were wearing bedroom slippers. Our bedroom had a solid wood door, and it was completely shut, but all of a sudden, this same woman came walking right *through* the door. If that won't scare you, nothing will! I yelled and pled the blood of Jesus again, and she left. When Sherry came home, I told her all about it. She told me she'd also noticed that items in the kitchen had been changed around again in her absence. This woman came walking through the door into our bedroom four or five times, always when Sherry was away. I would always plead the blood of Jesus, and she would leave.

"There is no way to describe how terrifying those 'visitations' were. Even though the embargo was over, there was still very little electricity available to us; Sherry and I would go for days without having any electricity, and it was always very dark at our house at night. That meant I couldn't even turn on the lights afterward to make me feel better. I knew this thing was a spirit, and that I knew it looked like a woman, but I didn't really know what in the world it was. But I became determined to put an end to what was happening, and I thought, *I'm going to be ready tomorrow. I'm getting my 'demon-chaser!'*—my .357 Magnum.

That night, I got out my .357 and hid inside my closet, keeping the door open partway. Eventually, I heard the woman coming down the hallway, with those slippers flapping. I wish I could say I was super-spiritual so that I knew the Lord was by my side and I wasn't afraid of anything, but let me tell you, I couldn't have been more scared! If I'd been any more scared, I would have died. But when I heard her coming, I jumped out of the closet, thinking, *I'm going to face this thing like a man.* I flung open the bedroom door, pointed my .357 at her, and said, 'In the name of Jesus, I plead the blood of Jesus.' Of course, when I said that, she left again. I had thought that maybe she would try to attack me that night, so if for some reason she kept on coming at me, I was gonna shoot her first. It probably wouldn't have done anything, but that was my plan!

"When Sherry returned, I described what had happened. We decided to fast and to pray about it for three days, binding that spirit—and it never came back. A little while after that, I happened to be talking to a Haitian man down the street when our conversation turned to the owner of my house and how I felt bad that his wife had been killed in an automobile accident. I mentioned how people said she'd been a beautiful woman. He said, 'Yes, she was.' Then he added, 'Bobby, his wife didn't get killed in a car wreck.' I said, 'Really?' He continued, 'No, because I worked for them then as their houseboy. They were both upstairs, and they got into a fight because she found out that he had gotten another woman pregnant.'

"My Haitian neighbor told me that he had been downstairs, and this man and his wife had been at the top of that winding staircase, and he said the husband had pushed the wife off of it. Those stairs were high, and there was no railing on them at that time, and she fell to her death, breaking her skull. My neighbor had mopped up the woman's blood afterward. When I asked him what she'd been wearing at the time, he said, 'She was wearing nothing but a long nightgown—and a pair of bedroom slippers that were too big for her.'

"Fre (Brother) Dodo, a former top witch doctor who became a Christian and is now an evangelist and a friend of ours, says that Satan has 'photocopy spirits.' It could be that the enemy had wanted to make us leave Haiti, so he'd sent an evil spirit that looked like that woman to scare us away. But whatever it was—whether it was a demon that looked like the woman or whether it was somehow the woman herself in spirit form—she looked at me at times as if she was trying to talk to me. I wondered later if she was trying to tell me that she had been murdered. But I never gave her a chance to say anything because I always pled the blood of Jesus right away. Jesus' power is greater than any evil spiritual being or any attack by Satan."

"The Lord Is My Shepherd"

Our friend Fre Dodo, the former witch doctor, has a remarkable story about how he was set free from voodooism. His father had been a witch doctor, so he had become a witch doctor, too, not knowing any other way of life. At that time, his name was Ajimal, and he became a *hougan*, or a chief witch doctor; in fact, he was the personal witch doctor for "Papa Doc" Duvalier, Haiti's brutal president from 1957–1971.

Duvalier had started out as a good physician who helped the poor, but he wanted a political career, so he became involved in a lot of voodooism to try to make that happen. He used voodoo and fear tactics on people, and he was vicious against his enemies. Under Duvalier's rule, the country of Haiti was organized into seven segments; one segment was controlled by the electric company, another by the water company, and so forth. The leaders of these segments wanted to hold on to their power in the midst of a very unstable political situation, so they gave Ajimal money to put spells on them that would keep them in power. Papa Doc was concerned about maintaining his power, too, so Ajimal would go to the palace and perform all kinds of voodoo and magic for him. Every year in December, Duvalier would call Ajimal to the palace to give him and his high officials a bath in the blood of a sacrificed animal, and to perform other voodoo rituals.

As a *hougan*, Ajimal would have to sacrifice one person to the devil every year. He had a wife and six children; each year, he would offer one of his children, and during that year, the child would die. After losing all his children, he sacrificed his wife in the same way.

In the late 1980s, when he had lost his entire family, Ajimal became attracted to a beautiful young woman. He knew that she was different from other women he had known, but he didn't know that she was a Christian, and he decided he was going to make her his "woman." His plan was to control her through voodoo; he would turn her into a donkey, put a rope around her neck, and lead her away to his own village. But this young Christian woman had God's protection over her life to preserve her from the power of the enemy; every night, before she went to bed, she would quote Psalm 121, which says, *"Behold, he that keepeth Israel shall neither slumber nor sleep,"*[19] and *"The LORD shall preserve thee from all evil: he shall preserve thy soul."*[20] Even while this woman was sleeping, the Lord was awake, watching over her.

Ajimal went into her hut one night with his rope and his voodoo implements, and he went all around her bed, performing his magic. Then he lay down on the floor beside her with his rope in his hand, waiting for her to turn into a donkey. He fell asleep, and when he woke up, he saw that she hadn't yet turned into a donkey. He went around her again, repeated all his voodoo rituals, and then lay down again. As he watched her, he noticed that she slept as soundly as a baby. But as time passed, she still hadn't become a donkey! So, he did his voodoo a third time and lay down once more, but still nothing happened. He couldn't understand it!

All of a sudden, the young woman opened her eyes, saw him, and screamed, "What are you doing here in my room?" He answered, "I'm Ajimal. I came to make you a donkey to take you out with me with this rope and make you my woman." She told him, "Well, there's nothing you can do to me. There's no magic that can hurt me because I'm a Christian, and Jesus takes care of me." She quoted several Scripture verses to him about God's protection.

This young woman was the first person Ajimal had ever met who wasn't intimidated by his fear tactics and couldn't be manipulated by his magic.

---

19. Psalm 121:4.
20. Psalm 121:7.

Suddenly, he got scared and asked, "Why is your power greater than mine?" She explained to him about the power of Jesus Christ, and he said, "Well, I want to know this Jesus, and I want to become a Christian, because I need a power that is greater than mine." The young woman went and got her pastor, and they prayed for Ajimal. That night, he accepted Jesus, and he turned away from all voodoo and witchcraft. He burned everything he had, including his house, his car (in those days, if you had a car, you were very rich), and all his clothes, because he had gotten them with voodoo money. The only things he kept were the clothes on his back.

Later, the young woman fell in love with him, and they got married and had six children. She was a very strong woman, and she still is today. Fre Dodo is now in his early eighties. He preaches at our church from time to time, and we support him every month so he can continue his ministry of traveling around and telling people what God has done for him. Fre Dodo preaches a great message entitled "The Lord Is My Shepherd, I Shall Not Want," which was one of the Scripture verses his wife had quoted to him when he came to her hut that night.

Madame Jean

If you're going to defeat the work of the enemy, you have to wholeheartedly trust God and not have one foot in God's camp and another in Satan's camp. Additionally, as long as you are afraid of Satan, he will try to exert control over your life—but God's perfect love can cast out all fear.[21] We had a worker named Tinev who lived with his wife, Madame Jean, in a mud hut right next to our ministry compound. Madame Jean became sick, and Tinev asked me to go over and see what I could do to help her. When I entered their hut, she was lying on a straw mat on the floor. She was sweating and in a lot of pain, her feet were swollen, and her stomach had swelled to the point that she looked like she was nine months pregnant. In fact, at first I thought that she was pregnant. I didn't know what was wrong with her, but I knew we had to send her to the local hospital right away.

Madame Jean was in the hospital for about four days, and we took care of all her hospital bills. The staff at the hospital did tests and took X-rays, but they sent her home because they couldn't find anything that was causing her symptoms. Her husband gave her more medicine, but she continued to be sick. From time to time, he would come to me, telling me that his wife was

---

21. See 1 John 4:18.

dying and asking me to please come quick and do something. I sent her to several different hospitals to see if anyone could help, but no one could.

Finally, I realized that I needed to look elsewhere for answers. In the early days of our ministry, one of the first students at our school in the village of Babylon was a boy named Wilson Barthelemy, whose nickname was Nelio. At that time, we never dreamed that one day he'd become our Haitian director for Love A Child, a position he still holds today. Nelio is a wonderful gift to us who came out of our school and ministry in Babylon, and he is one of the best guys you could ever meet.

Nelio had begun working with us by the time Madame Jean was ill, and he had often been able to give us insight into problems the Haitian people were having, so I explained to him about this woman's illness, saying, "Every time I send her to the hospital, they can't find anything wrong with her." He replied, "Sherry, it's voodoo. No matter where you send her, they won't be able to do anything for her." I have to admit, that answer was hard for me to accept. I went back to see Madame Jean again and got down on my knees next to where she was lying and took her head in my hands so I could talk to her and try to find out something that would explain why she was sick. I happened to look toward her feet and noticed that there were two red cords tied around her ankles.

When I saw those voodoo strings, I got very angry, and I said, "Oh, Madame Jean, I've spent all my money on you, sending you to the hospital and paying for your X-rays, and you have been going to the witch doctor, haven't you? *Haven't you?*" She said, "Yes." I still had her head in my hands, and I was so mad at her that I thumped her head on the ground a few times as I said, "Well, let me tell you what's going to happen to you. The witch doctor's going to eat you up. You're going to die, and it's not going to be my fault, because I have prayed for you, but you give all your money to the witch doctor, and he's laughing at you. I sent you to the hospital, and they couldn't do anything, so guess what? I'm just going to let you die and go to hell because it's clear that you don't want to become a Christian. I'm finished with you. I'm washing my hands of you. Do you understand me?" (I was *really* angry!)

She replied, "Madame Sherry, I will come to church on Sunday, and I will give my heart to Jesus." Because of their culture and traditions, most Haitians want to get saved and baptized in a church. And when they do, they are very loyal to that church; they never leave it. But over the years, I'd heard many different excuses from people for why they were going to delay giving their lives to God, so I was skeptical and thought, *That's what she says she's got to do, but I know she's not going to come to church on Sunday.* I told her, "I don't want to hear about Sunday. I want to hear about today." When she still wanted to wait, I finally said, "Okay, I've done everything I can do, and I'm not paying another dime. I've prayed for you, and I've told you about Jesus. If you don't come to church on Sunday, it's not my fault."

To my surprise, Madame Jean came to church that Sunday. Her stomach was still swollen, and she looked half dead. She sat down at the back of the church, but when the altar call was given, she slowly walked up to the front to be prayed for. I expected a great big miracle immediately. I thought she would look different and would raise her hands and praise Jesus, but I didn't see any outward change. She just said the sinner's prayer and then turned around and walked back to her seat and sat down. I was so upset that she hadn't been healed.

We had trees in the field behind our orphanage, and the peasants used to go there to gather the branches that fell from them; they would use the sticks for firewood to make charcoal. About two days later, I was in the field at the back of the orphanage when I heard a voice yelling, "Madame Sherry! Madame Sherry!" When I looked in the direction of the voice, I saw a woman who was carrying sticks on her head. She had both hands up, praising the Lord, and she was jumping up and down. "Who are you?" I asked. She said, "This is Madame Jean. I'm healed!" I couldn't believe it. I ran up to her, and I saw that her face looked different and that her stomach was no longer bloated; the Lord had completely healed her and changed her. She has been a member of our church ever since.

I learned an important lesson through this situation. I had been so mad at Madame Jean for using up all our money for her medicine and the hospital bills while, at the same time, putting herself under the influence of the witch doctor. And I had been very frustrated because I couldn't "get her saved." But God had a time and a place to bring her into His kingdom (maybe I knocked a little sense into her, too!). Madame Jean had accepted Christ by simple faith; and, in His perfect love, God had saved her, transformed her heart, and progressively healed her.

God's Love Is Greater Than Satan's Evil

Bobby and I deeply want the Haitian people to be set free from their terror of voodooism and to have peace and joy in their lives, and we take every opportunity to tell them about God's power to defeat the devil. That's why we were confused when, about ten years ago, God specifically told us *not* to preach to the people of the village of Le Tant. But we were reminded that His ways are infinitely higher than our ways[22] and that we have to follow His specific direction for any given situation.

Le Tant is a village of mud-and-grass huts near a salty lake. Bobby and I first started going there to see if we could help the people get a cleaner source of water. We drilled many wells there, but we found that the brackish water from the lake had seeped underground and contaminated the fresh water supply, so wells would not work there. I still wanted to do something for the villagers, so I thought I'd organize a big mobile clinic for them. I asked around to see who had the biggest hut, because I wanted to use it as the base for the clinic. Everybody I talked to said, "Go see Joel."

I spoke with Joel and found him to be a mean-tempered man. What I didn't know—and what I managed not to learn for quite some time—is that he was the village witch doctor. When I asked him if we could use his hut, he told me, "Yeah, you can use my *tonnel*." As soon as he said that, I should have realized who he was, because in Haiti, a *tonnel* is a round structure where voodoo services are held. But somehow, I didn't make the connection.

Before we held the clinic, we brought in food, clothing, and other items for the people of the village several times, giving them to Joel to distribute. We had no idea that he was keeping them for himself to sell, and never giving them out to anyone. The villagers were scared of him, so they never said anything against him to us; they were afraid he was going to put voodoo on them.

Only after we had everything ready for the mobile clinic did I go inside Joel's hut for the first time. He was helping me to arrange everything, setting up the tables and so forth, when I noticed a conspicuous, black, wooden voodoo cross that was two and a half feet wide, made out of mahogany. Joel had a lot of other voodoo things, too, but he covered them with sheets before the clinic started. Though I knew he was a voodoo person, I still didn't make the connection that he was the witch doctor. Bobby and I and the rest of our medical team prayed and held a gospel service in Joel's hut, and then we conducted the clinic.

After that first mobile clinic, we regularly went back to hold clinics. We learned later that all during this time, Joel was thinking, *They're going to preach to me and tell me how bad I am.* But the Lord had said to us, *Do*

22. See Isaiah 55:9.

not preach to him. Just live your life in front of him. Bobby wanted so badly to preach the gospel in the village—he thought it was his duty to preach—but still the Spirit of God told him, "Do *not* preach." God just wanted us to show the people His love—consistently. Whenever we told Joel that we would come back to help the village by holding another clinic or doing something else, we always kept our word.

We had been conducting mobile clinics in Le Tant for about a year when we arranged to do a joint clinic there with our friend and fellow missionary Donna Bryce of Feed a Child. But when Donna and I arrived, we were shocked to discover piles of ashes where all the huts had been. I stood there thinking, *God, where is everybody?* Then people started coming out of caves and from behind trees and piles of wood. Distraught and crying, they told us that somebody had come in and burned the whole village to the ground. The people were left with nothing. Donna and I cried with them, and we asked each other what we could do to help them. When we went back and told Bobby about it, we decided to have a meeting with the people of Le Tant in the small block building in the village that served as a kind of depot. Thankfully, that structure hadn't been destroyed by the fire. After everyone gathered, we told them we would help each family in the village, giving them some money to buy sticks so they could build new mud huts; we would also give them food, buckets, new furniture, and Bibles.

A Witch Doctor's Passport...to Heaven

Joel was sitting in the back row when we began to announce this, but then he moved to the front row, sat down, and just stared at me. I thought, *Wow, that's weird.* When the meeting was over and we went outside, Joel immediately came up to me and tapped me on the shoulder, saying, "Madame Sherry, I have to talk to you about something." I asked, "Joel, what is it?" He replied, "I want to become a citizen of the same country that you belong to." I told him, "Joel, I'm not getting you a visa to the United States," but he replied, "I don't want to go to the United States. I want to go to heaven."

Right there, this village witch doctor knelt down on the ground to pray; he crossed his arms and bowed his head—as if bracing himself because he thought the prayer was going to hurt! We started praying, but then he said, "Wait a minute. Not here." Joel got up and led me to where the big black voodoo cross was sticking up out of the ground in the remains of his burned hut. Because the cross was made of strong mahogany wood, it was one of the few things that had survived the fire. Joel knelt down beside it, and we continued praying. There were a few Christians in the village, and they came over, too, and we all prayed. The more we prayed, the more Joel cried; he started shaking as he wept and repented.

Afterward, he pulled the voodoo cross out of the ground. You could see anger in his eyes as he took out his machete and started hacking into that hard wood. He cut off the arms of the cross, and then he pulled some kind of wire voodoo object out of the ground. Picking up the broken pieces of the cross and the wire object, he dragged them away and threw them into the bushes. When he came back, dusting off his hands, he said, "The Joel that you saw before—you'll never see him again. This is the new Joel. You're going to see a beautiful Joel." Somehow, he'd had a revelation of how a person becomes a new creation in Christ, and about the kingdom of God. We had never told him about these things because God had not allowed us to preach to him.

Joel had never been taught to read, so he wasn't able to read a Bible, but he started to tell others about salvation in Jesus. That week, he took an evangelist to the village of Cotin, where some of his relatives lived, about forty-five minutes away. The two of them won 140 people to the Lord, and with those new believers, we started a church in that village.

"You Were What You Said You Were"

Months later, I asked Joel, "What really made you come to the Lord?" He told me, "You and Pastor Bobby came here for a year, and you never preached at me one time. You didn't know it, but I hated missionaries. Some of them came here to the village, took pictures, and made promises but never came back. I was just waiting for you to start preaching to me and telling me I was going to go to hell. I wouldn't have listened to you. You didn't know it, but I followed you to wherever you had a mobile clinic or wherever you held a feeding program, and I watched you. I followed you for one full year. I wanted to see if you really were what you said you were."

It's so important when you're working in a Third World country—or anywhere—to keep your word to people. If you don't, you hurt your Christian reputation. Sadly, a lot of Christians will visit Third World nations and, like Joel said, they will take photos and make promises but never follow through. Naturally, the people in those countries become angry at these missionaries. Can you blame them?

Joel also told us that, as a witch doctor, he'd had three evil spirits working for him. He had positioned them in a tree above his mud-and-straw hut so they could watch over it and protect it. But when the village was destroyed, Joel's hut was the very first to burn, and he figured that if the devil couldn't protect his hut, why should he serve him? That's when he started thinking about becoming a Christian.

The new Joel made a big impact on our lives. He was a living testimony of the supernatural power of God to completely transform a life. Joel became a preacher and a great evangelist. He was so honest, and he was really a genius; his brain was like a calculator. Although he couldn't read, he was great at memorizing the Word of God. And he helped with our food distribution (he faithfully distributed the food after his conversion!). If I gave him a certain number of boxes of food for his village but wanted to double-check that it was the right amount, I would ask him, "Now Joel, are you sure I gave you the full number of boxes?" He'd stand there counting them up in his head, and he was never off by even one box.

Bobby and I considered Joel a true gift from God to us. He has since died, and his death has made a big hole in our hearts. No one has ever been able to replace him. But even his death was a testimony to God's grace in his life. I saw him on a Wednesday at our depot, where our missions teams eat, and we sat and talked about the feeding programs and other matters, and then I left to do something else. After talking with me, Joel stood up and told someone else, "I have to go now, because I have to prepare everything for my funeral; I'm going to die tonight." Somehow, the Lord must have told him that it was his time to die.

Joel was only about forty years old, but that day, he went out and bought everything that would be needed for his funeral and for his wake (when a Haitian dies, people come to the home of the deceased and stay and cry all night, so the family needs to have food and other items prepared for the visitors). Then Joel went home, told his wife that he was about to die, and got everything finalized for his funeral. At about midnight, Bobby and I received a phone call that Joel had died. Everyone in the village grieved because he had meant so much to them. What a remarkable change from being a feared and mean-tempered witch doctor to being a beloved leader and brother in the Lord who was mourned by all the people of the village—and also by two grateful missionaries who kept seeing more and more evidence from God that *love is something you do.*

22

HAITIAN ZOMBIES

*"It's because the rat knows what he does at night
that he doesn't go out during day."*
—Haitian Creole proverb

Mythical stories of zombies are extremely popular today. You find them on the Internet and in television shows, movies, books, and graphic novels. But when Bobby and I moved to Haiti, we found out that there really were zombies there! The village where our first four orphans came from is nicknamed "Babylon" because it is so wild, and one reason it has that reputation is that it is known for its zombies. Bobby and I even had a close encounter with them. Bobby remembers, "Once, when we were ministering in Babylon, telling people about the blood of Jesus and preaching against voodoo and witchcraft, we stirred up the voodoo people. That night, we were staying in one of the mud huts in the village because it was too far to travel back home. At about two or three o'clock in the morning, several zombies came around outside our hut; you could smell their presence because of their stench, and people started screaming, 'The zombies are coming to get you!' They were coming to kidnap us and make us zombies, too. The voodoo people, who were controlling them, wanted to get back at us for preaching against what they were doing. When the zombies tried to open the door to our hut, we called out, 'The blood of Jesus! We plead the blood of Jesus!' They went away and didn't try to attack us again."

Victimized by Voodooism

Only recently have people come to understand more about what the Haitians zombies really are—and what has been done to them. There have even been a couple of television documentaries with interviews of people who have researched this. The "zombies" are people who have been victimized by voodoo witch doctors and others who practice voodooism. The witch doctors give them a drug that makes them appear dead—they don't register any heartbeat or other vital signs. Even though they're still alive, they are in a coma-like state. Fre Dodo, our evangelist friend who used to be a witch doctor, says that the drug they use includes an element from a blowfish, as well as other ingredients, which destroys part of the brain. After giving their victims this drug, the voodoo people put them in a coffin and literally bury them alive for three days. Then, in the middle of the night, they dig them up again, give them something to bring them back to consciousness, and do with them whatever they want.

Bobby wanted to see for himself what the voodoo people did when they dug up the "zombies," so he and a friend went out at night to a graveyard near one of the villages. Bobby remembers, "We hid behind bushes, like the time Sherry and I went down the mountain to see the voodoo ceremony. First, we saw the people chanting and doing other voodoo rituals. Then they took shovels and dug up a grave, pried open the cover of the coffin with crowbars, and pulled the person out of the coffin. After they put some kind of powder on him and poured liquid on him from a rum bottle, he woke up. I was told that after the people come out of the coffin, they can hear only the voice of the person who is their 'master.' Their eyes look like dead fish eyes, and even though a part of their brain no longer works, they can do physical labor, which is usually what their masters make them do. It's practically unheard of for anyone to recover after going through this zombie experience. You can't connect with them mentally anymore; they are the 'walking dead.'

"There was a principal at our school in Babylon who I had thought was a Christian, but later I found out that he wasn't. Sometime after we established the school, Sherry and I moved to a new location in Haiti that was many miles from Babylon, so I couldn't often get back there to check on things. But I trusted this man to take care of the school because I thought I knew him. We paid him each month, but after a while, I noticed that while all the other staff members would sign for their pay on a sheet that was sent back to us, he never would. Finally, I traveled out there to see him and to find out why he never signed for his money. The people there told me, "He was stealing the food from the children." We had regularly sent food to the school, but this man had begun to steal all the beans and rice, sell it, and keep the money for himself. The people of the village had gotten mad at him, so they had turned him into a zombie and put him out in the fields to work for them. (Meanwhile, someone else was apparently collecting his pay and not bothering to sign for it.)

"This story was hard for me to believe, so I went out to the field to check. As I looked around, I recognized the man who'd been the principal of the school; he was out there working, but he looked horrible and he smelled like a dead body. That was probably the closest I ever got to a zombie."

Back from the "Dead"

Another time, our Haitian attorney, Mr. Osner Fevry, who is a devout Christian, contacted Bobby and me after he received a call from a local Christian radio station. A girl had been brought to the station who said she had been a zombie. She had apparently escaped from her captors and become normal again, but now she needed help to find her parents.

This claim was extremely unusual, so I went to talk to the girl; her name was Sophania, and she was about sixteen years old. She told me that she had been living with her aunt, but about a year earlier, the aunt had sold her to some voodoo people who had turned her into a zombie and made her a slave. She claimed they had taken her to a white house in the middle of Haiti that was two stories tall and had a white picket fence around it. There were guards at the house, and in every room, people were chained to beds and subjected to voodoo rituals. She also said that during the day, her captors used to put her out in the sun, and snakes would bite her. Then, at night, they would put her in some sort of freezer, where it was very cold. It sounded crazy to me, and at first I didn't really believe anything this girl said. I didn't know if she had been given drugs so that she had hallucinated all this, or if it had really happened.

When our attorney, Mr. Fevry, had first heard about Sophania, he had immediately sent her to a friend of his who was a psychologist to be examined from a mental standpoint. The doctor who examined her said, "I've never seen anything like this, but she believes that what she is telling you is the truth. She's not intentionally lying to you, but I can't verify whether it is the truth or not."

Next, the attorney had sent Sophania to a hospital, which is where I first met her. The attending doctor told me that when she'd first arrived, her blood count was so low, she was practically dead. She was missing so much blood that he had given her many blood transfusions—more than he had ever administered to any other patient. He also told me that he'd had a dermatologist examine the markings all over her body, and the dermatologist had confirmed that they were bite marks, although he could not determine exactly what kind of bite marks they were. After I heard the doctors' reports and saw those marks all over Sophania's body, her story started to make more sense to me.

Sophania's case was being kept secret from the public for her own protection until the authorities could find out what had happened to her. Hardly anyone was allowed in to see her, and the hospital wouldn't even tell anybody her name because if people found out that she had been a zombie, they would have been afraid of her and might even have tried to kill her. However, the hospital did allow a pastor to visit and to pray with her, and Sophania accepted Jesus Christ as her Savior!

Nevertheless, the hospital bill was growing larger every day and needed to be paid. Our attorney took care of half the bill, and Love A Child took care of the other half. Bobby and I offered to take Sophania to our orphanage, where we would try to restore her to health as we attempted to contact one of her relatives. She stayed with us for about six months, and during that time, her behavior was completely normal; she was a sweet girl who loved God. Eventually, I learned that one of her uncles was a pastor who lived in the mountains, so she went to live with him. She is probably the only person we've ever heard of who was restored to health after being subjected to a zombie ritual.

23

OUR "LAND OF CANAAN"

"If it is God who sends you, He'll pay your expenses."
—Haitian Creole proverb

The Death Sentence

By September 1996, we had spent five full years in Haiti. We were so busy with our missions work that we didn't always stop to take inventory of ourselves. But during that month, I noticed a mole on Bobby's side that didn't look right, so we arranged to make a trip to Florida to have a physician take a look at it. Bobby remembers, "After the doctor examined me, his expression was pretty serious, so I said to him, 'Now, doctor, just tell me the truth. What do I have?' He answered, 'Bobby, you have third-stage melanoma cancer, and you have less than six months to live.'

"The doctor thought the cancer had spread to my brain and lymph nodes, because that's how the disease usually progresses, so I had to have some tests done. I also needed surgery to remove the mole, but because I didn't have any medical insurance or money to go to the hospital, the doctor did the surgery at his office. He had to cut very deep, taking out a large section of flesh to get all the cancer, and he told me, 'You really should be in the hospital.'"

I was in the examining room, standing by Bobby's side, when the doctor did the surgery. I thought I would be fine with it because, after all, I had seen a lot of blood while doing my mobile clinics; watching a mole being taken out wouldn't be a big deal for me—but it was! I could not believe that a doctor could take that much flesh out of anyone, especially right there in his office! I was really scared, but I could not let Bobby see my fear.

Miraculously Healed of Melanoma

Bobby tried to process the doctor's diagnosis. He remembers, "After the surgery, I called my son, Jonathan, and said, 'The doctors tell me I'm gonna die. I just wanted you to know, Son.' That night, I was sitting in my rocking chair, thinking, *Well, it's time for me to check out, I guess. Sherry will probably do better with the ministry than I've been doing with it.* All of a sudden, something like a breeze blew through the room. I knew that it was the wind of the Holy Spirit, and when that happened, I also knew that I was healed.

"I went right back to the doctor the next day. He sent me for some additional tests, including a CAT scan and an MRI. When the results came back, there was *no sign* of cancer in my brain or my lymph nodes. Their explanation was, 'Well, it must have moved to different lymph nodes.' The doctor referred me to an oncologist who wanted me to have chemotherapy and radiation right away. When I told him, 'No, I have to get back to Haiti,' he insisted, 'You *have* to have it.' Again I turned down the treatment. 'The breeze of the Lord came through,' I told him, 'and I just went back and had more tests done, and man, it's gone.' My dermatologist said he didn't know what had happened, and all the doctors kept insisting, 'The cancer has to be somewhere.' But the Lord had healed me; the cancer had left every part of my body. Finally, my dermatologist said, 'You must know the Man Upstairs!'

"My body has always healed very fast, so the incision from the surgery was healing very well. In just two weeks, I was back in Haiti, ready to continue our work. I still go back to the dermatologist every six months for a checkup. And I always have to wear a hat and use sunscreen. But several friends of mine have died from melanoma, passing away about two or three months after they were diagnosed, so the Lord gave me a real miracle. I knew it was because He still had work for me to do. Additionally, the Lord had given Sherry and me three important Scripture passages to stand on for healing. One of them was Psalm 41:1–3. The passage begins, "*Blessed is he that considereth the poor,*" and then gives seven supernatural promises, or blessings, for the person who helps the needy:

1. The Lord will deliver him in times of trouble.
2. The Lord will preserve him.
3. The Lord will keep him alive.
4. He will be blessed upon the earth.
5. The Lord will not deliver him to the will of his enemies.

6.   The Lord will strengthen him upon the bed of languishing.

7.   The Lord will make all his bed in his sickness (restore him).

"We stood on all the promises the Lord had given us, and He was faithful to His Word to heal me."

Wanted: A Permanent Ministry Hub

Bobby and I continued to minister in Haiti—taking care of our orphaned children, building churches and schools, conducting mobile medical clinics, drilling wells for clean water, and working on other projects—but we had always wanted to have a piece of land that we could use as a ministry base, a central hub that would become the heart of our Love A Child outreach. It would be like our own Promised Land—our Land of Canaan—where we could really branch out and do what God had called us to do in Haiti. We especially wanted to find a house in a safe area that would be large enough to accommodate all of our "extended family" of children. Bobby and I prayed for guidance, recognizing that finding a large piece of land where we could build a permanent orphanage would be the solution. But good land with clean water was scarce in Haiti—and had been for many years.

We looked at many pieces of property, but we couldn't find anything that was right for us. Either the land was too small, it cost too much, it didn't have water, there were too many owners to deal with, or the owner's deed wasn't legal. Finally, we stopped actively looking for property and just turned our need over to the Lord.

A Large Tract of Land in Fond Parisien

Then Bobby and I traveled to Orlando, Florida, to speak at a church service where we described our missions work among the Haitian people. An elderly, white-headed, Haitian-American man who had seen us on television found out that we would be speaking there and came to hear us. Afterward, he showed us a map of some land he owned in Haiti, drawn on a wrinkled old piece of cloth parchment. He had documents dating back to 1804—the year when France transferred its claim of land on Hispaniola over to Haiti—and he owned a large amount of property in an area called Fond Parisien in eastern Haiti, less than ten miles from the border of the Dominican Republic.

This landowner had been born in Haiti and had lived there when he was a young man. At that time, Papa Doc Duvalier was running the country under military rule. Under that brutal regime, there was little crime on the streets, and many people in the country lived in relative safety—but there were costs to their financial and personal freedoms. One of those costs was that, in lieu of paying certain taxes, landowners had to pay a percentage to Duvalier's military force, the *Tonton Macoutes*, as a tribute, in order to guarantee their safety. However, the man told us that, as a landowner, he had constantly opposed the government's policies. One time, he had even tried to drop a bomb on the National Palace, where the president lived—but missed! Because of his opposition to Papa Doc, he was eventually forced to flee the country for his life, taking his family with him, and leaving his land behind.

He had been living in the United States for forty years, and because his land had been abandoned, it was claimed by the Haitian poor. There was apparently an understanding among the Haitian people that if someone abandoned his land, after a certain number of years, the peasants had a right to occupy it and claim it. It would have been impossible for this man to have gone back to Haiti after four decades to reclaim his land; it would also have been very dangerous for him to try it because the people in that area did not like him and wouldn't have wanted to give him back the land. So, after hearing about our ministry, he decided to give his property to Love A Child. At first, he gave us the equivalent of about a hundred acres of land, and a short time later, he gave us the rest of the land, an additional sixty-two acres or so.

Giants in the Land

When Bobby and I returned to Haiti, we thought we would "spy out the land," taking along our Haitian pastor and our Haitian director, Nelio. With the parchment map in our hands, we drove up and down Fond Parisien, looking for the location of the property. When we found it and met the people living in the village near the land, they were hostile to us. None of them wanted any *blans* to come and take over the land, and many of the voodoo people threatened to kill us.

If that wasn't enough to scare us off, the land itself was dry, unsightly—and hazardous. It was filled with *pie bwa pikan*, which are huge trees with long, sharp needles. There were also bushes with long needles called "Flying Satan"; remarkably, the needles on this bush are heat sensitive, so if you walk within a few feet of them, they shoot needle daggers into you! All the Haitians were afraid of those Flying Satans. Additionally, there were huge tree-bushes called *kandalab* that were dark green and had long, thick, curved stems with prickly points. The Haitians told us that if you struck one of them with something, such as a machete, a milky white liquid would shoot out, and if that liquid got into your eyes, it would blind you. This white substance could also cause horrible swelling and inflammation. (We've treated children at our clinics who've been afflicted by it.) There were also *pikan tosh* trees, which looked like giant, thick, round cactus and had thousands of long, thin sharp needles sticking straight out of them. If you were clearing land and that tree fell on you, you would have to be taken to the hospital to be treated for serious stab wounds.

After having lain fallow for forty years, the property was practically inaccessible and seemed unusable for development. I thought it was the ugliest piece of land I had ever seen in my life, and I wanted to leave and never come back! Besides, the local voodoo people hated us and did not want us there. Nelio and our Haitian pastor were so frightened by the situation that they could not wait to get out of there. They told us, "Don't ever come back here. The people will kill us."

I was so discouraged. All I could see were the "giants" in the land—and the ugliness of it! But when Bobby looked at that land, he believed it was our Canaan, our land of milk and honey. He told me, "I can see what God is going to do here on behalf of the poor." After that, although I still had many misgivings, I trusted that Bobby was hearing from God about what He wanted to accomplish there.

Divine Favor

Bobby and I had always loved Scripture passages that talked about people having God's "favor." When Samuel the prophet was a child, he grew in favor with the Lord and with other people.[23] Joseph had favor even after being enslaved and falsely imprisoned.[24] Queen Esther had favor with everyone she met, but especially with the king at a crucial time when her people needed to be saved from destruction.[25] And the Bible says that when Jesus Christ was a boy, He *"increased… in favour with God and man."*[26] Knowing these examples, we prayed every morning for divine favor with the Haitians, with all other people, and with God.

---

23. See 1 Samuel 2:26.
24. See Genesis 39:1–5; 20–23.
25. See Esther 2:15; 5–8.
26. Luke 2:52.

Bobby wanted to go out and see the land again, but our Haitian staff wouldn't go with us, so we went by ourselves. The people living in the area were again very hostile to us and surrounded us as we talked with them. Even so, after we left, we trusted that the Lord would change their hearts and give us His divine favor.

A few days later, the people of Fond Parisien sent a young man from the village by the name of Reggie to our house as their representative. He told us, "We welcome you to come back. We want to talk to you some more." On our next visit, we met with the leaders of Fond Parisien, and Bobby told them, "God has sent us here to be a blessing to you, to help you, to build a school for you, and to be a benefit to your community and your children." God answered our prayer and gave us divine favor with these leaders, and they allowed us to have the land given to us by the landowner!

We were able to hire about thirty local men to cut paths with their "ma-che-*tees*," as they called them, through the thornbushes, the Flying Satans, and the other thick bushes, to allow the Haitian surveyor to come and measure the parameters of the property. The men were hacking and slicing their way through the lethal vegetation like a scene from *Raiders of the Lost Ark*! It was a nasty job! After the property was surveyed, we paid the people who believed they owned the land. We also met with the donor of the property several times and had all the papers related to the land legally transferred to Love A Child, Inc., in accordance with the laws of Haiti. Afterward, we dealt with various difficulties in regard to our ownership of the land that were eventually overcome through the grace of God.

A Man Called "Daisy"

We were so thankful to the Lord for providing us with the land, which we would call Love A Child Village. We wanted to minister to and bless the people of Fond Parisien, so we held open-air gospel meetings on the property. We used a small wooden platform, similar to what we'd used while preaching on the streets in Florida. On the day of the first meeting, Bobby got up to preach, but in the middle of his message, one of the Haitians whose name was Desir (pronounced "Daisy"), who had given us the most trouble over the land, came to the front and interrupted him. Desir was a tough, mean man who was famous for having killed two people at the same time and buried them in one hole! He jumped up on the platform and declared, 'I want to be converted, right now!'

Bobby was shocked and asked him, "Desir, *right now?* Can't you wait until after I finish preaching?" He demanded, "No, right now!" Desir accepted the Lord right there, and at the next service, the young man named Reggie who had been the people's representative came forward for salvation. God continued to move, and one by one, people came to the Lord that week. We built a small brush-arbor church on the site and started a Christian school there.

Clearing the Land and Building a Village...with "RoboCop"!

Soon after we obtained the property, Bobby and I taped one of our television programs at the site so we could share our plan for developing the first 100 acres of land with our viewers in the United States. Mark Ostrander was our one-man producer/cameraman for our programs, so he was there with us. At the same time that we were recording, some of the Haitians we had hired to clear the land were cutting down *pikan* trees and stacking them in huge piles to be burned. Some of the trees were already smoldering.

In those days, when we taped our programs, Bobby and I didn't use lapel mics; we shared an old-fashioned microphone with a long cord that connected to the camera that Mark held, so we had to remain pretty stationary when we talked. That day, it was especially hot, and Bobby and I were standing in the middle of this ugly land, trying to talk about our vision for building a permanent orphanage there. We were looking at the TV camera, but out of the corner of our eyes, we began to see huge clouds of black smoke rising all around us! Soon we heard flames snapping and popping, almost like a forest fire...and there was a strong burning smell. This wasn't just smoldering piles of brush—this was a spreading fire!

We stopped taping and spun around to see what was going on. One of our Haitian workers, resembling "RoboCop," had a tank of gasoline strapped to his back. In one hand, he held a long nozzle that was attached to the tank, and he was walking around squirting gasoline on all the piles of trees that were already burning! He didn't realize how extremely dangerous that was, not only because the fire could get out of control, but also because of the risk of an explosion. Fortunately, we got the fire contained. In those days, we weren't able to preview our television program; we just sent what we had taped to the TV station, and we didn't see the program until it aired. When we watched that worker squirting gasoline all around us and saw those flames rising up, we realized how really close to death all of us had been!

After that, we taped other TV programs explaining our project of developing the land for our ministry base, and John Boldt of Engineering Ministries International saw one of them. He called us afterward and said, "It looks like you will need some help from engineers to examine this large tract of land, so that you can design the layout, the buildings, and everything else you want to put on it." John and his EMI team offered to assist us, and they became one of the greatest blessings Love A Child has ever known.

When John first discussed the layout of the property with Bobby and me, he asked, "If you could have anything you wanted on this land, what would it be?" We immediately began to talk about an orphanage, a Jesus Healing Center clinic, four large school buildings, a carpentry shop, ware-housing, a Tilapia fish farm, and more. In January 2000, John and his team began the arduous task of surveying the land and doing all the topographical maps. They labored tirelessly alongside our Haitian workers with their machetes. That was the first of numerous trips that EMI made to Haiti to help with the buildings and other projects at Love A Child Village. They were "EMI Angels" to us, and Love A Child would not be what it is today without their help.

September 11, 2001

God had taught Bobby and me from the start that in order to fulfill what He had called us to do, we would have to walk by faith—and our faith was constantly being stretched as we expanded our ministry to help more people. While we developed the new property, we continued to travel to the United States from time to time to preach in churches and tell people about our work in Haiti. In 2001, we thought it would be helpful to obtain a motor home so that when we visited the States, we wouldn't have to stay in a hotel as we traveled around, saving us a lot of money. Then we found out that someone wanted to donate a motor home to us.

Bobby remembers, "One day, our office in Florida called me in Haiti and told me we'd had an offer from a woman in Louisiana of 'a very nice motor home' that was about thirty feet long. The owner wanted to hand it over to me personally. She was a good donor to our ministry, and one time she had even given us five thousand dollars, so I thought, *This is someone who is serious about an offer.* I asked one of our Florida staff members to call her back and get all the details for me—mileage, working condition, any liens on the vehicle, and so on. I wanted to find out everything I could about the motor home before flying to Louisiana to drive it back to our office in Florida.

"Our office staff talked with her, and she told them the trailer was in mint condition, with low mileage, and had been stored inside. I made a reservation on a commercial airline flying to Louisiana the morning of September 11. Our departure was smooth, but while we were in flight, the captain suddenly got on the intercom and said that we had to land immediately. I thought, *What's going on?* We landed in Tallahassee, Florida, and when I looked at the television monitors at the Tallahassee airport, I saw the World Trade Tower buildings burning and heard the reports of the terrorist attacks. In the midst of taking in this news, I immediately realized that I needed to rent a car quickly because all the planes in the United States had been grounded indefinitely. I ended up getting the last rental car available and drove the rest of the way to Lake Charles, Louisiana. Even though I still looked forward to receiving the motor home, I was stressed out about the 9/11 disaster. I also wondered, *With everybody's mind on the terrorists, who's going to support our ministry now? Everybody's afraid, we may go to war, and people may not be able to give any more donations. How can we afford to continue to live and minister in Haiti?* My mind was filled with all these questions, and I was also very tired and hungry. I just wanted to get the business done in Louisiana and head back to Florida.

"When I met the woman at her home, she said, 'Bobby, let's just kneel down and have a word of prayer in the living room.' Well, that dear lady prayed for about an hour, nonstop! I was so hungry that, after an hour of hearing her pray, I did some 'intercession' of my own, saying, *Lord, I'm so hungry…please let her stop praying!* She kept going for a little while longer, but then, when she finally ended the prayer and stood up, she called the mayor of her town because she wanted to introduce him to me! Thankfully, he wasn't there, and we went to a restaurant to eat. At last, we drove to see the motor home. I would soon be on my way.

"The report I'd received was that the motor home had been stored inside, out of the weather, but when we got there, I saw that it was out in the open—and it looked like it had been there for *years*. The roof had a large hole in it. The rain had come in, there was a thick layer of leaves inside, the seats were covered with green mold, and it smelled terrible. Besides that, all the tires were flat, and the motor wouldn't even begin to crank. The vehicle supposedly had a mileage of only 35,000, but it was obvious that the odometer had turned over several times.

"I was in a tight spot because I knew that this woman loved that motor home. Somehow, in her eyes, it looked as wonderful as the day she had bought it. I didn't want to hurt her feelings, so I prayed, *Thank You, Jesus.* Then I told her, 'Ma'am, this is such a beautiful motor home, but you know what? It would be expensive for me to drive it to Florida, ship it to Haiti, and then try to get it through customs.' (Actually, Haitian customs would have told me to ship it back to America!) I continued, 'It would be better if you just sold it and donated the money to Love A Child.' The woman seemed disappointed, but she agreed.

"After taking her home, I started driving my rental car to our home in Florida, but then I discovered that I was driving into the path of a hurricane. At that point, I got pretty depressed. I had taken a flight from Haiti to America, only to have to make an unscheduled landing in the middle of a national crisis and rent a car in Tallahassee to drive all the rest of the way to Louisiana, where the promised motor home turned out to be a piece of junk. The news about 9/11 was getting worse and worse by the minute. Gas prices along my route shot up to about eight dollars a gallon; either the gas stations were worried about shortages, or they were just taking advantage of the crisis, but they were certainly scalping gas that day.

"As I drove, I started worrying again that people would stop sending us donations. Maybe our ministry in Haiti was over. And now I had to deal with this hurricane blowing in. I made it into Florida, but the rain was pounding down so hard by then that I had to pull over and stay at a hotel. While I was there, Sandra Smith, who is Love A Child's executive director in the States, called me and said, 'Bobby, I want you to call back a man I just talked with. He was kind of grouchy, and he's never given anything to the ministry before, but he wanted to know why it is costing so much money to construct the school we are building in Haiti. He's just grumbling about it.' I thought, *Well, it's pouring down rain, and I'm in the middle of a hurricane, but I'll call him.*

"When I called the man back, he asked me two or three questions about the construction of the school, which I answered. Then he said, 'Well, good. That's just what I wanted to hear. As soon as I can get to the FedEx store after this storm, I'm going to send a check for twenty-five thousand dollars to your office.' The man did exactly that! It turned out that he was the owner of an electric company and wanted to help us finish building the school. But when he told me on the phone that he would send that large donation, I felt it was another sign from God letting me know that the work He had for us in Haiti was not yet finished and that, even in the midst of this crisis, and no matter what else happened, the support was not going to stop—in fact, it would be better than ever. And it was!"

Love A Child Orphanage

The generous donation from the electric company owner reminded us that we needed to keep walking by faith, not by sight, and trust God to provide the funds for the operating expenses of the ministry and for our ongoing building construction. When we were making plans to build the orphanage on our new land, we met with some people who were professional fund-raising consultants. They told us that whatever we did, we should build the orphanage so that it "looked very poor-looking and depressing." They claimed, "When people see that, they will cry and give you money."

Bobby and I didn't like that idea at all. We prayed about the kind of orphanage it should be and gave it a lot of thought. Then the Lord spoke to Bobby and said, *I want you to raise "thoroughbreds"—champions for Christ!* Bobby told me he wanted to build an orphanage for the children that was safe, comfortable, and attractive. Additionally, he felt that if the children grew up in a nice home, it would encourage them to get a good education and a well-paying job when they were older, because they would want to live in the same kind of house they had grown up in.

We knew that some people would criticize us for building a large and beautiful orphanage, but we felt it was our responsibility to raise these children and take care of them as we would our own. Bill Moore, an architect from Naples, Florida, flew to Haiti and donated his skills to develop the design. It would be 21,500 square feet and include special ventilation and other wonderful features. Then we hired R & R Construction in Haiti to build our orphanage. When we met with Philip Magloire, one of the partners of R & R, he said, "Bobby, you should spend a lot more money on the foundation, which will go about twelve feet deep, because one day, a big earthquake may come, and it will save your lives." Bobby and I prayed about it, and we felt that we should do this.

The construction continued, and after three years of hard work, our two-story Love A Child Orphanage was finally complete! We felt that the building of the orphanage was a miracle from start to finish, and we invited those who had donated generously to the project to come to Haiti for the dedication. The dedication celebration was a wonderful event, not only for us but for all the children. They now had not only a mother and a father but also a permanent home. They would be settled into a real family environment. Bobby and I, the children, and the staff moved in during April 2005. The orphanage became our home in Haiti, as it still is today. We live with the children, which is one of the biggest joys of our life, but we also recognize it carries a great responsibility.

We currently provide a loving Christian home at the orphanage for about eighty children who have either been orphaned, abandoned, enslaved, malnourished, or are in need of ongoing medical care. They have nutritious meals, new clothes, a warm bed to sleep in, and regular health care. There is a huge lawn and a playground where they can have fun and get exercise. And unlike the unfortunate situation of most children growing up in Haiti, they are able to attend classes regularly at our Christian school as they learn how important it is to develop a personal relationship with God. Many of the children finish high school and go on to earn college degrees.

We want each child who ever calls Love A Child their home to realize their dreams and to reach their full potential in God's plan for their lives. We show them lots of love and try to instill them with self-worth, giving them the capacity to dream big!

The Jesus Healing Center

It was amazing for us see how God was beginning to transform our "ugly" land into an oasis in the middle of a desert. The orphanage being complete, we next wanted to build the clinic. Two of the partners who had attended our orphanage dedication ceremony were Ron and Joy Sills, who, together with their family, had been big supporters of the project. Right after the dedication, this couple had come to Bobby and me and said, "We feel we are to give the first donation toward the building of the Jesus Healing Center!" We were stunned when they gave us a check for fifty thousand dollars! We had not even started preliminary work on the clinic, but God had already begun to move so that it could become a reality.

Following the completion of the two-story Jesus Healing Center, we were able to build the Love A Child Christian School, opening with an enrollment of several hundred children. Today, the school has six hundred students.

After this, we built our Tilapia Fish Farm and Training School, and we established a Christian radio station. Bob D'Andrea, president and owner of Christian Television Network (CTN), sponsored these two projects. To help start the radio station, he sent engineer Paul Garber, along with Paul's wife, Melody, and another staff member to install the equipment and to train local Haitians to work in the station. Love A Child's radio station, under general manager Eldon Bryce, provides Christian music, Bible stories and Bible readings, education, health information, and public service programming. In addition to our local broadcasting, Love A Child Christian Radio can be heard around the world in both Creole and English via the Internet.

The Lord faithfully supplied the finances for all these projects, but there was one unexpected provision that was especially miraculous. Back when our Jesus Healing Center building was nearly complete, Bobby had prayed, "Lord, the clinic is almost finished, but how will we ever be able to purchase all the equipment, medical supplies, and everything else that's needed to actually open its doors and help patients?" The miracle that God provided came from someone we knew about but hadn't yet met face-to-face.

David Meyer, the son of well-known Bible teacher and author Joyce Meyer, is the CEO of Hand of Hope, the missions outreach of Joyce Meyer Ministries. In May 2008, we received a call that David Meyer wanted to visit us but wouldn't be able to stay long due to his schedule. He wanted to fly in to Haiti to "check us out" and see what Love A Child ministry was all about. We were excited that David Meyer, representing Joyce Meyer and Hand of Hope, even knew who we were!

When David came on the scheduled day, his visit was short, just as he'd said it would be. But he toured our orphanage and then wanted to see the Jesus Healing Center, which was not yet open. "How much would you need in order to purchase the equipment for the inside and open the doors?" he asked. "And, how much will your monthly operating costs be? Send those figures to me, and I will let you know what we can do." We didn't have the answers to his questions, but we told him we would work on a budget and get back to him. "Let me know," he emphasized again, and then he was gone as quickly as he'd come.

When we figured the amount that would be needed to open the Jesus Healing Center, it came to ninety-five thousand dollars, and we estimated the monthly budget at fifteen thousand dollars. After we told David, he immediately sent us a check on behalf of Joyce Meyer Ministries/Hand of

Hope for ninety-five thousand dollars, enabling us to open the doors of the clinic! Hand of Hope also committed fifteen thousand dollars a month to cover the operating budget, including payroll for all the employees! Today, our medical center has a great Haitian staff of Christian doctors, nurses, lab technicians, and pharmacists. This team is committed to Love A Child's campaign against hunger and poverty in Haiti. They see up to 150 patients daily and treat an additional 200 malnutrition cases in outpatient care.

Joyce Meyer/Hand of Hope has continued to support the monthly budget for the clinic to this day. They also sponsor a container of food each month at a cost of ten thousand dollars, supplying two hundred seventy thousand meals for our feeding programs. We deeply appreciate all their help, including these tremendous gifts each month to the Jesus Healing Center, which allows us to give the best of medical help to those who are among the poorest of the poor in Haiti. In fulfillment of His promise, and because of His great love for the Haitian people, God provided everything we needed—*"pressed down, and shaken together, and running over"*![27]

---

27. See Luke 6:38.

24

"I WILL TAKE CARE OF YOU"

"A stumble is not a fall."
—Haitian Creole proverb

God had encouraged us that He would provide everything we needed for the ministry, and we witnessed His miraculous provision to make the Love A Child Orphanage and the Jesus Healing Center a reality. But God also gave us assurance that He was watching over us and would take care of us—no matter how bad things might get—after Bobby had a terrible accident.

Bobby remembers, "I had a big tractor with a Bush Hog, a piece of equipment with a spinning blade that's used for clearing land, which was generously donated to us by Pastor Lia Willets and the Christ United Methodist Church of Lehigh Acres, Florida. We were going to tape our television program that day at Love A Child headquarters, and I got up early because I wanted to cut the grass with the Bush Hog and make sure things looked nice around the compound. I thought it was strange when Sherry said, 'Oh, don't go' and told me she had a funny feeling about it. Meanwhile, a woman we knew in North Carolina, Angela Greffin, was trying to contact me to warn me that she felt my life was in danger, and to be careful—but somehow I never got that message.

"I went outside, got on my tractor, and starting cutting the yard slowly in low gear. I was almost done when I drove under a tree but didn't see a low-lying limb. It hit me hard on the forehead, and I was knocked off my seat, landing right on my head. The tractor had a built-in safety mechanism so that, if you left your seat, it would automatically stop. But the large limb that had hit me broke off and fell right on top of the tractor seat; because the tractor sensed weight there, it kept on going.

"As I was lying facedown on the ground, the tractor's big, left rear wheel started to run over me…slowly. I could hear my bones going pop, pop, pop as the wheel made its way across my back, my shoulder, and my arm. The next thing I knew, the Bush Hog was right above me, with the blade still spinning! The noise was deafening, and I just knew the blade would cut me to pieces. Finally, I felt the back wheel of the Bush Hog run over my head as the tractor drove away. My whole back was on fire! I thought the blade had sliced me like a piece of bacon. Some of our Haitian workers rushed over to me, and I asked them if I was bleeding. They told me I was bleeding somewhat, but not badly.

"Somehow, that rotating blade hadn't touched me! I knew God had protected me from it. The only natural explanation I can think of is that I was lying flat on my stomach when the front wheels of the tractor went over me, and they may have mashed me into the ground, pushing me just below the reach of that rotating blade, but I don't really know.

"The workers ran and got Sherry and Mark Ostrander; they lifted me into a truck and drove me to the house, where I was carried upstairs on a homemade stretcher made out of a board. After I was transferred to my bed, Sherry opened her Bible to Psalm 41:1–3, placed the Word of God on my chest, and prayed, 'Lord, You promised that if we would consider the poor, you would keep us alive.' And she continued to pray for my healing.

"I had broken bones and was badly injured, so they called for an air ambulance from Miami, Florida, which flew me and Sherry to a trauma center in New Orleans. The reason we had to go to New Orleans instead of Miami is that, to use the air ambulance, I first had to have a doctor examine me and write a report about the accident so the doctor at the admitting hospital could review it before treating me. But we had not yet opened the Jesus Healing Center, and the nearest doctor was a long way away in Port-au-Prince—and they never would have come all the way out to where we were. With no doctor able to examine me, the hospital in Florida would not accept me as a patient.

"But a friend of ours, Dr. Chester Falterman, a prominent cardiologist, had his practice in New Orleans. After seeing our television program, he had become one of our donors, and he had also gone on one of our missions trips. Dr. Chester and his wife, Debbie, had become very close friends of Sherry and me. He said he would write the report and take care of me if the air ambulance would bring me there. In fact, the building where he had his practice was connected to the hospital, where he held the position of head cardiologist.

"After I arrived at the hospital in New Orleans, I was told that I needed to have surgery. Every rib in my back was broken. (In fact, the huge tires of the Bush Hog had pressed into me so hard that you could see tire prints on my back for four or five months afterward.) In addition, my shoulder and my arm had been smashed, and I needed to have steel rods and plates put in them. I still have scars from those injuries.

"When I woke up after having the surgery, I was still groggy from the anesthesia. I had all kinds of tubes in me, and I felt like I couldn't breathe, so I started yanking out the tubes—causing the medical staff to come running. Because of my grogginess and the tremendous pain I was in, I imagined that I was still in Haiti and had been captured by the zombie voodoo people! I thought, *Oh no, they're here to get me!* But the head doctor came and calmed me down, telling me, 'Mr. Burnette, you can't breathe well on your own; you have to have these tubes.' I told her, 'Look, I'm breathing good now.' She said, 'You have to stay in this room longer, because you're not doing very well.'

"I was shaking because I was so cold, and I told her, 'If I stay here any longer, I'm going to die. I'm from Haiti, and I need to be where it's hot.' She said, 'No sir, you have to stay right here.' Sherry wasn't in the room yet because they had asked her to wait in the hallway. But when they allowed her to come in, I told her, 'I've got to get out of here. I'm freezing to death. Call Dr. Chester.' Sherry contacted him, and he got the head doctor on the phone and told her, 'Get him out of there immediately, and don't worry about it.' They had me out of there in five minutes. I told them, 'Forget the tubes, I'm fine; I'm not having trouble breathing.' So they just left the IV in me and moved me to a regular private room where the air conditioning was broken—which was perfect for me!

"My body had been badly crushed in the accident, but within the first week, the doctors were asking me, 'Why are you healing so fast? Things keep progressing overnight. Your body's coming back together.' I told them, 'It's the Lord.'

"I was determined not to just lie in bed and get sick. So, although my body was in a lot of pain, I forced myself to get up and walk, and I got better every day. In the midst of all this, Dr. Chester took special care of me. He was one of the most prestigious doctors in that hospital, with a suite of offices about as big as the hospital itself, but he would come twice a day and personally walk me down the hallway. He would even give me a shave every day. People noticed this, and at one point, one of the doctors came in and said, 'He never walks or shaves anybody. Who *are* you?' I said, 'I'm just a missionary from Haiti.' He replied, 'Well, put in a good word to Dr. Chester for us, because we'd like to work for him!'

"After I'd been there about a week, the hospital said they were ready to release me. Dr. Chester and his wife, Debbie, who used to be a physical therapist, kindly invited Sherry and me to stay at their home for as long as we needed while I recovered. But after only another week, I told them, 'I've got to get back to Florida and then to Haiti.' Their response was, *'What?'*

"I was determined to go home, so Sherry and I decided to drive from New Orleans to our house in Florida. I was still experiencing a lot of pain, and I could hardly make it out to the driveway. Dr. Chester and his wife were still trying to get me to stay as they accompanied us to the car. I finally got settled in the front passenger seat with some pillows behind me, and Sherry got behind the wheel and started driving. For the first twenty minutes of the trip, the pain was terrible, and I thought, *I'm not going to make it. I better turn around and go back.* I told Sherry I didn't know if I could do it. But all of a sudden, I started feeling better, and I said, 'Sherry, let's keep on going.'

"After we arrived in Florida, we stayed there for about five days. Then I got a wheelchair so I could travel by plane, and we flew back to Haiti. The doctors had told me I wouldn't be able to return for about three or four months. But within three weeks, we were back in Haiti, continuing to minister God's love to people.

"My rapid healing after the accident was a real miracle. Even today, people ask me, 'How do you feel? How's your back? How's your arm?' Everybody thinks I should be sick-looking. But I don't have one physical problem. Over the years, I've had a lot of bad falls; I've been thrown from mules and I've fallen down mountain slopes and concrete stairs. I was told I would have severe arthritis in my body, but I have no arthritis, and I feel fine.

"Shortly before the accident, I had been thinking, *Sherry and I take care of so many people in Haiti, medically and otherwise, but if something were to happen to me, who would take care of me?* About two weeks later, I had that terrible accident, and along came Dr. Chester, treating me like a king in the hospital, giving me the best of everything. Then I went to his beautiful house, and he and his wife took care of Sherry and me. Dr. Chester was really an answer to prayer for us at a critical time, and things couldn't have been better under the circumstances. (We really want to thank Dr. Chester and Debbie again for everything they did for us! To this day, they are our very dear friends.) Reflecting on this whole situation, we felt God was assuring us, 'I will take care of you.'"

25

ROLLER-COASTER RIDE

"The sunken boat doesn't hinder another boat from navigating."
—Haitian Creole proverb

With all the wonderful developments at Love A Child Village, our days became busier than ever. As we oversaw the various areas of our growing ministry, we continued to provide loving parental guidance and discipline for the orphans; supervise the staff; maintain the property; keep up-to-date with Haiti's laws and regulations; confer with customs officials for the release of cargo; communicate regularly with our partners; produce our radio and TV programs; direct the food distribution; conduct medical clinics in remote areas (often hosting volunteer medical teams from America); ensure that the Love A Child school, orphanage, and medical clinic were running smoothly; supervise the churches and schools we'd established in the remote regions; build additional churches and schools; greet a variety of visitors; address personal, medical, and spiritual issues of individual students and staff members; and many other things!

As we carried out these responsibilities and activities, there were times when we felt we were on an emotional roller coaster. While working closely with individuals, families, and entire villages to address their needs, our feelings alternated between joy, frustration, thankfulness, disappointment, happiness, anger, gratification, sorrow, and relief. We saw many children and adults grow stronger and healthier, find hope in Christ, and build better lives. But we saw others lose heartbreaking battles against disease, starvation, or other negative circumstances beyond their control.

The Naked Thief

Sadly, we also witnessed some people make poor decisions that caused grief not only for themselves but for their families. It was painful to see those whose lives held great promise throw away that potential. One case involved a young man named Bouji who had been caught cutting down trees on our land with his friend Neve to make charcoal that they could then sell. With the land erosion in Haiti, and for the safety of those who lived on the property, this couldn't be allowed. However, not wanting to cause these young men trouble, Bobby told them that if they would stop cutting down trees, he would forgive them and give them a job.

Neve said he wanted to get an education, so we began to pay for him to go to school as he worked at Love A Child. Bouji accepted a job with our groundskeeping crew, and at the beginning, he seemed to do well. But then he used his access to Love A Child Village to steal a large quantity of diesel fuel from our tractor and backhoe so he could sell it and make some extra cash. He removed the diesel a little at a time, hoping nobody would notice that the fuel was missing. The Haitians often like to buy an inexpensive juice called "Juno Drinks" that comes in a small plastic bottle, and Bouji found it easy to regularly fill an empty bottle of Juno with diesel and then walk around with it in his hand—with everybody assuming he was just drinking juice—until he could transfer it to a hidden bucket.

At first, we couldn't figure out where the diesel was going. Then, one night at about one o'clock in the morning when Bobby and I were sound asleep at the orphanage, we got a call from Nelio, our Haitian director. He told us that the security guard at our front gate was trying to reach us, but our walkie-talkie was off and he didn't have our cell number. Nelio asked us to go to the front gate quickly because the guard had caught a thief—and he was one of our own workers.

I grabbed my camera so we could get evidence of the theft, and then Bobby and I drove to the guardhouse. In Haiti, the authorities seem to allow people to fire their workers for very superficial reasons—with one exception: They consider it a very serious thing for an employer to fire an employee for stealing. As in America and other countries, you can't let someone go just because you *think* he or she is stealing; you must have specific proof.

At the guardhouse, we were startled to find that, except for a red voodoo *mouchoua* on his head, Bouji was completely naked and had greased his entire body! The security guard, who kept his gun pointed at Bouji, told us, "He was running along the wall with two five-gallon buckets of diesel." Bouji had planned to climb back over the wall with the buckets, and he had his "get-away car"—a donkey—right outside the gate. You could say that he got caught with his pants down, but he wasn't even wearing any pants!

When we saw Bouji standing there "butt naked" with the five-gallon buckets of diesel beside him, we knew he was guilty, and we were really upset. I asked him, "Why did you do this, Bouji, after we gave you a job?" With his hands on the two buckets, he answered, "I didn't steal anything, Madame Sherry."

The security guard reminded me to take Bouji's picture because the police and the judge wouldn't do anything without proof. Considering Bouji's lack of attire, that was a little awkward! But we documented the theft, and then Bobby and I and two other witnesses had to take Bouji to the police station.

The saddest part was that Bouji's mother was a devout Christian and a member of our church whose husband had left her to raise their eight children by herself. She met us on the road the next morning, crying because she was so ashamed of her son's actions. She said she'd had to put Bouji out of her house some time earlier because he was always out very late at night and getting into trouble. We gave her some money so that she could buy food and make meals to take to Bouji at the jail. In Haiti, they don't typically feed the prisoners in the local jails, so unless a family member or someone else brings them food, they won't get anything to eat.

Bouji's mother had tried to talk him into admitting his mistake and saying that he was sorry, but he'd refused, and he was due to appear before the judge in just two days. Bobby and I talked the problem over with Nelio, who directs all our projects throughout Haiti, and Reginal, or "Reggie," who oversees the projects in the area of Fond Parisien where Love A Child Village is located. Reggie told us that none of our other workers wanted Bouji back on the property, and they didn't even want him to return to Fond Parisien, because he was a thief. If we were to forgive Bouji for the theft and give him back his job, and then he were to steal from us again, it would cause resentment among the other workers, and it might even reflect badly on all of our workers in the eyes of the community.

After discussing our options, we all agreed that if Bouji would admit to the judge that he stole the diesel and say that he was sorry, we would drop the charges—but he would not be able to come back into the area. Nelio talked separately with both the judge and Bouji, telling them of our plans. For some reason, Bouji refused to admit his guilt or express remorse for his actions, and the judge sent him to jail. Going to jail in Haiti is not like being incarcerated in the United States. Most jails in Haiti are so overcrowded that the prisoners have to sleep in shifts, similar to what the workers in the crowded city of Port-au-Prince have to do. Inmates are woken up in the middle of the night to take their turn lying down while the others sit or stand.

Allowing Bouji to be sent to jail was one of the hardest things we've ever had to do. But we knew that if he wasn't sorry for what he'd done, he might try to sneak back inside Love A Child Village some night—perhaps bringing along others with him who had guns—and either steal something else or hurt someone.

Regrettably, Bouji had caused his mother much shame, and as the Haitian Creole proverb says, "Shame is heavier than a sack of salt." Because we didn't want his mother to suffer any more than she already had, we decided to give her the equivalent of Bouji's paycheck each week so that she could take care of her other children.

"Shoot-out at Le Tant Corral"

Another emotional ride for Bobby and me came in the summer of 2008 when we were trying to help the people of Le Tant, the same village where Joel, the former witch doctor, had come to the Lord. Le Tant is located on the shores of Lake Azuéi (also called Lake Étang Saumâtre), on land that the government of Haiti had donated to Love A Child. We were in the midst of completing more than fifty concrete block houses in the village so that the people, who were living in mud huts, could have healthier homes. We also hoped the new housing would make the villagers' lives more stable.

But several rich businesspeople operating in the area began to give us trouble. They had hired boatmen to sail their boats to the Dominican Republic for the purpose of buying charcoal, food products, and wood (which they would later grind up to make perfume and soap), and to bring these items back into Haiti. Because the business owners didn't want to pay customs fees, they told the boatmen to bypass the Dominican Republic border by sailing back across the lake and into Haiti with their cargo, landing right at the shores of the village of Le Tant.

The Haitians who operated the boats for these businesspeople were tough and mean. They stole sacks of cement that we were using to build the block houses, and they even stole a boat from one poor lady in the village. But the worst part was that the owners brought in large trucks to transport their cargo from the shores of the lake to their production areas and markets, and their drivers would plow in between the new houses we had built, breaking off parts of the roofs and never acknowledging it or offering to repair them. They would also speed through areas where the children played—putting them at great risk of injury or death.

One day, when Bobby and I were in Le Tant, one of the huge trucks came barreling through again. Then a woman and her husband who were part-owners of the smuggling business came along in a pickup truck. When Bobby tried to tell them they had no authority to come through the area and damage the houses, the woman said, "We give these 'little people' some money to carry the charcoal sacks off the boats, so we provide them with jobs! And besides, they are all just animals!" When she said that, Bobby almost lost it. I would love to tell you that we handled this situation in a sweet and gentle manner, but they really made us angry, and between my Creole and Bobby's "southern Creole," we really let them have it. (We hoped our anger counted as righteous indignation!)

Sadly, the poor in Haiti have been mistreated for so many years that they often believe they deserve it. And if a rich person abuses them, they're too scared to report it to the police. The Le Tant villagers reacted in the same way, and none of them protested the destructive actions of the truck drivers. Bobby and I felt like we were living in our own version of the "shoot-out at the OK Corral." The rich business owners and their henchmen were oppressing these villagers, and Bobby and I felt it was up to us to stand up to them. You have to be tough to work in Haiti!

We had already built three individual seawalls in Le Tant, fifty feet apart, to help keep the lake waters from flooding the village, and we thought that if we extended those walls, the businesspeople would have to use the other side of Le Tant for their activities, the boat people wouldn't need to use the area to unload their products, and the trucks would no longer come through and damage the houses. But when the boat people found out our plans, they went to the local judge and filed a suit against us! They told the judge that the lake was the property of the people of Haiti, and they had rights to it. (However, they failed to tell the judge that they and their associates had been destroying people's property and endangering the lives of the village children.) The business owners were making huge profits, especially from the charcoal, and they didn't want anyone interfering with their plans.

The judge ordered us to build a separate access road to the shore before extending our seawalls. We brought in thirty trucks of gravel and used our backhoe to spread it out, creating a road and a loading area. But even after we built the road, the trucks continued to drive between the houses, causing damage!

We instructed Nelio to invite the judge, the mayor, and the police to come to the village and see that we'd done everything we'd been asked to do, and to appeal to them to help us make the business owners use the new road. However, when the owners learned that the officials were going to visit Le Tant, they realized they were about to get into a legal matter they would be sure to lose. They went to the judge ahead of time and told him that they did not want any problems with Love A Child; they would move their piles of wood and charcoal to the other side of Le Tant, using the new road, and they would repair the damaged houses! Even though this was excellent news, we still brought the judge, the mayor, and the police out to Le Tant to see the new road and the damage to the houses—and all the officials were on our side.

Devastating Hurricanes and Floods

Unfortunately, our relief over the resolution to the conflict in Le Tant was short-lived. Soon afterward, Haiti was hit by the strong tropical storm Fay, followed by the destructive hurricanes Gustav, Hanna, and Ike. During August and September of 2008, powerful winds pounded Haiti with great force, and heavy rains created deadly mudslides and flooding. Our Love A Child Village was not seriously damaged, but hundreds of Haitians died in these storms; many people's homes were flooded or destroyed, and thousands fled on foot to try to find safety, carrying what meager possessions they had. These hurricanes have been described as the "cruelest natural disaster ever experienced in Haiti" up to that point. Flooding destroyed 70 percent of Haiti's crops, which later led to even more malnutrition among Haitian children. The damage was estimated at a staggering $1 billion.[28]

We learned that the roofs had blown off our schools in the mountains, the gardens of the poor had been destroyed, and many of their little homes

28. Jeffrey Masters, PhD, "Hurricanes and Haiti: A Tragic History," http://www.wunderground.com/resources/education/haiti.asp.

or huts had been swept away. Everything they'd owned was either gone or covered in mud. To the best of our ability, we started mobilizing emergency supplies for hurricane victims in various villages, regions, and cities, but we had to wait for the waters to go down and the roads to be cleared before we could actually transport any supplies.

Relief work requires careful logistics; it takes a coordinated effort just to gather and organize the materials to be distributed. But our Love A Child partners gave generously to hurricane relief, and we worked together with many wonderful ministries, including Hand of Hope, led by David Meyer, and Feed My Starving Children, headed by Mark Crea. We had first gotten involved with Feed My Starving Children in the late 1990s when they contacted us and asked if we wanted them to supply us with containers of food to distribute to the poor. This was a wonderful opportunity, and we started with one or two containers and grew from there. Through our association with Feed My Starving Children, we learned how to better organize our feeding programs and to reach more and more people—even whole villages—and we kept improving our methods. All this experience was so valuable as we coordinated the hurricane relief efforts.

At Love A Child Village, Bobby and I worked alongside our associate missionaries and many of our orphans and other workers to fill plastic bags with relief items and dried beans, which would be given out along with donated boxes of rice. A few days before bringing emergency relief to a particular location, Nelio would prepare the way by going ahead of us and organizing the people in the area. To avoid chaos when the supplies arrived, every family was issued a Love A Child food card that would allow them to receive the relief provisions. Assisting hurricane victims was an ongoing task, but we did as much as we could.

The people of Haiti suffered so much loss from the hurricanes and their aftermath, but one of the results that affected us most personally was the distressing situation in Le Tant, where we had just built the block houses, and where we had thought life for the poor villagers could now improve. The waters of Lake Azuéi rose higher than the seawalls, began to flood the houses, and threatened to overtake the whole village. We wondered if the outlet for the water was somehow blocked, but we found out that there actually was no outlet! Compounding this problem were two issues: First, the area had experienced many small earthquakes over the years that had opened up underground springs in the lake, causing the flooding that we'd been trying to stem with the seawalls. Second, Le Tant was only fifty-six feet above sea level. That meant that whenever there were hurricanes, floods, and mudslides, the lake would inevitably overflow. There was no way to get rid of the excess water except through natural evaporation or absorption. But the hurricane season had been so devastating that year, the lake couldn't keep up with all the extra saturation.

By November 2008, the floodwaters had reached more than half the block homes in Le Tant. Families had to walk through water to get to them, and then they had use whatever they could—including coconut shells and their own hands—to bail out the water each afternoon so they wouldn't have to sleep in a pool of water at night. But the water would always flow back overnight. What was even worse, the water was contaminated, bringing typhoid and malaria to the village.

Bobby and I decided to clear another area of land in Le Tant owned by Love A Child so that the families whose houses had been flooded could relocate and have a dry place to live. We gave each family money to buy sticks and palm straw to build new mud huts, but we were praying that somehow we could get new, temporary tents for the villagers to see them through this emergency.

Then, out of nowhere, the Hotes Foundation, endowed by Richard W. Hotes, called us and said they wanted to come and help. We had never met them before or even heard of them. They said that they had tents, buckets, and food for victims of the hurricane. Wow, what an answer to prayer! Each family in Le Tant was given a five-gallon bucket (a precious commodity in Haiti) full of food and supplies—and those with flooded housing also received a family-sized tent to live in. We were so thankful for this crucial help in the midst of the flooding crisis.

Bobby and I were still very concerned about the conditions in Le Tant, and we felt that God must have a more permanent plan for the villagers—we just didn't yet know what that was. For the present, we could only keep a close watch on the situation and continue to provide medical aid and other assistance.

Joy on the Mountain

In January 2009, following the devastating floods and relief work, Bobby and I took a volunteer medical team, made up of people from all over the States, up to the mountains of Savaan Pit. It was a trip that would fill us with joy once again as we ministered to the poor Haitians of that region who had no doctor, nurse, or other medical assistance available to them.

We had planned and prepared for this trip for months. Carole Stufflebeam, the director of the Jesus Healing Center, had spent weeks in the warehouse working with our Love A Child orphanage children to pack, fill, and label medicines. Often, our volunteer medical team members would help with this job when they arrived in Haiti, but since we would be traveling far into the mountains, we could not afford an extra workday, so we had to prepare all the medicines ahead of time.

The day the team members arrived from the States, we worked well past dark to load our big Mitsubishi truck with medical supplies and tents. We packed the truck all the way to the top until it became top-heavy! Early the next morning, we set out with the Mitsubishi and three pick-up trucks carrying staff, volunteers, and supplies.

Getting to Savaan Pit was no easy trek. That is the area where I'd had my "adventures" with the nine flat tires and the back wheels of my truck going over the cliff; it's also where Bobby and Mark almost went off the side of the mountain! The further our convey ascended the mountains, the worse the roads got, and the more dangerous it became. Bobby was driving our well-worn truck, and I was driving a four-wheel-drive pickup that had never before been taken into the mountains. (The light on my dashboard indicated that the four-wheel drive was on, but later we discovered that it had never engaged. It was a miracle that I was able to drive the vehicle through the rugged mountains without an incident!)

Bobby and I had traveled to Savaan Pit for the first time eighteen years earlier, in 1991, the year we moved to Haiti, and we had built a church and a school on the mountain. To put things into perspective, at that time, there were no roads to Savaan Pit at all. Our medical teams had to walk the last four hours in the tropical heat up the mountain. On one early trip there, we had to make the journey in the middle of a tropical storm! So, even though these roads were bad, at least they were roads!

At first, there had been only a brush-arbor school in Savaan Pit, set on top of the mountain. Mr. Occius, the wonderful man who owned the land where the school was, had hired a few school teachers by selling a goat or two, and he had tried to keep the school going. But high winds would whip around the mountain and tear off the tin-and-stick roof of the structure. In the rainy season, the roof would leak and water would collect inside, and many of the children would become sick. Even worse, during dry season, the sun would beat down on the stifling school until the students were nearly ready to pass out. Continuing to use it for the children's education finally became impossible. After we saw the horrible condition of that school, we happened to mention it to our friends James and Daphney Sanders. Soon, they told us that the Lord had spoken to them about sponsoring the building of a new school there. We were so excited for the children of Savaan Pit!

We hired a Haitian construction team to build the school and bought the needed supplies. With the lack of roads, it was a strenuous job to haul all the cement, wood, tin, and other materials up that mountain, but we managed to do it. Everything went well until a local witch doctor put a "spell" on a huge mango tree near the location of the school. Night after night, the witch doctor would make the mango tree catch on fire—or *appear* to burn with fire—and keep burning until the next morning when it would become a normal-looking tree again. When the construction workers saw this "burning tree," they became so afraid that they abandoned the job!

We had to hire another set of workers and send them out to build the school. These workers, too, saw the mango tree catch on fire and burn all night, only to become normal again in the morning. Terrified, they left the job site after only a few days. But the third construction team we sent was a Spirit-filled group led by a Haitian pastor. When the witch doctor made the mango tree catch on fire again, the Christian crew went over and began to rebuke the devil and pray over the tree. After that, there were no more burning mango trees; the group finished the job of building the school, while also preaching to the villagers during the week! This experience was another early lesson for us in how to deal with voodooism and curses.

Now, with our medical convey ascending the last steep hill to Savaan Pit, we could see the village up ahead, with the Love A Child church and several school buildings. We were in the "regions beyond" modern civilization—where there was no phone, electricity, or running water. There weren't even any clusters of huts or homes visible. Someone arriving in the area for the first time and seeing the barren-looking mountains might have thought, *Where are all the people?* But there would be no reason to worry—the people would soon show up from all over the mountains! These mountain people worked hard in their gardens, even though the soil was poor and rocky. Many of them sold small items in the marketplace down at the river, but their income was barely enough for them to survive on. The people were so poor that they would never be able to afford even aspirin. They desperately needed any medical help we could give them.

As we arrived, we looked into the precious faces of people who had already come to wait for us. Our team had brought portable wooden racks where we could hang up our bags of medicines, which we called our "pharmacy." These medicine bags had been rolled up and packed into durable travel bags for the trip. Now, part of the team assembled the racks and hung up the bags as the rest of the group unloaded other supplies, like medical tables and cots, into a school classroom.

After setting up, we had time for a quick dinner over charcoal fires before the evening church service. We planned to hold a gospel crusade meeting every night. Most of us ladies had packed mainly scrubs to wear, so we pieced together "church clothes" by borrowing articles of clothing from each another, whether they fit or not (mostly not)! We had a wonderful time as the local people came to the meeting to pray, sing, and praise the Lord. Afterward, the people returned home, and we retired to our camping tents, climbing into our sleeping bags for a little rest before our first big clinic day.

The next morning, we got up early to be ready for the first patients. It didn't take long for word to get around that there was a clinic in Savaan Pit, and a large crowd gathered. Our interpreter and our nurse were stationed at a registration table where they could talk to the mountain families and fill out triage forms for them. People waiting in line would often become disorderly because they wanted to make sure their families would be treated. We understood that desperate people do desperate things to get help for their babies and children, and we had to keep creating order so things could proceed.

Our team worked hard treating hundreds of children and adults who had a variety of diseases and injuries. Some of the babies had terrible skin infections or suffered from malnutrition. We immediately sent one little girl to the nearest hospital because she had developed Kwashiorkor, a severe form of malnutrition, and we were afraid she was about to die. We also saw a fifty-year-old man with many cancerous tumors. Since we couldn't do anything to help him, either, we gave him money to go to the nearest hospital, and our driver took him there the next day.

Each day, the crowds grew. Those who had come on a previous day and received medical help went back to their homes in the mountains and told their friends and neighbors about it. And now, more people were coming. On the last day, we knew we had to see all the families that we'd already triaged, but we wouldn't be able to treat all the newcomers.

After our nurses had seen the last of the triaged patients, we decided to give out "Family Packs" that families could take home to their huts in the mountains. Each packet contained various kinds of medicines and first-aid items that would serve as a medicine cabinet for them. When a child became sick or injured, the family would have a much better chance of being able to treat them right away. Carole Stufflebeam and I asked all the mothers who were standing in line but had not been triaged to come into the church. Then we shut the doors and began to explain in Creole exactly what was in the Family Packs. Each mother listened intently and was excited to receive medicines for her family that could help keep them healthy and perhaps even save their lives.

With the clinic concluded, we ate a quick supper before heading to our last gospel meeting. Some families had given their hearts to the Lord during the clinic, and they all came to the service. The crowds grew until there was not enough room to seat everyone in the church, and people had to stand outside. But everyone had a wonderful time praising the Lord!

At one point in the service, the pastor of the church asked Bobby and me to go outside the church from a back door and to return through the front door, because they had a surprise for us. When we came in through the front, we were shocked to see a table full of fruit, eggs, and beans. Then we heard some noises at our feet and looked down to see two goats and a rooster! We knew these gifts were a huge sacrifice for such poor families, and we were speechless and humbled at their generosity.

By this time, we were overwhelmed with gratitude to God, and, along with the goats, the rooster, the church people, the overflow crowds, and the rest of the team, we began to sing and dance! We all made a "*joyful noise unto the LORD*,"[29] and from those mountains in the middle of nowhere, our praise went up to heaven.

---

29. See Psalm 98:4; Psalm 100:1.

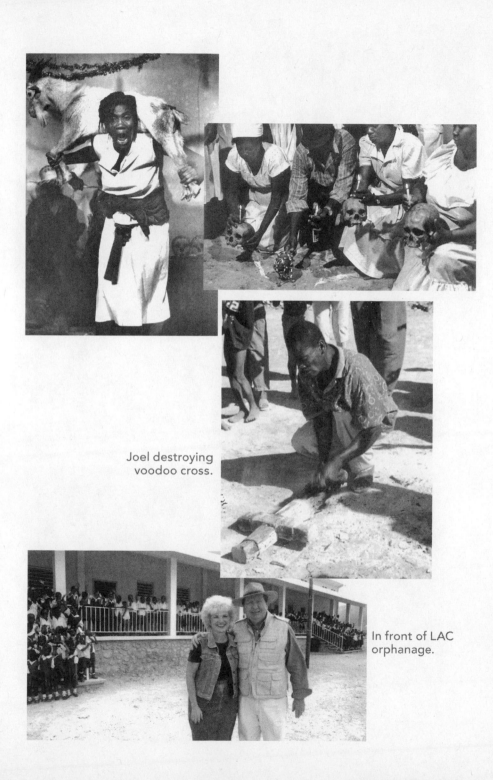

Joel destroying
voodoo cross.

In front of LAC
orphanage.

PART 3

AN EARTHQUAKE SHAKES A NATION

26

VISIONS AND DREAMS

"For the vision is yet for an appointed time, but at the end it shall speak."
—Habakkuk 2:3

Bobby's Vision

During the second week of November 2009, Bobby decided to take a break from our ongoing missions projects to do some thinking and praying about the future of the Love A Child ministry. He got into one of our pickup trucks and drove over to our undeveloped sixty-two acres of property—the second donation of land from the Haitian-American man after the first hundred acres—which we had never been able to get a handle on what to do with. He parked the pickup and began to walk between the thorny trees and scrub brushes.

Bobby remembers, "I looked out across all this property that belonged to Love A Child and wondered, *What does God want for this land?* All of a sudden, I clearly saw before my eyes many houses painted in different colors—pink, yellow, blue, and green. I was stunned. I had no idea who the houses would be for, but I knew God would make it happen in the very near future. I got into my truck and drove back to Love A Child Village. Donna Bryce was working out in the yard. She and Eldon had joined us as associate missionaries, and they lived right next to our orphanage. I told her about the vision, and she believed that this was what the Lord wanted for the land, too. Then I went to tell Sherry the same thing, saying, 'I just saw a vision, and God showed me the property's going to be filled with rainbow-colored houses, and He said they were going to be for poor people, and we're going to build them. It's going to cost a lot of money, and I don't know when it will happen. But God said we're going to do it, and I've already seen what the houses will look like.'"

When Bobby told me about his vision, I immediately knew it was the right plan for that land—we were supposed to build homes for the Haitian people there. But which people? And when? We didn't know the answers to those questions, but we knew that the vision was for *"an appointed time"* in the future:

> *And the* LORD *answered me, and said, Write the vision, and make it plain upon tables, that he may run that readeth it. For the vision is yet for an appointed time, but at the end it shall speak, and not lie: though it tarry, wait for it; because it will surely come, it will not tarry.*
> (Habakkuk 2:2–3)

Pastor Narcisse's Dream

For most of our ministry, we have had to walk one step at a time in faith and trust the Lord to work through us and carry out His plans as we obeyed His Word and followed the Spirit's leading. But a few times over the years, God has given us a glimpse into His will in a special, supernatural way, as with Bobby's vision.

Another such time occurred when Bobby and I had first moved to Haiti and didn't know exactly what God had planned for us except that He had called us there as full-time missionaries. During the difficult early years of the embargo, we received spiritual and emotional encouragement from a wise, elderly Haitian pastor named Pastor Narcisse who oversaw a large church in Petionville, a suburb of Port-au-Prince. We enjoyed talking with this wonderful man, and we wanted to glean any bit of wisdom we could from him.

Pastor Narcisse would frequently have dreams with a spiritual meaning—and they always came true. One day, long before we were given the land in Fond Parisien, we went to visit him, and as we sat in his living room talking together about God's will for our lives, he told us something surprising: "I had a dream about your work in Haiti. God said it's going to grow very, very big! I saw a big piece of land that God is going to give you, and many buildings. I saw you blessing and helping many people." After telling us about the land, he added, "I saw helicopters coming down, many helicopters, and landing on that big piece of land. They will be corning and going, back and forth. I saw dignitaries, generals, important people coming in from the north, the south, the east, and the west. They will all be coming to the land that God will give you, and everyone will know all about what you are doing for the Lord, and God will receive the glory."

Bobby and I didn't want to doubt the word of the Lord in the pastor's dream, but it seemed very far-out. For one thing, it was difficult for us to imagine owning a big piece of land. Second, our ministry wasn't very large or well-known. Third, all the schools and churches we were building were far up in the mountainous regions where no helicopter would ever want to land. So, we kind of put the dream on the shelf and kept moving in the direction we thought God wanted us to go, to the best of our understanding and ability.

But about nine years later, when we received the large piece of property from the Haitian-American landowner, we recognized that this was a fulfillment of Pastor Narcisse's dream. Bobby remembers, "Soon after getting the property, we held a big gospel crusade on the land under a huge tent someone had donated to us, and we asked Pastor Narcisse to be one of the guest speakers. The meetings were wonderful, and many people came to the Lord. Pastor Narcisse preached on the second-to-last night, and before he left the following day, he reminded us again about his dream. 'You will never see me on this land again,' he told Sherry and me. 'I have seen God's plans in my dream, and I know what God is going to do here on this property, but I want to remind you of the dream that God gave me: Helicopters will be coming to this place...from the north, the south, the east, and the west. Don't forget what I am telling you; it will come to pass....God keeps His word. They will land *right here* at Love A Child. They will bring in many important people, generals, and dignitaries from all over the world, and everyone will know of this work here.'"

Our dear friend Pastor Narcisse died in his sleep two weeks later. Though we still didn't understand what the second part of his dream meant, his words rang in our ears for several years afterward—awaiting the appointed time.

27

THE DAY THE EARTH SHOOK

"The rich and poor meet together: the LORD *is the maker of them all."*
—Proverbs 22:2

"God has only one measure for all people."
—Haitian Creole proverb

Tuesday, January 12, 2010, began as a normal day for Bobby and me—children to care for, hungry people to feed, and problems to solve. Pastor Jentezen Franklin and his family from Free Chapel in Gainesville, Georgia, were scheduled to fly in for a visit the following day. They were in the middle of a twenty-one-day "Daniel Fast," which required special food, so we drove about an hour to Petionville to shop at the Caribbean Market, a huge supermarket made of concrete that many missionaries in Haiti used. After we came home, Bobby stayed with our children at the Love A Child Orphanage while I went with Carole to the village of Le Tant, where several sick children were in need of medical care.

Without Warning

Just after we arrived in Le Tant, at 4:53 p.m., a magnitude 7.1 earthquake suddenly struck Haiti. We were standing by a hut near the lake talking to some of the mothers when we heard what sounded like a freight train, coming out of nowhere. The earth beneath us began to move violently. We thought that the land was going to break away and we would be flung into the lake and killed. All of us, including the villagers, threw ourselves prostrate on the ground and prayed. I looked around and saw *every single mud hut in the village* bow down to the right and rise up again together; then they all bent over to the left and touched the ground before coming back up again! After this, the ground moved in waves, followed by another shaking; this time, the tremor acted like a dog shaking its head when it has something clenched between its teeth—growling and thrusting it back and forth violently. Then, suddenly, everything went quiet. When we got back up and found out that everyone was still alive, we began praising God. No one had been injured, and none of the huts had even been damaged. Because the huts were made of sticks, straw, and mud, they had "given" with the force of the quake, much like palm trees do, and remarkably, they were all intact.

Trapped!

At exactly the same time the ground started moving in Le Tant, the entire two-story, 21,500-square-foot orphanage at Love A Child Village began to shake forcefully. Bobby remembers, "The children were on the first floor with their 'mother workers,' who were taking care of them. They all ran outside as fast as scared rabbits, making it out safely, along with their caregivers. I was on the second floor with our main cook, Nini, and both of us were thrown to the floor on our backs. The walls moved about two feet back and forth, and the floor began to roll in waves. Everything on the walls came crashing down. We were afraid that the building was going to fall on us and crush us, but we were trapped inside because the steps going down to the first floor were swaying back and forth. I yelled, 'Jesus, save the children! Jesus, save the house!'

"When the earthquake stopped, and I was finally able to go outside, I saw that all of our children and workers were safe and unhurt. Jesus had protected us. Our church building and several of our schools had cracks in them, but there was no major structural damage."

Immediately after the quake, I returned to Love A Child Village, where Bobby told me about his experience, describing the same tremors I had seen and felt in Le Tant. Later, we learned that stairways—especially cement ones like we had at the orphanage—are among the most dangerous places to be during an earthquake because they lurch, grind, and throw off anything that is on them, so it was a blessing that Bobby and Nini were not on their way downstairs when the shaking started!

We felt so grateful that during the construction of the orphanage, we had taken the advice of Philip Magloire from R & R Construction and spent the extra money for a deeper foundation for the building. We remembered him saying, "One day, a big earthquake may come, and it will save your lives."

The Worst Disaster in Haiti's History

None of our communications devices—our TV, radios, and cell phones—were functioning, and Fond Parisien was about fifty miles from the epicenter. Safe at Love A Child, Bobby and I had no idea how appalling things were in Port-au-Prince and other parts of Haiti. The earthquake had lasted only about forty seconds, but the damage to the nation of Haiti—particularly in the south—was incalculable; it was the strongest quake Haiti had experienced in two hundred years, and it was the worst disaster in the country's history. The earthquake had occurred along the Enriquillo-Plantain Garden fault—the epicenter being a town just west of Port-au-Prince. The fault had been dormant for a hundred and fifty years, but when it woke up, it brought widespread devastation—toppling huge concrete buildings, bridges, houses, hospitals, schools, and other structures for miles around. It also triggered mudslides and flooding.

In less than a minute, approximately 316,000 people had been killed (some estimates say one out of every 45 Haitians[30]), 300,000 had been injured, and more than 1 million had been left homeless.[31] Later, tens of thousands of bodies would have to be buried in mass graves.[32] Haiti's government would have been unprepared to deal with a disaster of this magnitude no matter where it had occurred, but it was especially incapacitated since the capital of Port-au-Prince was one of the hardest-hit areas. The massive Presidential Palace—which had been considered the safest building in Haiti—and other government buildings exploded and collapsed. Nearly all the buildings had been built with concrete roofs but without any building codes, so they had immediately been reduced to piles of rubble and fine powder—killing and choking people. One missionary later said, "It looked like an atomic bomb had exploded." The disaster had reached from the Presidential Palace to the poorest of the poor.

The quake buried many people alive under collapsed buildings. Rescue attempts started immediately, especially by family members, friends, and

---

30. See http://www.eoearth.org/view/article/153237/ (accessed August 22, 2015).
31. See http://www.cnn.com/2013/12/12/world/haiti-earthquake-fast-facts/index.html (accessed August 26, 2015); http://abcnews.go.com/International/years-earthquake-haiti-feeling-aftershocks/story?id=28165070 (accessed August 26, 2015).
32. See http://news.bbc.co.uk/2/hi/8469800.stm (accessed August 22, 2015).

other survivors; but nightfall soon came, making it too dark to see. Haiti's neighbor on the island of Hispaniola, the Dominican Republic, was the first nation to respond with emergency aid. Because both the airport and the seaport of Port-au-Prince were damaged and unusable, any international aid would also have to come across the border from the Dominican Republic into Haiti.

Over the following days and weeks, Haiti endured fifty-nine aftershocks with a magnitude of 4.5 or higher, sixteen of them having a magnitude of 5.0 or more. Of the two largest, a 6.0 aftershock followed only minutes after the initial earthquake, and a 5.9 aftershock struck about a week later, on January 20.[33] Even with all the devastation, one scientist later told Bobby and me, "The 'big one' has not come yet. You think it's over, but the plates have never come together. So we're still on the fault line." That knowledge was—and still is—almost too much to take in.

Right after the earthquake, most of our staff members at the Jesus Healing Center, including our doctor, as well as other workers from Love A Child Village, left to go to Port-au-Prince or elsewhere to check on the safety of their loved ones. They didn't think our clinic in Fond Parisien would be seeing many wounded people, so only two local nurses remained. That night, our orphanage children were still very afraid and wanted to sleep outside rather than go back inside the building, in case another earthquake or aftershock came, so we spread coverings on the ground, and everyone huddled under sheets and blankets beneath the stars. Tomorrow, we resolved, we would go out to assess the damage in nearby areas.

33. See http://earthquake.usgs.gov/earthquakes/eqinthenews/2010/us2010rja6/#summary (accessed August 22, 2015).

SEEKING THE LIVING...
AMONG THE DEAD

"The dead don't know the price of the sheets."
—Haitian Creole proverb

*"Withhold not good from them to whom it is due, when it is in the
power of thine hand to do it."*
—Proverbs 3:27

It was not until the next morning—when wounded people began to arrive at the front gate of Love A Child seeking help—that Bobby and I began to realize something really terrible had happened. With most of our medical personnel away, we were working with a skeleton staff. After helping to get the victims with the worst injuries stabilized, we took a driver and went out to look for more wounded in Petionville and Port-au-Prince.

Indescribable Destruction

Nothing could have prepared us for the devastation we drove into. Buildings we had done business in for years had crumbled into unrecognizable heaps. Roads were blocked, and no businesses or stores were open; there was nowhere you could buy food or gas. Some buildings that had been severely damaged the previous day but had remained standing were now collapsing before our eyes. On the streets, volunteers were bandaging the injured and trying to make them comfortable until more help could come.

Tens of thousands of people were still buried under tons of rubble. Some had survived simply because when their homes or buildings had collapsed, they had landed on piles of dead bodies that had broken their fall. They were trapped together with those corpses in tombs of concrete. Those who had escaped the falling buildings were standing outside piles of debris with cell phones to their ears, trying to reach loved ones, many of whom were imprisoned underneath the wreckage. We saw hands and arms reaching up from beneath fallen buildings, desperate for someone to rescue them; we heard muffled groans and cries for help. The sights were beyond shocking. In our many years of rewarding but challenging ministry, we had faced struggles, difficulties, heartaches, threats, and dangers, but we hadn't experienced anything like this. Our lives would never be the same.

In Petionville, we saw the collapsed remains of the Caribbean Market where Bobby and I had shopped the previous day. Many people were trapped inside, alive—people who had been working or shopping there when the quake hit, people Bobby and I had frequently talked to. They were communicating with the outside world using their cell phones from inside the debris. I stood there and fought back tears as I realized that if Bobby and I had done our shopping just a little bit later the day before, we would now be under that giant pile of concrete blocks—killed or injured—entombed. We still keep our cash register receipt from that day to remind us of how thankful we are to be alive.

No heavy-duty machines were available to remove the tons of rubble, so volunteers worked relentlessly with their bare hands, lifting block after block of concrete in hopes of finding one more person. Others with rags wrapped around their hands dug through concrete, rebar (a steel rod with ridges for use in reinforced concrete), and broken glass, looking and listening for survivors. If they found a dead body, it was dragged away and put into a pile.

Makeshift Ambulances

In Port-au-Prince, we were horrified to see scores of bodies just lying in the streets, which had become a makeshift morgue. Even on the sidewalks, you had to step over dead bodies as you made your way. Quietly, people would walk by and place a sheet or a cardboard box over a body—someone's child, parent, grandparent, brother, or sister. Sometimes, the body would be marked with a name. (A few days later in Port-au-Prince, I heard someone looking for their little girl named Espelancia. I was stepping over dead bodies when I suddenly saw the name "Espelancia" written on the side of a sheet covering a body. I was devastated for that family member who was looking for her.) Bobby and I also saw wounded people filling the vast lawn of the crumbled National Palace. Some were groaning, and some were barely breathing. All were hungry, thirsty, and in shock.

Still stunned but spurred to action, Bobby and I began to gather as many severely wounded children and adults as we could to bring back to Love A Child Village. One man named Sony was lying under a tree. He had lost three children in the quake and his legs were badly mangled and swollen, so we found a metal door to use as a stretcher to carry him to our truck. After we had lifted Sony into the back of the pickup, we fit in as many other adults and children as we could. One little girl was still in horrified terror as we lifted her up, her broken leg wrapped with cardboard and twine. Some of the other victims we helped into the pickup also had broken legs or arms and were wearing makeshift splits made of tattered license plates and other materials. When our pickup was full, we drove home with our precious cargo. At the Jesus Healing Center clinic, the nurses triaged the worst cases, got them comfortable, and put them on pain killers, stitching whatever wounds they could.

Because many other hospitals and clinics were demolished in the earthquake, our Jesus Healing Center was one of the few medical facilities still standing, and it became a makeshift hospital. For days after the quake, every able-bodied person from Love A Child Village was out looking for survivors. We went back and forth between Fond Parisien and Port-au-Prince using our pick-up trucks, our dump truck—anything with wheels—as portable ambulances. We had to use sheets, blankets, or whatever else we could find to lift people into our trucks. As we transported the wounded to Fond Parisien, we would spread other sheets and blankets as canopies over the backs of the pickup trucks to shield the wounded from the blazing sun.

The first week after the earthquake, we had nearly a thousand patients at Love A Child, and we had never seen suffering like this in our entire lives. We saw everything from terrible gashes, deep cuts to the bone, head injuries, broken or missing limbs, missing eyes, serious burns, and much more. We were trying to comfort heartbroken mothers whose children were still back in Port-au-Prince trapped under concrete, or victims who were missing half a face. We were crying with a woman who was about to lose her foot, which was in pieces and had been tied together with fishing line. We were shocked at the condition of an old man who had been burned so badly that his skin was sticking to the vinyl mattress. There were many wounded whose arms and legs were crushed and would need to be amputated, while some people's arms and legs were literally ready to fall off by themselves.

Before long, there were wounded lying all over the floor of our clinic in every room, including the bathrooms and the hallways. We were constantly trying to find cots, sheets, blankets, pillows, and clean clothing. We were tearing up sheets for bandages and assisting in triage. Meanwhile, more wounded people kept pouring through our front gate. We helped everyone we could—but some people died right in our arms. Bobby and I wondered how anyone in the States could ever understand how devastated and helpless we felt.

We decided to take the patients who were in the worst condition—those who were near death or in need of lifesaving amputations—across the border of the Dominican Republic to the Good Samaritan Hospital, because we had no doctors or surgeons at our clinic. Exhaustion began to set in as, around the clock, LAC staff and volunteers drove to and from Port-au-Prince to bring back the injured, as well as to and from the hospital in the Dominican Republic with patients in critical condition—many of whom probably wouldn't be coming home alive.

We tried not to let our hearts get involved with the devastating stories we heard every day from the survivors, but sometimes we just became overwhelmed with emotion. I couldn't help thinking about how frightened all the children in Port-au-Prince and other areas must have been while the earthquake was rumbling and buildings were falling around them or on top of them. Later, when I would ask the children or their parents if they had known what was happening when the quake hit—when the earth, the ground, the buildings, the cars, and everything else began to tremble violently—they would all shake their heads no and look down. Even a month after the earthquake, a mother could be telling me her story and tears would be streaming down her face in raw pain.

"We Left Him Behind!"

On one trip to Port-au-Prince, our Fond Parisien project overseer, Reggie, drove Carole and me to locate the worst cases to bring back to the clinic. We had our truck completely full of wounded and were about to head home when a large group of injured people and parents carrying children rushed toward us, wanting to get into our truck. We knew we had to leave quickly or it would be chaos and nobody would be helped; but one young man about twenty-five years old came running toward us, screaming and crying. In his arms, he carried a child covered with concrete dust. "Take my brother, take my brother; please, he'll die," he pleaded. Carole and I jumped out, literally pulled some people out of the back of the truck who didn't look as bad off as the little boy, quickly placed him in the truck, and then raced back in again as Reggie quickly pulled away.

The journey back was difficult and dangerous as we made our way through looters, rubble blocking the roads, and bodies piled up in the streets. It was after dark by the time we arrived at Love A Child. Carole and I bolted out of the truck to get the little boy and the rest of the people into the clinic. As we helped the patients down, we began to panic when we discovered that the boy was not there—but those we had pulled out of the truck had somehow gotten back in! Exhausted and at the breaking point, we both burst into tears, saying, "We left him behind!"

God bless Reggie. He saw our grief, and he said, "Madame Sherry, don't worry; I will go back and find him." As I waited for Reggie to return, I was overcome with anxiety about what had become of that little boy. Later that night, we saw the lights of the pickup truck coming toward the clinic. When Reggie climbed out, he looked exhausted. He went around to the back of the truck, lifted out the little boy—we learned his name was Edmonson—and carried him inside. Reggie had filled his truck with additional wounded people, and we helped them into the clinic for treatment also.

Worrying about Edmonson's fate was one of the most emotional experiences I have ever been through. The thought of leaving a child behind created a fear inside my heart. To this day, I still have nightmares about leaving a child behind—a child injured in a disaster or dying of hunger. Little Edmonson ended up losing half his foot, but he survived.

The Little Blue Truck

Another little boy was brought to our clinic in the arms of his father. He was about five years old, seriously wounded, and having such difficulty breathing that he repeatedly needed CPR. We knew he needed advanced medical care, so we placed him in the back of our truck to go to the hospital in the Dominican Republic. His father got in beside him and began blowing air into his mouth to keep him alive. I stood next to the truck, and the boy reached up to take my hand. As he did, I placed a little blue toy truck into his hand. With tears rolling down my face, I thought of our own twin grandsons in the

States. They were about his age, and I thought my heart would break into a million pieces as I saw this boy's suffering. Later that night, I received a phone call from our driver saying that the boy had died on the way to the hospital.

One of the most difficult things I dealt with in the aftermath of Haiti's earthquake was guilt—guilt that Love A Child had not been better prepared for something like this...guilt that we could not rescue someone from beneath the rubble...guilt that the little five-year-old boy did not reach the hospital in time...guilt that while so many people had been horribly injured, and masses of people had been buried under the concrete, we had somehow survived—unhurt.

Bobby and I had to keep telling ourselves that God had kept us alive and positioned us with resources so we could provide aid to the earthquake victims. He had placed these wounded people in our lives for a purpose, and we could not look the other way. We could not pretend we didn't hear them or see them; they were the very ones God called us to help. If someone were to ask me the most important thing I learned from the disaster, it would be this: *"Withhold not good from them to whom it is due, when it is in the power of thine hand to do it"* (Proverbs 3:27). We never know when we will have another chance to do good for someone.

On the Verge of Collapse

A few days after the earthquake, Dr. Mardy, our Haitian doctor from the Jesus Healing Center, and our other nurses on staff returned from Port-au-Prince and immediately jumped in to help care for the wounded. When the Jesus Healing Center filled up with patients, we moved some of the injured into our church, which quickly became another hospital. Trucks were constantly bringing in more injured people—even throughout the night. The medical team worked endlessly, and we were so grateful to the volunteers—from physicians to local Haitian Scout troops—who continually arrived at our compound to help. They did many different tasks, from helping us unload the wounded from the trucks and transporting them into the clinic to sanitizing rooms to prevent infection. Our Haitian director, Nelio, seemed to be everywhere at once, helping everyone.

In the midst of the nonstop work, we thought about how, with the hundreds of thousands of people killed in the earthquake, there would now be many more children growing up in Haiti without a mother or father—or both. Additionally, a number of orphanages had been damaged in the quake.

The Rescue Children Orphanage near Port-au-Prince had been destroyed, and in the first few days after the earthquake, we took in thirteen of their children. Pastor Randy Landis of Life Church in Allentown, Pennsylvania, who has a wonderful heart, flew to the Dominican Republic and crossed the border into Haiti to help move these children to Love A Child Village. The orphans had thrown everything they owned into garbage bags when they'd left their former home. It was touching to see how our orphanage children welcomed the newcomers and helped them to unload their mattresses and other items. We quickly took pictures of the new orphans, recorded their names, and got them settled in.

But the survivors of this earthquake needed even more than medical help and shelter. So many people throughout the region also desperately needed food and water. Bobby worked with our LAC staff to get food, water, clothing, and other necessities ready to distribute. They packed everything they could find from our warehouse into white Love A Child rice sacks and sent the supplies out with our Haitian workers to the worst areas where there was no food at all.

All of us continued to work around the clock until we were on the verge of collapse. We knew that it would be impossible for us to continue to function like this, given the numbers of wounded we were receiving. We were doing everything we could, but we were struggling with not having enough medical personnel and supplies to care for all the patients. Furthermore, there were never enough vehicles to transport the severely injured to the hospital in the Dominican Republic.

Just when we were about at our breaking point, we got a phone call from David Meyer of Hand of Hope saying, "What do you need? Just tell us." I replied, "We need surgeons, doctors, nurses, medicines, X-ray equipment, vehicles, and much more." When he immediately responded, "You got it," I burst into tears of relief and deep gratitude. Hand of Hope quickly put together a team of doctors and nurses to send to us. Pastor Randy Landis and Life Church also sent in medical help.

The wonderful Christian medical professionals who came, along with the donations of a portable X-ray machine and other equipment from Hand of Hope, were among the first of many miracles we received that kept us going during this horrific time. "[God] *giveth power to the faint; and to them that have no might he increaseth strength.*"[34]

---

34. Isaiah 40:29.

29

HELICOPTERS AND GENERALS

*"And God sent me before you to preserve you a posterity in the earth, and
to save your lives by a great deliverance."*
—Genesis 45:7

"With many hands, the load is not heavy."
—Haitian Creole proverb

On January 20, just a week after the earthquake, we heard a loud noise overhead at Love A Child Village. Once you experience a natural disaster, any loud noise makes you jumpy. Earlier that morning at about six o'clock, we had experienced a 5.9-magnitude aftershock, causing terrified patients to run outside the clinic—or to crawl out if they couldn't walk—dragging their IVs with them. Now we braced for more shaking, but this time, the noise we heard was not an earthquake or an aftershock. It was a huge helicopter that got closer and closer until it began to descend right next to our Love A Child Radio Station. Apprehensive, we all came running. A helicopter, landing here?

Mere Minutes to Decide

The copter landed in a whirlwind of dust and a blast of air that nearly blew the door off the radio station. Two men got out and hurried toward us. One turned out to be Dr. Douglas Bournigal, a well-known cardiologist from the Dominican Republic (DR). He had been commissioned by the president of the DR to come and speak with Bobby and me, and he had an army general with him. Dr. Bournigal began talking very fast because they had left the helicopter running, and they didn't have a lot of gas left in it.

Bobby remembers, "They told us that the Dominican Republic could not handle all the medical emergencies from the earthquake. They were trying to treat thousands and thousands of critically hurt people, and their hospitals were overflowing. They were running out of beds, and they needed to bring in more doctors right away. They wanted to partner with Love A Child and use our land and buildings to set up a field hospital for earthquake victims. The Dominican Republic felt that our compound was a secure place near their border where they could bring in surgeons and other doctors and nurses from all over the world to help the wounded."

As soon as I heard the men's hurried request, I shouted over the deafening noise of the propeller, "Hold it, hold it! You are running over us like a steamroller! We need to pray about this." But they told us the need was urgent and that we had to make a decision quickly.

With the helicopter engine still running, Bobby and I had only minutes to make up our minds. We already had hundreds of wounded in our Jesus Healing Center, all over the floor of our church, and even outside under the trees—patients were everywhere. We were under a heavy burden as it was, and now they wanted to bring in many more wounded.

Questions swirled in our minds: *How could we feed all of these people three times a day? Grocery stores were crumpled. Gas stations were smashed. There was no cooking oil available. Electric lines and poles were lying in the streets. What about water, toilets, showers, clothing, blankets, tents, and security? Who would oversee this huge field hospital?*

But we also understood the tough situation the Dominican Republic found itself in. It had been inundated with earthquake victims and refugees, and there were not many secure locations in Haiti near the Dominican Republic border where a large field hospital could be set up. With our medical clinic, our other buildings, and our extensive property, Love A Child had everything they needed, and we were just seven miles from the border. Bobby and I were being presented with an opportunity to do great good for the Haitian people in their crisis. Bobby recalls, "In those few minutes, as Sherry and I talked, we remembered that God had led Moses and a million Israelites through the desert wilderness every day for forty years—feeding them, supplying them with water, and caring for them. If He could do that, He could take care of whatever we might need for this field hospital."

Dr. Bournigal urged us, "We've had our eyes on your compound for a long time. It is perfect for disaster victims. We need an answer right now."

There seemed to be no other choice. Still half-dazed, we said, "Yes, we will do it." The two men immediately climbed back into the helicopter and disappeared as quickly as they had come.

After they left, the thought of strangers moving onto our land and of helicopters coming and going all the time scared me. However, after Bobby and I called our LAC board members to discuss it, and after we had prayed over the situation, we both had a peace about it.

More Helicopters Descend

The next morning, January 21, more helicopters began to descend. When the first one landed, men in camouflage jumped out, followed by some generals from the Dominican Republic. Even though we knew that more officials would be coming, it was unnerving to have helicopters landing and men in military gear leaping out carrying weapons. One of the men from the first helicopter was General Pena Antonio, Chief of Armed Forces in the Dominican Republic, who had several other high-ranking officers and an interpreter with him.

They repeated their urgent request and told us that a humanitarian organization wanted to bring in large tents to house the wounded during their recovery process following their surgeries. We were told we could expect one to six thousand wounded to arrive on a daily basis as the crisis continued. "How soon will this all start?" we wanted to know. "Immediately," they replied. With that, they all jumped back into their giant, grasshopper-looking helicopters and flew away.

Bobby and I stood there, speechless, suddenly recognizing what was happening. Pastor Narcisse's words echoed in our minds: *Helicopters will be coming to this place...from the north, the south, the east, and the west.... They will land right here at Love a Child. They will bring in many important people, generals, and dignitaries from all over the world, and everyone will know of this work here.* We turned to each other and said, "This is Pastor Narcisse's dream." That was the moment of grace when we knew for certain that God had planned for us to do this. God had chosen us for this assignment "*for such a time as this.*"[35]

Crisis Across Haiti

Meanwhile, makeshift field hospitals were being set up in other places in Haiti, as well. Some of the wounded were being flown back and forth for

---

35. Esther 4:14.

surgery on the *USNS Comfort* (a United States Navy ship). But in Port-au-Prince and other areas hardest hit by the earthquake, new problems were developing. Hundreds of thousands of people who had survived the quake but lost their homes and possessions had created haphazard "tent cities," most of which had popped up in some of the worst places—rocky riverbeds, public parks, open streets, and even in front of the crumpled National Palace. Many were using mere tarps for shelter, often made of sheets and sticks. Survivors sifted through crumpled piles of concrete, scavenging for materials they might be able to make use of, such as rebar, small chunks of concrete, pieces of cardboard, wire—anything.

As the dust and smoke from crushed and burning buildings hung in the air, respiratory problems became a great concern. Sanitation was another critical issue; people had nowhere suitable to go to the bathroom or take a bath, and the bodies and body parts buried underneath crushed buildings had begun to decay. Worse, thousands of dead bodies were still lying aboveground and also decomposing. The majority of the bodies were unidentifiable, and there were no DNA teams coming to Haiti. Numerous mortuaries lay in ruins, and many hospital morgues had also been demolished, so there were few places to take bodies even if they were identified.

The odor of the dead filled the streets, and people with masks worked day and night to clear away the bodies. Heavy equipment was slow to arrive, so bodies were carted away on pickup trucks or even thrown over donkeys to be collected into piles for burning. Later, it became common to see bulldozers and dump trucks, brought in from many foreign countries, working to dispose of the bodies. Some bulldozers dug massive holes for graves while others scooped up hundreds of bodies from the streets to deposit in dump trucks that hauled them to the gravesites and dropped them in the holes. Steam rollers would then push piles of dirt over the dead to cover them quickly. But contamination had already settled into the dust, and any small wind would carry it throughout Haiti. There was a great danger that diseases would spread and that the dwindling water supply would become tainted.

The mass burials were not only a health issue but also an emotional and psychological trauma for the Haitians, for whom funerals are extremely important. Even the poorest families will sell, borrow, or do whatever they can in order to provide a nice funeral for a deceased loved one. Often, funeral expenses far exceed what the average Haitian can make in years of hard work. For Haitians to think that they would never be able to retrieve the body of a loved one from beneath tons of gravel and concrete, or never be able to give a family member a proper burial, was as painful as their sorrow over the death itself.

Already a struggling nation before the earthquake, Haiti had become even more a land of broken lives and broken hearts. As Bobby and I prepared to lend our Love A Child buildings and property as an emergency field hospital and relief center, we prayed that we would be instruments of God's healing and comfort in the midst of the brokenness.

30

THE LARGEST FIELD HOSPITAL
IN HAITI

"The rock in the water does not know the pain of the rock in the sun."
—Haitian Creole proverb

"For all the law is fulfilled in one word, even in this;
Thou shalt love thy neighbour as thyself."
—Galatians 5:14

Several years before the earthquake, I had started an online blog on our Love A Child website called "Sherry's Journal" in order to keep our partners and the public informed about our ministry work in Haiti. Ever since the earthquake hit, I had been sending out urgent updates as often as I could to ask for prayer and donations for our disaster relief. However, I didn't know how widely those journals were being read until January 22, when more helicopters landed at Love A Child Village. Out jumped men and women in blue jackets and hats who turned out to be a group from a Washington, DC, humanitarian organization. Bobby remembers, "I walked up to greet them, and they suddenly seemed to recognize me and became very excited. One woman said, 'We were sent by President Obama. Washington reads "Sherry's Journal" every day—it's hot! That is how we have been keeping up with the news about the earthquake and whether the border of the Dominican Republic was open or not.'"

Somehow, this group had discovered my blog; and, remarkably, "Sherry's Journal" had become Washington, DC's link to what was going on in Haiti's earthquake disaster areas! These representatives explained that they were in partnership with Harvard University and Harvard Humanitarian Initiative (HHI), as well as Partners in Health, to provide disaster relief for Haiti and to help establish the new field hospital and recovery area at Love A Child. Many of the field hospital's doctors would be coming from the Dominican Republic, but a number of other medical volunteers would be arriving from all over the United States and the world. Our medical staff would be working alongside the international doctors, nurses, and other volunteers. Mobilizing and organizing this international staff would be a huge task, requiring interpreters, an extensive communications system, and much more. But the group told us that they were sending their very best person from the United States to direct the entire field hospital—Dr. Hilarie Cranmer from Harvard University.

"The General" Arrives

In essence, all of us at Love A Child would be operating under the authority of Dr. Hilarie Cranmer as the director of the field hospital—someone we'd never even met before—and we didn't know what sort of person would be leading us. We were a bit nervous the day she was scheduled to arrive, but when this tall, warm, capable woman stepped out of a helicopter to meet us, Bobby and I were immediately impressed. She was very interested in partnering with Love A Child to build a wonderful field hospital, and we soon felt the calm reassurance we needed for what we were about to undertake. In addition to exhibiting strength, Dr. Hilarie Cranmer had a way of letting us know that we would all be working together, and that everything was going to be okay. Our entire staff instantly loved her, and soon we were all calling her "Dr. Hilarie"—or her affectionate nickname, "the General."

Dr. Hilarie went right to work—with little to work with—to prepare and equip the field hospital. Nothing seemed to take her focus away from her goal of providing the earthquake victims with the best possible care. Other US universities and medical staff came and volunteered, working under Harvard. Like a commanding general leading a campaign, Dr. Hilarie organized her volunteer surgeons, doctors, and nurses to use a systematic way of caring for all the wounded. She had a schedule for patients, surgeries, night-time checks, and everything else that was required. Soon, she had the surgeons, doctors, nurses, physical therapists, and other volunteers checked into their tents. The volunteers lived without any conveniences as they gave of their time and skills to take care of the wounded. Throughout the duration of the field hospital, over nine hundred of these medical volunteers would come to Love A Child to help out.

"The General" seemed to know exactly what to do at every turn. For example, she realized immediately that we needed full Internet service. Bobby remembers, "We knew the best Internet people in Haiti—Joel Trimble of Haiti Satellite, as well as his friends who had specialized uplink Internet equipment. They donated sixty-five thousand dollars' worth of equipment and worked very hard to provide Internet service to our remote area. This allowed all patient records to be logged; a program was set up so that doctors could just tap their smartphones to check on any patient at any time. It could have been chaos, but there were efficient organizational and communications systems in operation."

We had no idea that Dr. Hilarie had volunteered to come to Haiti even though Harvard had not yet raised any money to run the relief effort. Only later did we discover that she had actually started the Love A Child–Harvard Humanitarian Initiative (LAC–HHI) Field Hospital with her own money. It would take a while for Harvard to obtain that funding, especially at the levels that were needed; until then, we were on our own. But that didn't deter Dr. Hilarie, who went right to work to require the necessary resources.

One of our immediate needs was for numerous tents for both the volunteers to sleep in and the patients to recover in. We also needed medical equipment and other supplies, along with tons of food and water. Bobby and I and our staff had used up everything in the Love A Child warehouses during the first week of the crisis: cots, blankets, towels, food, clothing, electrical cords, generators, tables, chairs—the list goes on and on. Everything needed to be replaced.

A businessman friend of ours, Mike Wneck from Palm Harbour, Florida, donated many items for the field hospital, such as laptops, wheelchairs, crutches, and solar lights. The Hotes Foundation, which had previously given tents to help the flooded villagers of Le Tant, brought in three Quonset-hut tents to be used as the operations center for the field hospital. Hotes also donated three air-conditioned surgical tents. Other donations— water, medical supplies, clothing, blankets, soap, toothpaste, and much more—came pouring into Love A Child Village via the Dominican Republic. Bobby and I were reminded again of how God had strategically placed our

Love A Child Village just seven miles from the border of the Dominican Republic so we could be a channel of relief for those who were suffering.

Surgery in the Classrooms

The Love A Child church and all of our school buildings became vital components of the field hospital. The day before the earthquake, our orphanage children had been in their classrooms learning lessons that could still be seen written in chalk on the blackboards, frozen in time. Now those classrooms had become operating rooms and laboratories. One classroom served as the pharmacy, and nurses and women volunteers from the Dominican Republic worked long, hard hours to set it up; the quantity of medical supplies needed was incredible.

Even with the many wonderful volunteers and donations of equipment and supplies, working at the field hospital felt like medical care "in the trenches." Hundreds of wounded continued to arrive daily by helicopter, by bus, by truck, by ambulance, and on foot. All the patients were taken to the triage tent to have the severity of their wounds assessed. The worst cases were prepped for surgery in the pre-op/post-op tent, while the rest of the patients were attended to in other treatment tents. Every day, the camp surgeons suited up for major operations. Now that we were a field hospital, we were able to do amputations on site instead of sending patients to the Dominican Republic for the procedure. (With the high number of these surgeries, and for sanitary reasons, the field camp had to have special incinerators to burn body parts.)

After surgery, patients were returned to the pre-op/post-op tent while their anesthesia wore off so the medical team could keep an eye on them before assigning them to a regular patient tent for recovery. Many people needed multiple surgeries to treat their injuries, which required the staff to do special planning and follow-up care. All patients who had undergone surgery or other medical treatment shared a recovery tent with five or six others, where they were monitored for signs of infection or other problems. There were rows upon rows of such patient tents, and the comparatively few nurses made caring for the wounded very challenging.

Family members looking for their missing loved ones regularly arrived at Love A Child to see if a relative had been admitted to the LAC–HHI field hospital. If they were fortunate, they found their loved one there and stayed to help care for them during their recovery. But if a patient had no family members present, we attended to them during their recovery period and even afterward. Thousands of families had been separated by the earthquake, and scores of small children, older people, and others were all alone. Taking care of everyone was an enormous task, but whenever we felt overwhelmed, we would think of all the injured Haitians around the nation who were trying to survive in their devastated cities and villages without any medical care at all, and we would renew our determination to help all those we could.

Sometimes, it was hard to believe that our Love A Child Village had become a fully functioning field hospital. Not only that, but LAC–HHI had become the largest field hospital in Haiti! One reason was that thousands of patients—most of them amputees—who had been operated on by doctors on the *USNS Comfort* or on a Mercy Ship docked at Port-au-Prince needed to be taken somewhere nearby for post-op recovery and extended care. The LAC–HHI Field Hospital became one of several critical care and convalescent centers they were sent to.

Going to the hospital each day was emotionally demanding for Bobby and me. Before the earthquake, we had felt we were on an emotional roller coaster as we daily ministered to people, but this was a hundred times more intense. It was the children who tore at our hearts the most. Some were crying for their parents who were dead, some were in pain, and some had received amputations and were in horrible discomfort. We will never forget their screams and cries and groaning, which echoed in our ears for weeks afterward.

Then we would walk down the rows of patients inside the tents and see people with missing arms and legs, with open wounds—and with crushed spirits. Along with thousands of others, they had been in the wrong place at the wrong time. We tried to put ourselves in the place of our patients, to "love our neighbor as ourselves."[36] There is a Haitian Creole proverb that says, "The rock in the water does not know the pain of the rock in the sun." We were the rocks in the cool water, and these earthquake victims were the rocks in the scorching sun.

Imagine what it would feel like to be an earthquake victim with a broken leg or a head injury or a terrible burn. Suppose you also no longer had any home, you couldn't find any of your relatives (and didn't know if they were alive or dead), you had no money, and you had no way to get to a hospital.

---

36. See, for example, Matthew 22:39.

Then someone comes along in a truck and offers to take you to a medical facility. Once you arrive, you receive food, water, medical care, clothing, comfort, and prayer. It would be such a relief to finally have your needs cared for so you could begin to look ahead toward healing and renewed hope. So, despite our exhaustion, we knew we had to keep ourselves going for the sake of the earthquake victims. Knowing that God could take even the worst things and cause something good to come out of them,[37] we visited, prayed with, and comforted as many people as we could.

Mara's Story

During the first week that the field hospital was in operation, I noticed a woman sitting outside one of the surgery units, looking down at the ground. I almost walked past her, but the desolate look on her face stopped me in my tracks. As I began to talk with her, I learned that her name was Madame Lesoinises and that her seven-year-old daughter, Mara, was undergoing her fourth surgery in two weeks. My heart broke as I listened to her story.

Madame Lesoinises and her little daughter had been at home in Port-au-Prince stirring a pot of rice when their small dwelling started to shake violently. "The few dishes I had began to rattle," Madame Lesoinises told me, "and things began to fall to the floor. I didn't know what was happening. Then, our home collapsed around us."

A huge metal door fell on Mara, crushing her leg and foot to the ground. Not only did Mara sustain a serious injury, but her leg and foot were trapped under the heavy metal door; if that wasn't bad enough, several large, concrete blocks came crashing down on top of the door, making the pressure even greater. Madame Lesoinises couldn't pull her daughter out from beneath the wreckage; Mara had to remain under the rubble, with all that weight pressing on her leg and foot, for two full days before she was finally freed. Madame Lesoinises had also been hurt, but not as severely as Mara.

After being rescued, mother and daughter ended up at a public hospital in the Dominican Republic. I'm not sure exactly how they got there—maybe by a bus used to carry the wounded for medical treatment—but a trip from Port-au-Prince to that Dominican Republic hospital by car would have taken about two hours along very rough roads. I can't imagine what that ride was like for them in their weak and injured condition. At the public hospital, Mara underwent surgery to amputate her leg because infection had set in,

37. See, for example, Genesis 50:20; Romans 8:28.

and her life was in grave danger. Then she was transferred to another medical facility where her leg was sutured and dressed. Several days after Mara's leg was removed, the medical staff saw that another infection was developing where the incision had been made, so they sent her back into surgery. Sometime after that procedure, Mara and her mother were transferred to our LAC–HHI field hospital. Now, the little girl had been taken into surgery once more because her incision was again showing signs of infection. (I couldn't help thinking what a blessing it was that she was under anesthesia. I had heard a story of one little boy who'd had his foot amputated without anesthesia because there was none available and his life was in danger.)

Mara's mother jumped up when she heard that her daughter was out of surgery and was waiting in post-op. She ran to be by Mara's side, and the doctors assured her that this fourth surgery had gone well.

An Outpouring of Help

It wasn't long before Dr. Hilarie ran out of money to keep the field hospital running. There were so many costs, including purchasing fuel; making payroll for some of the workers; stocking pharmacy items; obtaining additional cots and water basins; ordering PVC pipes and truckloads of gravel; buying portable toilets; ordering electrical wiring; and much more. Bobby and I were so grateful for the many donations that came in from our partners and others who heard about our field hospital and relief efforts. Funds also came in from large organizations and ministries. We were so humbled by everyone's sacrifices and generosity. We could not have done what we did without the help of so many people. Every gift was precious and miraculous to us.

In early February, Pastor Jentezen Franklin came to Haiti with his wife, Cherise, and his daughters, Caressa and Caroline, along with other members of his church. Bobby remembers, "They'd been scheduled to visit Love A Child on January 13—the day after the earthquake—but the disaster had suddenly cancelled their plans. Pastor Jentezen has always had a tender heart for the poor, and along with his church and his *Kingdom Connection* television and Internet viewers, he had already been sponsoring two containers of food each month through Love A Child—totaling 540,000 meals per month. This food was going to the poorest of the poor in the mountains. But with the many needs of the earthquake victims, Pastor Jentezen and his supporters helped with extra gifts toward feeding the patients at our LAC–HHI field hospital. They gave fifty thousand dollars to help keep the field hospital going during the first month and later gave an additional fifty thousand to keep it running. They also donated two large trucks for hauling food and supplies. Pastor Franklin, his family, and his team met some of the patients and served them food alongside our LAC staff members. Pastor Franklin joined us in praying with recovering patients, and the entire Franklin family visited with Haitian families in their tents, offering encouragement and hope.

"Then David Meyer from Joyce Meyer/Hand of Hope called again and asked me, 'What do you need? Give us a wish list!' I gave him a long one! Most people would not have understood why we needed a large forklift to move heavy pallets of food, additional trucks, generators, and so much more, but Hand of Hope understood—and they gave it all. We were thankful that Hand of Hope had already been supplying 270,000 meals a month before the earthquake. This really was a blessing at this time of great need. And the Hotes Foundation donated an additional fifteen hundred high-quality tents for the earthquake victims, as well as more supplies."

Before long, the team of those who were helping to fund and supply the LAC–HHI Field Hospital quickly grew. It was led by the Dominican Republic government, in association with HHI, Partners in Health, and Love A Child and its partners—such as Jentezen Franklin/Kingdom Connection, Joyce Meyer Ministries/Hand of Hope, and Feed My Starving Children—but many other organizations also came together to lend a helping hand. Among them were World Vision, AmeriCares, America Refugee Committee, Pan American Health Organization, UNICEF, World Health Organization, Operation Smile, Operation Blessing, the University of Chicago, Cooper University Hospital, Medical Missions, and the government of Mexico. Without all these groups working together, the field hospital would never have been possible.

The Orphans Reach Out in Love

We also wouldn't have been able to keep things going without all the volunteers who personally helped out—including the local Scout troops that came every day to assist with many different tasks. Additionally, the earthquake brought out the very best in all the children at our orphanage, whose lives had been completely disrupted by the quake and the disaster relief. Bobby and I had always made it a priority to teach our Love A Child orphans the importance of giving back to their country and of helping others. Every day following the earthquake, we watched the children jump in and help in many different ways. We never once asked them to do anything—they just knew what to do, and we were so proud of them! As Bobby always says, "Love is not something you just talk about; love is something you do!"

Julianne, who was one of our original four orphans, always enjoyed working in our remote medical clinics, and she wanted to go into the medical field. (She is currently in medical school, studying to be a pediatrician.) Julianne started helping at the field hospital right away as a translator so the doctors and nurses could communicate with the patients about their treatments. Another of our orphans, Clepson, spoke English very well and enabled the doctors to understand what the patients needed. Dimelia helped to transport medical supplies, and several other children went every day to pray with children who'd had amputations.

Dana, another of our older daughters, helped to lead the kitchen staff in preparing hot meals for the patients. Frantzo, one of our older boys, carried heavy pots of food into the Jesus Healing Center and then dished out the food for the patients. Julia helped to get everything ready to serve the patients, and then she and Florence offered patients a big smile as they handed out plates of nourishing food. Frantzo passed out donated bottles of water to the earthquake survivors. These are only a few of the orphans and some of what they did to provide assistance during the crisis.

Bobby even organized our younger orphans to walk through the camp and make sure everything was litter-free. From the oldest to the youngest, they did what they could to help, working day after day for months, and we greatly appreciated everything they did. (We don't know what we would do without our orphanage children. When our hearts are broken in Haiti, they bring us so much joy and hope!) We had no doubt that our children would grow up to be a huge blessing to the people of Haiti as they carried on the legacy nurtured at Love A Child by their "Poppie" and "Mommie" and as they followed the path the Lord had prepared for them.

"Where There Is Broth, There Is Encouragement"

So many details went into the running of the field hospital—including providing daily meals for the whole camp. Right after the earthquake, Love A Child had supplied nearly all the meals for the many hundreds of victims at our compound. At first we used our own supply of food, and then we relied on immediate donations that enabled us to continue feeding the people. But with the creation of the field hospital, we took on the responsibility of feeding the influx of thousands of new patients, as well as the doctors, nurses, and other volunteers. This was in addition to the meals we were providing for the children in our orphanage and our own staff! More than ever, we relied on the gifts of our faithful partners and the contributions of other generous donors in order to feed this mass of people.

We didn't have a kitchen near the field hospital, so, in the beginning, we would set up charcoal stoves in front of the orphanage and cook the meals in huge pots, and this was hot, hard work for our cooking staff. After the food was ready, we would put the pots in the back of trucks—the pots were so heavy, it took two people to lift them onto a truck—drive them to the Jesus Healing Center, haul them inside, and put the food onto plates. Then we distributed the food to the wounded and often to their family members. We did this three times a day—an exhausting but necessary process.

We needed to make sure the patients were getting nutritious food during their recovery, full of vitamins and minerals that would promote healing and enable them to regain their strength. This food was donated by the organization Feed My Starving Children, with a rice and beans mixture that was a special recipe designed for those who are malnourished.

We found that a kind word and a plate of nourishing food went a long way toward the recovery of the earthquake victims! As a Haitian Creole proverb says, "Where there is broth, there is encouragement." I was greatly moved when I saw many people giving thanks for their food not only before eating their meal but also before *every bite* of their meal. When Dr. Hilarie saw how we were feeding the patients, she told us how wonderful it was for them to receive three meals a day, especially since no other hospitals in Haiti were able to do this. "What dignity this gives these people," she kept saying over and over again. I hadn't really thought about how it gave dignity, but when Dr. Hilarie put it that way, I thought, *How true.*

"Big Mama"

After a few weeks of cooking on charcoal stoves, we were blessed to receive several wonderful propane stoves from the organization Rice Bowls. Then Richard Hotes heard about our logistical struggles to feed the patients. Bobby remembers, "He called me and said, 'Help is on the way. We are sending a fully-equipped kitchen on wheels.' He donated an amazing mobile kitchen with huge, stainless-steel stoves that were large enough to cook meals for the multitudes at the field hospital."

The Hotes Foundation had paid fifty thousand dollars for the kitchen (which we soon dubbed "Big Mama"); however, we had many problems trying to get it shipped to us, so it took a little while for it to arrive in Haiti. First, we were told it was too big for a shipping container; then we couldn't get a military plane to fly it in; and so forth. But when we told Richard Hotes about our dilemma, he said, "Let me take care of it"—and within twenty-four hours, the mobile kitchen had arrived in Port-au-Prince!

We had hired a towing service to haul the kitchen to Love A Child Village, but it was so heavy that the towing company's vehicle could not handle it. We had to find a Plan B. That's when we discovered that only our specially designed, all-terrain ambulance was powerful enough to pull the kitchen all the way from Port-au-Prince to the Love A Child compound. So, after many delays, "Big Mama" finally arrived to feed her "children"!

Keeping Up with Our Ongoing Work

Even though Love A Child was in the midst of helping to run the field hospital, we still needed to continue all our regular outreaches, including our mobile clinics, because those needs hadn't gone away—and many of them had gotten worse. When the relief work became a little more stabilized, we were able to resume our clinic activities for the Fond Parisien community at our Jesus Healing Center. Because our buildings were being used to full capacity, the Hotes foundation donated large tents where we could conduct our additional services—our preventive malnutrition program, our vaccination program, and our ob-gyn care clinic.

We also continued supporting our schools in the outlying areas—including lunch programs for more than five thousand children a day—as well as our food programs for families living in the mountains. Additionally, we had previously taken on the responsibility of distributing food to about forty other missionaries and orphanages each month so they could carry on their outreaches, and we couldn't leave them without a lifeline.

We also needed to help feed hundreds of earthquake survivors throughout Haiti who still had no access to food or no money to purchase any. We tried to help as many of them as we could until they were able to help themselves again. In total, with all our food distribution projects, we were providing over a million meals per month. Staff members from the Love A Child office in Florida flew down to help out. Our Love A Child staff worked long hours unloading pallets of food to distribute to hungry people. There is a Haitian Creole proverb that says, "Hunger makes the caterpillar eat tobacco leaves," meaning "Hunger makes one desperate." At the food distribution sites, it was heartbreaking to see so many hands reaching out to grasp the food. I had never witnessed such desperation in my life.

Pressing Needs

We were now some weeks into our disaster relief efforts, but many pressing needs remained. When the earthquake first hit, there was extensive news media coverage of the disaster, with announcements about where donations could be sent; however, it wasn't long before most of the reporters and news crews went home, and the world was no longer focused on Haiti and its crisis. But Bobby and I and the rest of the volunteers and humanitarian workers in Haiti were with the earthquake victims every day, and we saw their ongoing struggles and pain. Our Love A Child staff continued to make trips to the areas of greatest devastation in Port-au-Prince to bring back more wounded to be treated. In front of the National Palace and in the marketplaces, thousands of people still begged for rides to a hospital—a pitiful sight.

But as we've said before, the Haitian people are remarkable. No matter what happens, they just keep adapting, improvising, and starting over. We saw people on the streets of Port-au-Prince, with tragedy all around them, managing to sell things such as fruit, charcoal, and other items in order to survive each day. Others sold used clothes brought in from the Dominican Republic. Still others set up Haitian "Goodyear" stands where they repaired tires. *Machanns* (sellers) in Haiti were setting up stores anywhere they could—on an old wall, against the side of a building, on a pile of stacked chairs. Still others without any resources had to resort to earning a little money by carrying buckets of water or hauling extremely heavy loads on carts. Bobby and I determined that somehow, someway, we would help more Haitians to regain their health, become self-sustaining, and live prosperous lives—spiritually, physically, and economically.

31

"WHO WILL CARRY
YOUR HEAVY LOAD?"

"God is good."
—Haitian Creole proverb

"God is our refuge and strength, a very present help in trouble."
—Psalm 46:1

Although many Haitians follow superstition and voodooism, there are a number of practicing Christians in Haiti, and Bobby and I saw patients and other refugees praying and praising the Lord in the field hospital, even in the midst of their troubles. These people were so strong, and their faith in God and their smiles helped to sustain us as we dealt with our enormous responsibilities after the earthquake.

Church at Field Camp

After the trauma they had endured, we wanted to help bring peace to the lives of all the patients, as well as to the family members who were caring for them as they recovered. Many Haitians love going to church, and because the earthquake victims and other refugees could not go to their own churches, we regularly held church services for them.

We began to hold Sunday services about a week after the field hospital opened. Since our church and school buildings were being used by the field hospital, we borrowed a tent and brought in our own musical instruments. The pastor of our Love A Child church, Pastor Varius, and our entire congregation invited all the earthquake survivors to come and worship with us under the tent. We were in need of seats, so some of the patients and their families carried their chairs on their heads into the tent, while those who could not walk were transported there on their own mattresses.

At the first Sunday service, it seemed as if we were conducting church for people who had been wounded in a mine field. Everywhere you looked, there were people without arms and legs, but there was hope on their faces as they praised the Lord! Many of the volunteer doctors and nurses from the various countries also came to the service. Afterward, the members of our Love A Child congregation walked with patients and prayed with them. It was one of the most touching services I have ever attended.

"You Have Given People Faith and Hope"

After a few weeks of Sunday services, Dr. Hilarie told us, "We notice that the people in this field hospital are healing faster than in other places. We think it is because of the church services. You need to have more than one service a week. Please have one every day—the people need it. We doctors from Harvard University study disaster relief assistance and how to take care of people in crisis. We thought we knew it all, but you have managed to give these people something that we didn't realize they needed—faith and hope."

When Dr. Hilarie told us this, we started holding church services several times a week, under the trees. A number of patients and their families attended; additionally, many doctors and nurses who normally didn't go to church kept attending every service, listening reverently to the preaching of the Word of God, some with their hands raised, some crying, some singing, and some just standing in quiet amazement.

The relief efforts had thrown together into one field camp people of various backgrounds and religious persuasions—Jews and Christians, Democrats and Republicans, liberals and conservatives, and everything in between. I remember one of the doctors saying, "When they told me I was coming down to work with a Christian organization, I said, 'Those stupid people don't know what they're doing. I'm not going down there.'" But when he came, he was amazed at how efficient everything was and how well we all worked together, regardless of our differences of opinion. Bobby and I had such a wonderful working relationship with everyone who came and volunteered, and we loved them all.

While many patients attended the services, others would worship the Lord privately as they listened to the meetings from their tents. I noticed that while people's eyes might be stained with tears as they worshipped, they were also filled with joy and hope. I even saw people with broken legs hobbling outside their tents to sing and praise the Lord!

"Come to Me, All Who Are Heavy Laden"

A number of the patients and their family members accepted Jesus Christ as their Savior while at the field hospital. The earthquake had stirred the hearts of many people who might never have been touched by the preaching of the gospel alone, awakening them to their spiritual need. As people's wounds healed, we thought we could hold a special baptismal service for anyone who wanted to be baptized. Baptism in Haiti is treated very seriously as a sign to relatives, friends, and everyone else that you are making a complete change in your life to follow the Lord. Because we didn't have a river or a baptismal pool near us, we would use the next best thing—our Tilapia Fish Farm tanks (moving the fish out first, of course!).

Many patients, family members, and medical personnel throughout the field hospital became excited and intrigued about the upcoming baptismal service, which would be held at the end of May, and they planned to attend. When the day arrived, every patient who was able, including the handicapped; and many of the medical volunteers, including doctors and nurses, headed to the Tilapia Fish Farm tanks for this unique service, and the crowd grew even larger as the service began. All these people from various backgrounds, beliefs, and nations had come together to focus on thirty new Christians who were to be baptized that day!

Bobby remembers, "Before Pastor Varius and the pastors assisting him performed the baptisms, many people gave their testimonies, and then I delivered a special sermon. I like to preach messages that are easy for people to understand, and I gave a sermon entitled 'Giving Your Heavy Load to Jesus,' based on Matthew 11:28: '*Come unto me* [Jesus], *all ye that labour and are heavy laden, and I will give you rest.*' I talked about the heavy emotional, psychological, and physical burdens that everyone at the camp was carrying, while an interpreter translated my message into Creole.

"I had asked our Fond Parisien project director, Reggie, to wait behind the scenes and then enter the service at a certain time carrying a large, heavy white sack. Reggie is a *big* guy, so when I gave him the signal, and he staggered in with his 'heavy load,' every eye was on him. Then Reggie dramatically fell to his knees under the weight of that load. I had placed boxes inside the large sack, and on each one I'd written a different confession of need, like 'I have no job,' 'My house was destroyed,' 'I am sick and in pain,' and 'I lost one of my limbs and can't provide for my family.' I began to pull out these boxes and read what was on them. Then, looking out at all the earthquake victims and those who had been working so hard to help them heal, I asked, 'Who is going to help you carry that heavy load? The answer is easy—Jesus!'

"After I said that, everyone began singing, 'Jesus is high above; here is my load. I have no mother or father or friend to help me carry my load, but here it is, Jesus!'"

"It Doesn't Matter If You Don't Have a Leg or an Arm"

At the end of that wonderful service, many more people wanted to be baptized. That day, people of all ages were baptized in those Tilapia fish tanks, including young boys and girls and older men and women. Every single one was precious, but no one touched people's hearts more than one beautiful young woman in a wheelchair who was missing both an arm and a leg and who had been a patient at the LAC–HHI field hospital from the time it first opened.

During the service, this woman had shared her testimony. She had been in Port-au-Prince when the earthquake hit, and she had ended up under a mountain of concrete, trapped for a day or two before being rescued. After being pulled from the rubble, she had been transported to the public hospital in the Dominican Republic, where she was taken into surgery to have her limbs amputated, similar to what little Mara had gone through. But during the surgery, she had a remarkable experience. "It was like a dream," she said. "Jesus was standing right beside me. He told me it didn't matter if I didn't have a leg or an arm, that He loved me just the same, and that I could do His work without my leg and arm. Jesus told me to tell others to follow Him, or else there will be even worse disasters to come. He told me to go back and to bring others to Him."

After that experience, the young woman had given her heart to Jesus, and she deeply loved the Lord. She wasn't feeling sad or depressed about the loss of her limbs; instead, with a glowing face, she praised God for giving her life and hope. When it was time for her to be baptized, I told Pastor Varius,

"We need to put plastic garbage bags around her wounds, because we don't want them to get infected in the water." After her wounds were wrapped securely, she was pushed in her wheelchair toward the tank. As she approached, she was crying and praising the Lord. All of a sudden, she ripped off those plastic bags, lifted her one arm, and said, "Put me in the tank! Let me go down in the water with Jesus."

As the pastors helped her into the tank to be baptized, there was not a dry eye in the crowd. Everyone was praising God and thanking Him for sparing this young woman's life. Bobby and I have had some great moments in our years as missionaries, but this was one of the best.

32

"HOPE MAKES US LIVE"

"Hope makes us live."
—Haitian Creole proverb

"Tribulation worketh patience; and patience, experience;
and experience, hope."
—Romans 5:3–4

Ever since late January 2010, the patients in our field hospital had received the very best of care, thanks to Dr. Hilarie, who had continued to maintain and improve the hospital, and all the other wonderful medical volunteers. When Dr. Hilarie would occasionally go back to the United States for a short rest, another doctor from Harvard Humanitarian Initiative would fly in to take her place. All of the field directors did an excellent job at overseeing the camp, and we couldn't imagine any other field hospital in Haiti being run better than ours.

The patients were healing very well. Many of the amputees and other wounded needed physical therapy, and volunteer physical therapists, including Hands of Light in Action, came to Haiti to help both the children and the adults. They had to learn to walk again using only one leg and crutches, or to do daily tasks using only one arm. Also, a number of the amputees were fitted for prosthetic limbs, and they had to learn to adjust to them and use them in daily life.

Nowhere to Go

As spring came, the immediate medical crisis of the earthquake disaster was abating. After doing months of surgeries, follow-up care, and rehabilitation, it would soon be time for the doctors, nurses, and other volunteers to go home, and for the field hospital to close down. However, there were nearly two thousand earthquake victims—three hundred and eighty families—still living in the hospital tents on the Love A Child Village compound. Most of them were homeless or displaced and had nowhere to go. Additionally, many of the amputees or other injured people were still undergoing the process of healing. They had no jobs, and they needed a safe place where they could be housed and fed until they could recover enough to become self-sustaining. Where would they go?

The organization American Refugee Committee (ARC) wanted to partner with Love A Child to help these refugees by setting up a tent city for them, and Bobby and I offered the sixty-two acres of raw, undeveloped land that adjoined the hundred-acre portion of our property. We knew that God had told us there would be permanent housing on that land one day, but we still didn't know exactly how that would unfold or who would be living in the multicolored houses of Bobby's vision; for the moment, we felt that the Lord would have us use the land for the refugee tent camp. These families had an urgent need, and we had the land.

Preparing the Tent City

Creating a tent city wasn't just a matter of setting up tents. First, the land first had to be cleared of brush. Also, since thousands of people would be living in close proximity, constructing a proper infrastructure was essential. We had to put roads between the tents, requiring tons of limestone gravel that would give protection against flooding during the rainy season. Community toilets and bathing areas had to be installed, which UNICEF provided the funds for. Wells for water had to be drilled, and Operation Blessing sponsored seven of those wells. A clinic and a rehabilitation center for the amputees were also needed. More tents would be required, and the Hotes Foundation came through again to provide them.

Reggie and another LAC worker named Philomen worked with our bulldozer and front-end loader to start clearing the land. We also hired twenty Haitian workers to help clear the brush with their machetes. While this was going on, many of the refugees came and gathered up every tree limb and tree stump they could find to make charcoal to sell or to use for cooking their food. Sometimes, a fight would break out over possession of a simple tree stump! But soon the land and the infrastructure were ready to receive the refugees.

Pulling up Stakes

The earthquake survivors had to start their lives over again with practically nothing, so we gave each family a "starter kit" when they moved to the ARC–LAC tent city. This included a tent; pots and pans; a cook stove; some food, water, and clothing; household items; and Bibles. The Haitian Christians had lost their Bibles along with everything else, and Bibles in both Creole and French were donated by groups like Joyce Meyer Ministries/Hand of Hope, the Hotes Foundation, and LeSEA Broadcasting. The refugees were grateful to have a place to live for the time being, with enough supplies to begin to set up their new households.

Many churches and organizations donated toiletries and other items for the families. In addition, a lot of clothing had been donated for earthquake victims at the field hospital, and this continued as the refugee camp took shape. World Vision gave one thousand pairs of wonderful tennis shoes. Sometimes, we received some unusual articles of clothing, too, but we still distributed them because we knew the people would make use of them somehow, regardless of their size, shape—or pattern. Once, we received a whole truckload of men's boxer shorts—with red hearts all over them! (The ladies loved them!)

A Difficult Adjustment

We set up a system for transferring the families to the ARC–LAC camp. As soon as ten or twenty families were medically discharged by HHI, they would pack up their tents and belongings and board our trucks, which took them to the tent city. Going to the camp was a very difficult adjustment for most of the earthquake survivors during first few weeks. While they were happy to have a place to go, the move itself was emotionally tough for them. They had been fed and nurtured in our field hospital, and they had made friends who had shared their hospital tents. Now they would be living in a different environment. The routine of field hospital life had given them a sense of security, and now they felt that security was being ripped from them.

Furthermore, it took a while for everything to get set up properly at the tent camp. For example, at first, there were no lights outside at night, and it was extremely dangerous for the amputees to find the latrines in the dark. They often fell into holes or tripped over tent stakes .We were finally able to provide some small flashlights for all of them, due to someone's kind donation. Sometime later, we were blessed with solar lights from Germany, thanks to LeSEA Broadcasting and Feed the Hungry.

"Just Let Them Be Haitians Again"

Another difficult adjustment was that they weren't permitted to cook their own food over charcoal fires, as most Haitians do. The ARC organizers said that it was unsafe to cook outside near the tents, and they also did not want people cutting down trees on the property to make fires.

They took away all the pots, pans, and cooking utensils that had been given to the families when they'd left the field hospital and locked them away. In their place, they gave the refugees "Meals Ready to Eat," or MREs. These organizers meant well, feeling that they were responsible for protecting everyone at the camp. But they didn't realize what the consequences would be. Haitians were not used to eating foods that contained a lot of preservatives, especially over a long period of time, and it caused intestinal problems. (Intestinal illness is not fun anyway, but imagine dealing with it in a huge camp with community latrines?)

Bobby and I would walk through the camp to see how the people were doing, and we would see their anger and hear their grumbling about not being able to cook for themselves. The refugees just wanted to cook their own hot meals on their own little *charbon rechos* (charcoal grills). We knew this could develop into a dangerous situation for the ARC workers, and we felt that the Haitians needed to get back to their normal way of life as much as possible.

We talked to the ARC organizers, explaining that as far as we were concerned, it would be fine to let the Haitians gather sticks of wood for their fires and cook their own food. "Just let them be Haitians again," we urged, and ARC finally agreed. Soon, we were regularly distributing rice and beans and other food for the people to cook, thanks to our friends at Feed My Starving Children and Feed the Hungry.

Camp Life

We tried to help the refugees establish as normal a life as possible under the circumstances, and they soon began calling the ARC–LAC tent city "Camp Hope," because, they said—quoting a Haitian Creole proverb—"Hope lets us live." The children were able to attend school, thanks to USAID, which provided new tents for classrooms, as well as new school books and the funds to build schools desks and chalkboards. Also, we were able to hire many of the refugees who had healed enough to do various necessary jobs around the camp so they could earn money and start recovering economically.

Additionally, since the people of Camp Hope were no longer near the tent church at Love A Child, they needed their own church. James and Monica Satcher heard about that need and donated a large red-and-white gospel tent. Soon, songs of praise filled Camp Hope Church. Some people would meet every morning under the big tent for a prayer meeting, praying for two or three hours.

Rain, Wind…and Deteriorating Tents

A tent camp can be difficult to maintain under the best of conditions, but with the late spring and early summer came the rainy season, and the tents started getting tattered and torn from exposure to the wind and the rain. Our volunteers sewed the torn tents back together; when they ran out of thread, they used dental floss. There is a Haitian Creole proverb that says, "The straw house can fool the sun, but it cannot fool the rain," and the tents were beginning to feel like "the straw house."

At night, when I was in bed at the Love A Child Orphanage and woke up to hear rain pounding down, I would start to cry because I knew what the people in Camp Hope were going through. Bobby and I would often get up, ride over to Camp Hope, and walk around in the mud with flashlights to check on how the people were doing. Fathers would be struggling to tie down pieces of tents flapping in the wind, and mothers would be shoveling out mud that had slid into their living spaces. Some people were on their hands and knees, scraping up mud with their bare hands. Bobby was always so kind to everyone at Camp Hope, walking around the tents and greeting people in his "Southern Creole," kissing grandmas on the cheek and hugging the children, and always reassuring them that everything was going to be all right. One tent we checked on was occupied by a lady who was still recovering from two horribly injured legs. She had no bed, so she would sit up at night. The next day, we made sure that she had a nice, soft bed to sleep in.

Bobby and I felt so guilty seeing these men, women, and children of Camp Hope battle not only the rain and mud, but also the tropical heat, the mosquitoes, the rats, and sometimes even thieves—let alone the monotony many people experienced from having practically nothing to do. Many refugees were experiencing depression.

Bobby and I wondered, *What would they do with their lives now? How could they continue to live in conditions like this? How long would these tents last?* We had an overwhelming feeling of helplessness, and even though we did everything we could do to assist them, we knew that they could not keep living this way much longer. Thankfully, Richard Hotes sent in brand new tents when they were needed the most. But Bobby and I felt such a burden for the people as we began to research housing solutions for the earthquake victims.

The Vision's Appointed Time

As Bobby and I prayed about the situation, it became clearer and clearer to us that the people living on our land were no longer temporary refugees. The earthquake and its aftermath had turned their lives completely upside-down, and while the earthquake survivors had originally come from Port-au-Prince and many other areas, they had all ended up in Fond Parisien. This is where they were—and this is where they were welcome to stay, if that is what they wanted. Those rainbow-colored houses of Bobby's vision, which he had seen just weeks before the earthquake, would be God's gift to them to enable them to create a new life of blessing and stability after all the tragedy and upheaval. They would have a new village to live in—a Miracle Village.

We were excited when we realized that this was God's purpose for the land, and we quickly began drawing up plans for permanent housing for the refugees. The housing project would be built in phases. We decided it was imperative to do something to move the amputees and others who were most physically disabled out of their tattered tents as soon as possible. Phase One, the first fifty houses, would go to all amputees (with their families), as well as to families with children who were critically ill or who had deformities.

We asked John Boldt of Engineering Ministries International, which had laid out the original plan for our Love A Child property, to draw up plans for developing the sixty-two acres into Miracle Village. John and his team of volunteer professional engineers were amazing! They planned an entire housing subdivision in a Third World country and worked very hard surveying the land and planning the layout of the new village. Mark Ostrander, who has been the construction manager for all our major projects, worked with EMI to plan the housing and design all the infrastructure. Each house would include a small yard for a garden, and there would be community toilets, kitchens, and showers. The village would also have a school, a church, a Jesus Healing Center satellite clinic, a fire station, a playground, a soccer field, and a security wall around the entire sixty-two acres to protect the families from intruders.

We began to think about what type of Haitian house to build—and how to build it strong enough to withstand hurricanes and earthquakes. We knew that the Haitian earthquake survivors were scared to death of concrete buildings, so Mark Ostrander, who is next to a genius when it comes to design and construction, came up with a wonderful design. We would build wooden houses, twenty-fix feet by sixteen feet, using strong, T-11 siding on the outside and OSB wood for the inside. Each house would have two bedrooms, a living room, and a front porch. (Oh, yes, the houses would also have louvered windows to enable the Haitians to close up everything tightly at night so they would be assured that no lougarous would get in!) The houses would be sprayed to protect against termites, and they would have special hurricane clips. These well-constructed houses would last about forty years. Additionally, the houses in Phase One would have ramps for the physically challenged.

Bobby and I wanted to see what the houses would look like before we started building them. Mark and his son, Jesse, actually built the first "Miracle Village house" behind Mark's church, The Mission, in Palm Bay, Florida. It looked beautiful, but we soon realized that in order to build each family a home, we would need enough wood to fill several Home Depots! Finding that much wood to purchase would be impossible due to the deforestation; and even if it were possible, the costs would be four to five times greater than the cost to buy it in the United States. The wood and other materials would have to be imported; which would involve huge shipping costs, but it was the only way to do it.

We estimated that it would cost three thousand dollars to construct each house. (This was just for the house—it did not include the costs of clearing the land, creating the infrastructure, laying the foundations, digging the wells, buying furniture for the houses, paying the shipping fees, constructing the huge concrete-block security wall, and building massive drainage canals to divert water.) That meant that the first fifty houses for Phase One alone would cost a hundred and fifty thousand dollars. We would need a miracle! But, as Bobby says, "Faith never wonders, *What if it doesn't happen?* Faith doesn't think about defeat. It just puts one foot in front of the other, and it keeps on movin'!"

As we moved forward, the miracle happened. David Meyer from Joyce Meyer/Hand of Hope called us to say they wanted to sponsor the first phase of houses for the full amount! The Lord also began to speak to many other people who gave what they could—from the "widow's mite" to larger gifts, so we could cover all the other costs associated with building three hundred and eighty houses (later adding even more). Our Love A Child partners also continued to give sacrificially to keep the miracles coming for the infrastructure, the gravel roads, the wells, and the security wall.

We would rely on volunteer teams to come from all over the States to help build all the houses. Our very capable missionary Mark Rose became the foreman of the earthquake housing project at Miracle Village, and over the months he was in the trenches every day, right beside the volunteers.

In mid-June 2010, we were able to start Phase One of the project. The first group of volunteers to come to Haiti to help build the houses included Mark Ostrander and his son, Jesse, along with members of the Crosspoint Church of Georgia. They were a wonderful, hard-working team. It was a tough job building those houses from scratch. Nothing was prefabricated; each board had to be cut and put together like a jigsaw puzzle.

Each day, the amputees made their way over to the construction site to see how their new dwellings were progressing. When the first house was going up, they looked at it in awe. "How many families will you put in each house?" they wanted to know. "Each family will have their own house," Bobby told them, "One family to each house." When they heard that, these brave men, women, and children suddenly realized what a great miracle the Lord was about to do for them. He was going to give them a better house than they'd had before the earthquake! We stood there with tears in our eyes as they began to praise God.

At the end of the first week, after much hard work in the tropical sun, the team had completed only two houses. Bobby remembers, "When Mark and I realized this, we calculated that in order to build all the houses, it would take four and a half years! It would take a long time just to finish the first fifty houses. We became discouraged, thinking of the amputees having to stay in their tents for months or years longer. I told Mark, 'I don't know if

I can take five years of organizing the logistics of a new team coming in every week, getting them in and out, feeding them, housing them, taking care of them, getting all the materials, and coordinating everything else.' But we also knew we served a big God who '*is able to do exceeding abundantly above all that we ask or think*'!"[38]

Just when it seemed impossible to get the first fifty houses done quickly, Bobby got a call from Carolyn of the Hotes Foundation. She said simply, "Hi, Bobby. We see that you are building some earthquake houses. Could you use some help to build them fast?"

We would never have been able to complete Phase One as quickly we did if it were not for our dear friend Richard Hotes. Bobby says, "Richard Hotes has such a heart for the poor, and when he helps them, he does it first class. His foundation is set up with his own money, and he doesn't accept any donations. He and his core 'dream team' are always there to help when there's a disaster or a need, as they'd been for us so many times in the past. He knew we were in the heat of the battle, and he had the ability to help. The Hotes Foundation paid professional carpenters to fly to Haiti along with Richard's core team to help with Phase One. They worked alongside our volunteer teams and helped out in many other ways.

"After the Hotes crew came and started working, David Meyer called and asked me, 'How many houses have you built in Phase One, Bobby'? I replied, 'Well, David, not many…it's going along slow, only about two houses a week.' He said, 'Well, we want to come out and shoot TV footage of them.' I told him, 'Okay, but you may see only about ten or twelve houses finished.' David already knew that things were going slow with Phase One, and I could tell that he was really concerned, but I didn't tell him about the Hotes Foundation coming and helping! I thought I would surprise him. So David came to see how things were going."

David Meyer expected to see only a few houses built, and when he arrived, he was shocked to see so many completed homes! Then he asked Bobby, "How much money would it cost to build the second fifty houses and to put furniture in the one hundred completed homes?" Bobby said, "Two hundred and twenty-five thousand dollars." David immediately took out his cell phone, called the Joyce Meyer/Hand of Hope office, and said, "Send Love A Child another check, overnight, for two hundred twenty-five

---

38. Ephesians 3:20.

thousand dollars, and have it there by 10:00 a.m." The next morning David was gone but the money came via FedEx by 10:00 a.m.!

Bobby remembers, "People from the US volunteered in droves to come help build the houses for Miracle Village. They would come in on a Monday and leave on Saturday. Up each morning at 4:50, they would work on the homes until dark. While many of the volunteer team members did not know how to build a house, they all had big hearts, and they worked hard and learned a lot under the supervision of Mark Rose. We are deeply grateful to all the church teams who gave their time and money to help build Miracle Village.

"Richard Hotes called and told me he was bringing his core team of thirty people, in addition to a large team of a hundred and fifty professional carpenters, which he had gotten from Craigslist and hired for pay, including expenses. I remember telling him, 'A hundred and fifty carpenters? I only have about two ladders!' It takes a generator to run an air compressor, and I had only one air compressor for one nail gun. But Richard told me, 'Don't worry about it.' I don't know how he did it, but in two or three days, he shipped in two whole containers of brand-new generators and air compressors, as well as two hundred ladders.

"The Hotes team arrived with a number of very long tents that slept multiple people, each with a four-ton air conditioner. These tents had nice cots with sheets and pillows. They were a blessing from God because with all the teams that were arriving, we could now house two hundred people! With these facilities and the use of our 'Big Mama' mobile kitchen, all the teams were well taken care of.

"Richard Hotes and his Hotes Foundation were truly the 'muscle' behind getting all the houses done! Not only did he supply manpower, but he also spent about two hundred fifty thousand dollars on tools, air compressors, generators, shiploads of wood, and security to guard all the materials."

A Surprise Visitor

While we were working on Miracle Village, we had a surprise visitor. "John" was an eighty-six year old man from New York who somehow became acquainted with Love A Child and decided to help us, so he set about collecting a container full of items and sent them to our Love A Child office in Florida. Then he decided he wanted to come to Haiti himself to see them distributed. Rad, our assistant executive director at our office in the States, tried to explain to him that we had so many teams coming into Haiti that it wouldn't be possible for him to go in by himself. But John decided to come anyway!

All his relatives, including his wife and his children, told him not to go, but John was determined. He secretly packed his bag, had his secretary buy him a plane ticket, and made his "getaway" at 5:00 a.m. While his wife was still sleeping, he wrote her a note saying, "I'm going to Haiti!"

Bobby and I didn't know he was coming until we went to the airport to pick up our daughter, Julie, who had flown in from Texas to see us and to help out at the field hospital. (Julie is a nurse and was such a blessing to us during her visit!) While we were walking amid hundreds of stacked suitcases and a sweaty swarm of about five hundred people waiting for their bags, we suddenly panicked when we saw older man wearing a yellow tee shirt and a "Bobby Burnette jungle jacket"—a style of jacket with pockets that Bobby always wears in Haiti—exclaiming, "What in the hell is going on around here?" We soon found that we had met our match with this cantankerous eighty-six-year-old New Yorker! Bobby and I took John with us to Fond Parisien, where we soon put him to work with the construction team building Miracle Village.

We were a bit worried about John because he was older, and the tropical Haitian sun was hot. He was sitting under a tree, cutting wire for the foundations, when Julie asked him, "John, are you working today?" He replied, "What do you expect me to do? Sit here on my a—?" Later, when we called the Love A Child office in Florida and spoke with Rad, he told us, "John's family is looking for him. He is missing in action!" We replied, "Tell them that we are looking at John right now—he is in Haiti!"

That week, John helped us with food distribution in Le Tant. During the visit, he stopped by a pile of charcoal to hug a few poor children from the village. He had never seen a mud-and-stick hut in his life, so I took him inside one of the huts to show him how many people live in Haiti. I took his hand and rubbed it over the dry mud walls, and he watched as the mud just crumbled in his fingers. Then he put his face to the wall and wept as he realized how many poor Haitians live.

Everything went reasonably smoothly with John that week until he insisted on being taken downtown to Port-au-Prince to see the earthquake destruction. We told him he couldn't go there because all our people were too busy with the construction teams, and besides, that area of Port-au-Prince was extremely dangerous. John got mad and went on a hunger strike until Reggie felt sorry for him and drove him there! After this, John went back to New York, and we all went back to our work. We weren't really sure why the Lord allowed him to come to Haiti. Maybe He wanted to do a work in his life, or maybe he was sent to us because we needed more patience! (Every time I would tell John, "Sit down in the back of the truck," "Stay out of the sun," or "Watch your step," he would always reply, "You're worse than my wife!") But whatever the reason, John's visit was a unique experience for us!

Kingdom Connection ("New Le Tant") Village

In the midst of the preparations for Miracle Village, the people of Le Tant received their own miracle through Pastor Jentezen Franklin. Pastor Jentezen had been helping to feed the villagers of Le Tant, as well as many other Haitians, for some time. He had visited Le Tant and had a great burden for these people whose houses had been swallowed up by the flooding that was overtaking their village. The situation had gotten so severe that all the concrete houses we had built for them were completely underwater; only the tips of some of the roofs were visible. The tents from Richard Hotes had gotten the villagers through the crisis of the hurricane flooding, but all the people were living in mud huts by the time of the 7.1-magnitude earthquake. With that powerful quake, the lake had risen even more, causing additional flooding.

Pastor Jentezen's right-hand man, Brian Smith, called and told us, "Pastor Jentezen would like to talk to you. He has a burden to build home for the one hundred Le Tant families where you are building earthquake housing. He will be raising the money to sponsor a hundred houses and will be sending you three hundred thousand dollars for this project." When we heard this, we could hardly speak. This was the permanent solution for the people of Le Tant that we had been praying for and seeking for so long. Not only would the earthquake survivors be living in Miracle Village, but the poor people from Le Tant would have their very own village of wooden houses nearby!

Cholera Outbreak!

As we neared the completion of Phase One, tragedy struck Haiti again when widespread cholera broke out. It had been decades since Haiti had been through a cholera epidemic, but now the disease was sweeping the country.

Bobby and I had worked in Haiti since the early 1970s and had lived there since 1991. In all that time, we had dealt with malaria, typhoid, dengue fever, and many other sicknesses, but never cholera—until now. All of a sudden, men, women, and children had symptoms of severe vomiting and diarrhea, and many were dying. (This outbreak continues even today. There have been over seven hundred thousand cases with nine thousand deaths.[39])

Our Jesus Healing Center was immediately hit with cholera patients, and we also began to have cases in Camp Hope. Many of the Haitians were frightened over the outbreak, and when we made plans for a cholera clinic in our area, none of them wanted it. Some even said they would burn down the hospital if we built such a clinic anywhere near them. However, they soon realized that no one was immune from the disease, and they accepted that the clinic was necessary.

Love A Child partnered with the local Mennonite clinic, Dlo Lavi ("Water of Life"), as well as a second local Haitian clinic and World Vision to come up with a plan. The Mennonite clinic would offer their land and their medical staff. Love A Child would donate a large hospital tent, pour the concrete foundation, buy a generator, and supply food to the cholera hospital. World Vision and the other local clinic would cover the staffing costs.

In no time at all, a cholera hospital was set up just about a mile from our Love A Child Village. Tons of disinfectant, Clorox, IV solutions, oral salts, and other supplies were donated. Special care had to be taken to bury those who died from cholera; otherwise, contamination would spread. It was rough for a while, but we rode the wave until the cholera subsided. It has returned again each rainy season since the earthquake. Ironically, the disease may have been brought to Haiti by UN workers who helped with earthquake rescue efforts. We are so thankful that the Lord helped us through that terrible time.

Finishing Touches

It was now time for the finishing touches on the Phase One houses! All the amputees helped to complete their new homes and neighborhoods. One of the projects was to construct "curbs" out of rocks and stone. It was so moving to watch these amputees—young and old—moving rocks, while others

---

39 See http://www.bostonglobe.com/opinion/editorials/2015/08/12/must-step-apologize-and-help-drive-cholera-from-haiti/ZZ2f9CGMl7kullUNz9bimM/story.html?event=event25.

sat on the ground, putting the rocks in place. Still others raked gravel or painted the sides of houses as they balanced on their crutches with one leg. Everyone helped out in some way, and everyone looked forward eagerly to celebrating the dedication of Phase One, the handicapped section of Miracle Village.

33

MIRACLE VILLAGE COMPLETED!

"Neighbors are family."
—Haitian Creole proverb

On October 30, 2010, we had a wonderful dedication service for Phase One of Miracle Village. David Meyer and his wife, Shelly, and Dennis and Sheila Hammond were our special guests. After a short service and prayer, and with lots of tears of joy, we cut the ceremonial ribbon. Then it was time to give the keys to the new homeowners, our precious amputee families.

It was such a delight to watch these families settle into their new homes. The little children, some of them amputees themselves, excitedly explored the rooms and climbed onto their new beds. Some of the Haitians—not only the children but also the adults—had never slept on a bed in their entire lives. Many of the amputees, with tears running down their faces, lifted arms in praise to God. It was a day we will never forget.

Emergency Evacuation of Camp Hope

After that celebration, our strength was renewed to move forward on Phase Two. But only a few days later, our work was suddenly interrupted when a hurricane threatened. The people in Phase One, with their hurricane-resistant houses, would be fine; but we would need to evacuate everyone still living in tents in Camp Hope—approximately fifteen hundred people—and bring them to a safe area of Love A Child Village. That meant uprooting all the refugees once again.

We gave each family a card with a particular color and advised them that when the time came, we would announce the various colors, in sequence, and when their color was called, they needed to come forward to be directed into one of our vehicles for the ride to Love A Child. In the meantime, we scrubbed down large, hurricane-proof tents that we had used for the field hospital, which we would use to house all the evacuees.

In preparation for the evacuation, all the people had to roll up their mattresses and then take down their tents, securing them on the area where they had stood. They could pack only one bag of valuables—besides some clothes, sheets, and blankets—and had to wrap all their important documents in plastic. All their earthly possessions were then packed into small tubs or bundles. Taking down all those tents was a huge job, but everyone helped each other. Breaking camp—even temporarily for the duration of the storm—was emotionally difficult for the refugees. Those little torn tents were all they had to call "home."

Our medical staff was right in the middle of the evacuation, making sure the most fragile people—some on crutches, others in wheelchairs—were evacuated first. When the hurricane approached, we systematically loaded the families onto the buses and trucks. However, we noticed several small children standing alone, with tears in their eyes, looking around for their parents. They seemed foggy about where their mother was or who was responsible for them. We waited and waited for their parents to come back for them, but when no one came to claim them, we put them on a truck, assigned them to families, and headed back to Love A Child Village. Somehow, we thought, we would figure out where their mother was, or she would figure out where they were.

After several days, the danger of the high winds passed, and we loaded everyone back into vehicles to return to Camp Hope to set up their tents and unpack all over again. Although the evacuation had gone well, the parents of those little children never returned to claim them. It was heartbreaking. The last we knew, the children were living with relatives.

"I Have Given You a Mandate"

By November 8, we were back at work on Phase Two, and we were starting to clear the land for the one hundred new houses of Kingdom Connection Village, also called "New Le Tant." A volunteer team from Orlando's Way of Grace Church was flying in to help build the houses. Bobby always made a point of greeting all the teams, giving them a warm "Bobby welcome" in his Southern drawl and letting them know how much we appreciated everything they were doing. When the Way of Grace group arrived at Love A Child, Bobby was at the orphanage, and he started to downstairs to welcome them, but our staff had just been scrubbing the front of the carport area, which has little pieces of tile in it, and as he made his way down the two flights of concrete tile stairs, his feet slipped out from underneath him. He went flying up into the air, with his feet higher than his head. When he landed, his back hit the edge of the cement steps. Bobby was in excruciating pain, and he couldn't walk.

I immediately started praying for him as Dr. Mardy and other medical personnel from the Jesus Healing Center rushed over to help. Somehow, they got Bobby into the courtyard and onto an army cot. They were almost sure he had broken his back. After several shots of morphine and other painkillers, Bobby's pain level still hadn't decreased, and they decided he would have to be flown back to the States for treatment.

Our Love A Child ambulance transported Bobby from Fond Parisien to the Port-au-Prince airport, now in operation, where he was flown by Air Evac to a trauma center in Tampa, Florida. Bobby was in such pain, he was almost screaming.

We arrived at the hospital in Tampa at about three o'clock in the morning, and the trauma doctor said to me, "We'll, he broke his back in three places. We'll just put a brace on him, and you'll just have to take him home." I said, "Do *what?* And with what? I don't even have a car." I was so angry at that doctor. I called my daughter, Julie, and she told me to ask the doctor to do a specific test on Bobby. When I asked the doctor to do the test, he said, "Well, that's going to take about another week."

Bobby remembers, "Another doctor came in and examined me, and he said, 'He's not going anywhere. He's not in any shape to do that.' I was able to stay in the hospital and rest so I could begin to recover. After a week, they were getting ready to transfer me to a rehabilitation center. The hospital gave me a back brace that went from my chin to my waist—which I called my 'mummy cast'! The doctor told me I had to stay at the rehabilitation center for at least three months in order to learn to walk again.

"They had arranged for an ambulance to come and take Sherry and me to the rehabilitation center, but I wanted to go back to our house in the country in northwestern Florida. Well, after living all those years in Haiti, I had learned that to get anything done, you have to pay people off; that's just how business is transacted there. I thought I would use some Haitian bargaining.

Even though I was still in great pain, I told Sherry, 'I'm not going to rehabilitation; I'm going to go to the great *Rehabilitator*—Jesus. Have five hundred dollars cash on you when they come to transport me.'

"Two young guys came in an ambulance to pick up Sherry and me, and as we drove toward the rehabilitation center, I said to the driver, 'Sir, can you take me to my place? It's about three hours from here. I have a therapist friend who volunteered to help me, and she will be there.' That was true—although she wouldn't be able to arrive until the next morning. He replied, 'No, we can't do that, sir. We have our orders.' Then I said, 'Look, I'll give you five hundred dollars in your hand.' They said, 'Which way, sir?' The ambulance guys called their headquarters and made some excuse, and then they took Sherry and me to our house.

"The first night, I was in almost unbearable pain, and I was on strong painkillers. Throughout the next day, I was very discouraged. The second night, I was lying awake at about one o'clock in the morning, with my whole body, but especially my back, racked with pain. I couldn't stop thinking about all those refugees at Camp Hope still living in tents. I thought about the winds blowing and the rain pouring through the rips in the tents, the mud coming inside, and the mothers and fathers on their hands and knees, trying to clean out the mud and the filth. I thought about the little children who had suffered so much, and my heart just broke into a million pieces. Here I was in the States, with a broken back, unable to assist the refugees and unable to help raise the rest of the money needed to build their new houses. I felt so helpless and alone.

"All of a sudden, I felt the presence of the Lord come into my room. He came around the foot of the bed and up to where I was lying; I could feel His presence standing beside me. He told me, *Bobby, I have given you a mandate to get those people out of those tents and into houses.* Then it felt as if liquid from a bottle was being poured right into my mouth. The Spirit of the Lord entered me and went into my spirit, and I instantly knew that I was healed!

"The next morning, I said, 'Man, I'm feeling better.' I still had that big brace around me that went from my chin to my waist, but I told our therapist friend, 'I'm just going to try to stand up'—and I stood up. Then I said, 'Take this thing off me.' Our friend said, "Oh, no, we can't take that off. I own my own therapy business, and I've never seen anyone with back injuries as bad as yours in my life. So you get back into bed.'

"Well, I didn't go back to bed, so Sherry called our daughter, Julie, and gave me the phone. Julie told me, 'Daddy, you're going to tear up your back, and it will never be right.' I loved my family and respected our therapist friend, but I insisted, 'You all just take this cast off of me. Take this thing off of me.' When they still wouldn't do it, I raised Cain! Finally, they took it off, and I said, 'Let me hobble around with a walker.'

"I was still in a little bit of pain, but I felt 95 percent better than I had. I made it to the door and then outside. The therapist told me, 'You're not going anywhere,' and she started walking with me. Then I put the walker aside and said, 'Let's just walk down to the river.' The Suwannee River was just ten minutes away along a dirt road. We started walking, and as we went, the therapist, who was a smoker, was running out of breath just trying to keep up with me. I told her, 'Just wait here. That is what smoking will do to you, Doc.' I went all the way down to the Suwannee River, and then I came walking back. The next day, the therapist told me, 'You don't need me anymore. I'm going home.'

"Within a week, we were back in Haiti, even though I had been told that I wouldn't be able to return for six months. God gave me a big miracle in the middle of all the other miracles happening at Miracle Village!"

While Bobby had been nearly incapacitated in the hospital and at our house in Florida before his healing, the work had continued on Phase Two with construction and infrastructure work, as well as on the security wall. The Hotes team was there in force, and Mark and Jesse Ostrander were also there, bringing in teams, pouring cement, building houses, and much more. They were diligently helping us to fulfill God's mandate to move the refugees into their new homes—as quickly as possible.

With the help of Richard Hotes and his remarkable crew, as well as all the wonderful volunteer teams, the three hundred and eighty houses, plus the one hundred Kingdom Connection houses, were all finished in just *one year*. It would soon be time to hold our second dedication service to celebrate the completion of Miracle Village!

The Miracle Village Contract

Before moving day, Bobby and I met together with the Haitian leaders of the Miracle Village Housing Committee, who had oversight of the affairs of the community. Then we all sat down with each family that was about to move into their new house and explained to them the housing contract and the rules very carefully; we had done the same thing the previous October for the families who had settled into the Phase One housing.

It might seem uncomplicated to move earthquake survivors into a housing subdivision, and it might seem strange that they had to sign a contract beforehand. But in the United States and other nations, renters and condominium owners have to sign contracts and agree to certain community rules. It was the same for Miracle Village. Additionally, for many reasons, it could be a difficult transition for these Haitian families to move into Miracle Village housing; they couldn't simply go back life as they had known it prior to the earthquake.

Two thousand people would now be living together in long, straight lines of houses instead of in the various neighborhoods they were familiar with before the disaster. Some of the people had lived in Cité Soleil, one of the poorest areas of Haiti, near Port-au-Prince. Others had lived in nice houses in the city, while still others had lived in old, dilapidated buildings. Most of the poor people had lived in lean-tos, mud huts, or stick-and-tin sheds. In addition, some of them had lived in the same community all their lives, usually in homes near their extended family members. Now, they would have to get used to setting down roots next to neighbors they had known only since the earthquake.

With all these new elements, everyone would have to learn to cooperate with one another and follow rules that would benefit and protect them all. The lawyer who had been consulted on the language for the housing contract had written the agreement in French, so when we sat down with each family, everything needed to be translated into Creole for them. They were instructed to keep their yards and streets clean and trash-free. They could not go back to certain practices common to them before the earthquake—such as bathing naked on their front porches or going to the bathroom against the side of the wall! Abusing alcohol or drugs, or using bad language, would not be acceptable.

There were additional requirements for safety that didn't make sense to many people at first. It took a while for them to understand how dangerous it would be for them to use candles or cheap Haitian wick lights filled with gasoline inside their new wooden houses or to build fires indoors. Instead, they would be using solar-based lighting.

Bobby and I had to smile when Patrick, the leader of the housing committee, explained some of the requirements of community life in his own terms: "Madame, if you find your husband with another woman, you cannot beat him, and there is to be no yelling or screaming at the other woman. You must handle this problem, but you can't kill your husband!"

Such instructions might seem overstated, but living in close proximity with others could make for some interesting situations, especially when neighbors "got acquainted" a little too well. In fact, the first case that was brought before the housing committee within six months of the opening of Phase One dealt with just such a scenario involving a one-legged man!

"Hanky Panky"

Mister Jean Louis had lost a leg during the earthquake. He was a poor, timid man who had a wife and eight children, with another child on the way. His wife, Madame Jean Louis, was also a timid person, but she would leave the house every day to try to find work to help support them. Sometimes she would wash clothes for other people, and sometimes she would sell items at the local market.

The Louis's next-door neighbor, Madame Silfie, had lost her husband during the earthquake, and she had six children. The two ladies got along very well until Madame Louis went out of town for a couple of weeks, and her husband was feeling "frisky." He decided to leave his younger children at home and go next door and visit Madame Silfie, whose children were all in school.

The visit turned out to be profitable for them both: Mister Jean Louis left Madame Silfie's house with a smile on his face, and Madame Silfie had some Haitian cash in her hands. The affair lasted until the one-legged man was no longer able to pay, and Madame Silfie wasn't about to give him "credit." She got very angry at Mister Louis and threated to tell his wife, and they got into a heated argument.

The fight was interrupted by a knock on the door by a woman selling beautiful white tablecloths. Mister Louis purchased a tablecloth on credit and gave it to Madame Silfie, who accepted it in exchange for continuing "visits." Mister Louis thought he was safe; however, a few days later, while he was away from his house, the woman who'd sold him the tablecloth came to collect what he owed her—and his wife was at home and found out about it! That's when the explosion began. From that day, Madame Louis and Madame Silfie were constantly fighting over the tablecloth and the one-legged man.

That's when the Miracle Village Housing Committee had to be called in to stop the commotion. The committee handled their first challenge well. After sternly reminding the women—and Mister Louis—that they were violating their housing contract and would be asked to leave if they did not comply, they gave each woman enough money to start a small business to help them out financially—and to keep each of them busy! That was enough "hanky panky" to last a while!

Phase Two Dedication

After all the families in Phase Two had reviewed the housing terms and agreed to them, they signed their contracts and were ready to move into their new homes. On July 1, 2011, we celebrated the completion of Miracle Village! All the remaining families from Camp Hope met under the big church tent for the dedication service. We had a joyful time singing, praying, and praising the Lord together; then we again cut the ceremonial ribbon, and each family was given the key to their new house.

As a prayer of blessing was said over their homes, the people sat very quietly, with their wrapped bundles of belongings lying on the ground next to them. At the final "Amen," the fifteen hundred men, women, and children headed off to their new homes and a new life.

Haitian "Homes and Gardens"

For many of the residents, one wonderful feature of living at Miracle Village was that they could grow their own gardens. There was plenty of space to do that because all the houses were spaced thirty feet apart. (Bobby and I were traveling in mid-Florida recently and noticed that all the brand-new houses were only fifteen feet apart, and Bobby said, "The people in Miracle Village live better than that!")

Vegetable garden plots were also provided for each family in a special gardening section of Miracle Village. Some of the earthquake survivors were city slickers who knew nothing about planting vegetables, while others were farmers who had gardening skills that they could pass along to the others. Everyone was encouraged to work together for their community. Before the people moved in to their homes, our Love A Child nurses had prepared a two-day program to teach them all about gardening and nutrition.

As soon as the program began, everyone was mesmerized. They listened intently as the nurses explained all about planting a garden and the nutritional elements of plants that the people themselves could grow. It was a very informative talk, and you could see the refugees taking it all in. Then the nurses showed them a DVD that featured a zippy song on nutrition, and the people were hooked! The second day, we gave them garden tools, showed them how to tend a garden, and gave them packets of seeds to plant.

After they moved into their houses, the people's gardening successes surpassed anyone's greatest expectations, turning Miracle Village into "better homes and gardens" in Haiti! Colorful flowers sprang up throughout the community, and the vegetable gardens produced abundantly.

The Miracle Village community also featured a Love A Child Christian school for educating the children, as well as a Jesus Healing Center satellite clinic, just as we had laid out in our original plans. (What a blessing for these families to be able to seek help from medical professionals rather than voodoo witch doctors!) Other important community buildings soon followed.

From Land of Desolation to Land of Promise

The earthquake and its aftermath had been harsh reminders that bad things can happen to good people. But that was not the end of the story. No matter what happens, the Lord will never leave us or forsake us.[40] His presence was with the refugees, and with us—even in times of fear, in times of pain, and in times of despair. What the devil had meant for evil, God had turned into good, just as He did for Job in the Bible. Never in their lives had these precious Haitian people imagined that God would provide them with a brand new house—as well as a beautiful new community to live in!

The land that Bobby and I were given and that we hadn't known what to do with for so long was part of God's plan for the earthquake survivors from the beginning. The Lord had laid this project on our hearts, and through the remarkable contributions of so many people, He had enabled us to turn a desolate land into a beautiful village of permanent new homes for the Haitian refugees who had suffered so much.

---

40. Hebrews 13:5.

34

LOVE IS SOMETHING YOU DO

"It's not giving that is not good at all."
—Haitian Creole proverb

"Driving Lessons"

Back in late October 2010, just before we were about to move the first fifty earthquake victims into their new homes in Miracle Village, Bobby and I thought we would take a little break and go for a test ride in one of Love A Child's new specialized vehicles, the Pinzgauers. The Canadian organization Empower Global (through Jeff Hageman) had given us three Pinzgauer ambulances and a sixteen-passenger Pinzgauer to reach our mobile clinics in the mountainous regions and for other transportation needs in the rugged Haitian countryside. Pinzgauers are high-mobility, all-terrain, six-wheel-drive vehicles that were designed for military use. Not only are they built like a rhinoceros, but they also have the agility to practically climb up a coconut tree. With these incredible vehicles, we would be able to reach many more people in the far regions and save more lives, and we were excited about the possibilities.

Maurice from Empower Global was staying at Love A Child fine-tuning the vehicles, and he had invited Bobby and me for a driving lesson in the sixteen-passenger Pinzgauer. When he said "a driving lesson," I thought he'd take us out for a spin on the property and maybe climb a little mountain near our village, so we took along two of the children from our orphanage, Julianne and Ezekiel.

Of course, I should have realized that Bobby and Maurice had a more adventurous plan in mind! (You know what happens when you give boys a new "toy"!) First, we took off up a mountain behind Camp Hope, one of the highest points in our area, where the towers for our radio station are located. Everything went smoothly until the rocks under our tires started rolling down the mountain, dragging us backward with them. But Maurice was an expert driver, and he quickly put the Pinzgauer in low gear and climbed right up to the top of the mountain. The view was beautiful from up there. We could see glimpse Camp Hope and see Miracle Village just beyond it in the distance. Although we were at a pretty high elevation, I wasn't worried, and I thought, *Okay, let's go home now.*

As we descended the mountain, Bobby said, "Turn right here." We turned onto what was basically a goat path that wrapped around the side of the mountain, finally ending up in a flat area. Again, I thought, *Okay, this is good; I love this vehicle. Now, let's go home.* But before I knew it, Maurice was driving up a steep incline, with rocks and other hazards right in front of us. This was no road or path; it wasn't even a goat trail—he was actually making his own path up the side of the mountain! As I turned around to check on Julianne and Ezekiel, I saw that Julianne was hanging on so tight that her knuckles were almost white. Ezekiel appeared to be looking for a way to jump out. "Stay put!" I ordered him. There is a Haitian Creole proverb that says, "Before you climb a tree, look to see if you can climb down." In other words, "Make sure you know what you're getting into"! I wished we had taken that advice!

The Pinzgauer continued going right up the mountain, plowing over bushes and scrub trees. Pikan trees were all around us, and because the vehicle was open on the sides, we were all ducking and dodging thorn bushes. Considering our "route," things went fairly well as we bounced along the rough terrain, when all of a sudden we heard a hissing noise—sounding very much like air escaping from a tire.

We looked toward the noise and saw that a huge thorn had stabbed right through one of the giant tires of the vehicle. We were in the middle of nowhere with our tire leaking air and the thorn still stuck in it. Fortunately, the tire wasn't flat yet, so we kept driving and ended up on a very narrow dirt path that we knew would eventually take us back to the orphanage. But as we came off the mountain onto that dirt path, the thorn popped out of the tire, and the tire completely deflated. There we sat in that remote area with a flat tire—reminding me of one of my early treks to Savaan Pit. (Too bad there was no Haitian AAA to call!)

Happily, Maurice was not only an expert driver who could handle mountain terrain, but he also could quickly change a gigantic Pinzgauer tire without any trouble at all. In only a few minutes, we were back in business. When we finally reached a wide-open road, Bobby said, "Oh look, the interstate!"

We all laughed, and then I actually took a turn driving as Maurice gave me lessons on shifting the gears. I really did love that vehicle and could not wait to take it to the regions beyond on our next medical clinic trip. Driving "off road" is what I did most of the time, anyway. And as we rode home, I thought, *Hmm…this Pinzgauer would look good painted pink….*

Bumpy Roads, Hazards…and Beautiful Vistas

Our adventure with the Pinzgauer on the mountain roads is a lot like the adventure Bobby and I have led with the Lord from the early days of our street evangelism and gospel tent meetings to our missions work and full-time ministry in Haiti. We accepted the Lord's offer to giving us His "driving lessons" in loving and serving Him as we loved and served others in His name. Not knowing where we were going, we climbed aboard His "Pinzgauer" and let Him set the course!

The Lord has taught us to always walk by faith and not by sight. To do that, we have to be willing explore new territory, and often that is like driving straight up a rough mountainside with no clear path to follow. The ride can be scary, but God is doing the driving, so we know we'll be all right. As we learn those lessons, we may be in the passenger seat holding on for dear life, but He's at the wheel, handling it expertly. And even when the trip is bumpy and hazardous, it leads us to beautiful vistas. We wouldn't have it any other way.

Bobby and I want to share with you some of the new territories the Lord has been leading us into during the last few years.

Three Assignments

After Miracle Village was complete, Bobby sought the Lord about the future of Love A Child, and the answer he received was completely unexpected. He remembers, "The Lord spoke to me, saying, 'There are three things I want you to do. I want you to build a thousand-seat church in Miracle

Village, I want you to build a thirty-thousand-foot food distribution center, and I want you to build a multi-acre marketplace so Haitians can have jobs and sell their goods and make a living.' I'd never thought about doing any of those things before, except for building a smaller church building at Miracle Village, but these projects were our next assignments from God. All of them required supernatural financial miracles—and all these projects are a reality today.

"The cost for the church was about a hundred and fifty thousand dollars; soon, two main sponsors donated funds, Robert Tiberio and Pastor Gregory Dickow from Life Changers International Church, and other partners sacrificed and gave even the 'widow's mite.' The Food Distribution Center, which would be as long as a football field, would cost even more—several hundred thousand dollars—and that wasn't including the money it would take to replenish it with food on an ongoing basis to be distributed to the poor.

"While I was still in the process of building the church, I was walking the floor again, praying about the money for the distribution center because I wanted to start it as soon as possible; I wanted to keep all these projects moving. Right as I was praying, who should call me but Jentezen Franklin, who immediately said, 'Bobby, I feel led of the Lord that you have a need and that I'm supposed to call you; and God told me, "You're supposed to meet his need."' I hesitating, thinking, *Maybe he thinks I need a thousand dollars or ten thousand dollars for a container of food.* But I told him that we needed between three hundred seventy-five thousand and four hundred thousand dollars for the Food Distribution Center, and he said, 'Bobby, good. I'm going to raise the money, and I'm going to send it all to you.' He started sending money right away, allowing us to start building the Food Distribution Center at the same time we were building the church. When we finished both projects, donations of food started pouring in; in addition, Feed My Starving Children increased their food contributions to us.

"It was now time for the biggest project—the marketplace. Our Love A Child board of directors asked me, 'Bobby, where are you going to get the money for the marketplace?' I told them, 'Well, I feel like one person is going to give the money to begin with, and I'm waiting on that person. I don't feel right raising a hundred dollars here and a hundred dollars there, because we're going to need at least a million dollars.'

"Once more, I was walking the floor, praying about the money, when Pastor Jentezen and his right-hand man, Brian, called me. Pastor Jentezen asked, 'You're praying about a need, aren't you?' I said, 'Yeah.' He asked, 'Well, what is it?' Again, I wondered which need I should tell them about, because we had several—the five thousand dollar need, the ten thousand dollar need, or the million dollar need. But I recognized that there was a kingdom connection; God had told them to call me right while I was praying. I knew the Spirit was directing them, and I replied, 'It's a million dollars to build the marketplace.'

"Jentezen said, 'You got it. I'm going to send you a hundred thousand dollars a month.' And that's exactly what he did. He gave us a hundred thousand dollars monthly until he had given the million dollars, never missing a month. We added projects to our original plan for the marketplace, and we keep adding to it, and it ended up costing more than a million dollars—between 1.5 and 2 million—but without that first million, it never would have been built."

Before the marketplace opened, a Christian organization called Open Hand contacted us about doing a lending program, as well as offering classes to teach the Haitians about teamwork, about presenting their products, and about the best ways to sell their goods. The participants learned valuable information that they would be able to continually apply to their businesses. The marketplace is designed to help the needy in Haiti on a long-term basis.

Jentezen Franklin was our special guest at the dedication of the marketplace—*Gwo Maché Mirak* (Grand Miracle Market)—on December 9, 2014. God sent us the very best management team for the marketplace, and we are so thankful for them: Villy Choute, President of Metro Management; Oriol Vatelia, Marketing Director; and Saralla Valliere, Public Relations.

There are now seventeen buildings connected with this endeavor. We recently arranged for our Love A Child radio station to be broadcast at the marketplace, so everyone can hear the gospel when they go there to shop and visit with friends and neighbors. *Gwo Maché Mirak* is really still in its infancy stage; it continues to expand and grow.

The earthquake that hit Haiti crippled an already failing economy in one of the poorest countries in the world. After all the relief efforts, what the Haitian people needed were jobs and dignity. Every day, Bobby and I will continue to feed the hungry, clothe the naked, and care for those who are helpless. However, the people also need employment and economic security. Ultimately, we believe this is the most important project for the earthquake families and for all the impoverished of Haiti.

The marketplace has the potential to create thousands of jobs. And this will help expand our food distribution to other areas. The more Haitians become self-sustaining and no longer need food distributed to them, the more we can use that food to feed desperate villages where there are still no jobs and the need is great. And the Haitian people don't want to receive free food for their entire lives. They want dignity. They want jobs; they want to be able to feel good that they are providing for their families. This is a sustainability project—helping Haitians to help themselves.

Feeding people gets people from point A, which is thinking only about survival, to point B, thinking about employment and the future. When you're hungry, it's difficult to think and to plan, and you also don't have the strength to work. Many poor Haitians are not thinking, *How can I go to work? Where can I work? Can I start a business?* There's only one thing on their mind, especially if they're a mother with children: *Where can I get some rice?* But once they get to point B, we can help them with development and sustainability—help them to support themselves, regaining dignity and pride. Bobby and I are committed to demonstrating that providing aid can and should be a progressive process. The highest form of helping people is to help them develop their own full potential for creating sustainable improvement in their living conditions.

Three Major Sustainability Projects

In addition to the marketplace, Love A Child is working in many other ways to help Haitians to help themselves and to become self-sustaining. We have a number of sustainability projects, but here are three of the main ones.

Tilapia Fish Farm

The Tilapia Fish Farm teaches Haitians how to provide their own food, develop a sustainable product, and produce a marketable commodity; it also provides important meat protein to their diet. Special thanks again to Christian Television Network (CTN) President Bob D'Andrea for sponsoring the Tilapia fish project. Bobby remembers, "When we first started this project and received our initial batch of fish, we asked expert Hans Geissler of Morning Star Fishermen to give a three-day class for teach Haitians on how to raise these fish. Thirty of the Haitians were so poor, they had no shoes. But I could tell that two of them in particular were picking it up quickly. I told them, 'Dream—this is what you can have.' They graduated from the class, and that year, they each raised Tilapia in their backyard, sold twenty thousand fish, and became wealthy. That led to another sustainability project, the chicken farm."

Chicken Co-op

Bob D'Andrea, President of CTN, also sponsored our very first chicken farming project at Love A Child Village. The purpose was to teach Haitians how to help themselves through a small co-op business. Our Haitian children also got involved and learned responsibility and hard work. This was a test project to see if it would be a success, and it was.

After that, Mike Welch, who runs Harrison Chicken, the third-largest chicken company in the United States, joined with World Poultry Foundation (WPF) to provide financial and technical support for a large chicken co-op project. The co-op is located behind the Marketplace, *Gwo Maché Mirak*, but on a separate piece of land. It currently has ten large chicken houses stocked with chickens. Pete Roberts, the broiler supervisor with Harrison Chicken, who has fifty years of experience, has been to Haiti twice with technical support.

Again, the Haitians working this business keep all the money; we don't take any of it. This is a large project, but we're going to expand it to help more Haitians learn a trade and become self-sustaining. At the writing of this book, Mike Welch and the WPF are working on plans to put in an egg hatchery.

Farm and Agricultural Training Center

A third sustainability project is a large farm and Agricultural Training Center located behind Miracle Village. There are about three hundred vegetable plots, each thirty by thirty. We are the first people in Haiti that we know of to put in six-foot-high sprinklers everywhere, so the vegetables won't wither when there's no rain, which happens too frequently in Haiti. Johnny and Shelby Mahon and their son, Paul, worked very hard putting in the sprinkler systems and all their pipes. Pastor Gregory Dickow of Life Changers International Church sponsored the well that provides life-giving water for the crops. Through this project, the Haitians are learning to raise large quantities of vegetables, sell them, and earn a living.

In the back of the farm is an ever-expanding Agricultural Training Center. Every Thursday and Friday, we offer classes on agriculture, how to grow better crops, how to experiment with different vegetables, which vegetables grow best in which kind of soil, how to sell the crops, and so forth. The first day the students are in the classroom, and the next day they're out in the gardens.

The Agricultural Training Center enables Haitians to learn gardening methods that are simple, affordable, and will improve their quality of life. This is really a "living classroom" that demonstrates and teaches the best sustainable farming practices for improving food security in Haiti. There is also a reforestation program that equips Haitians with the knowledge and techniques needed to grow trees and reclaim their environment. Going forward, we're going to do more with sustainability while expanding the sustainability projects we're already doing. We want to give special thanks to Rad Hazelip, assistant executive director of Love A Child, for his visionary insights in developing new ideas and technology for the Agricultural Training Center, whose instruction extends to the work in the Tilapia Fish Farm; the Chicken Co-op; the reforestation efforts, including the planting of Moringa trees; and much more. We also want to thank David Balsbaugh and his family who are moving to Haiti to help supervise these sustainability projects.

Churches, Schools, Feeding Programs, and Orphanage

Our Love A Child ministry has grown so much over the years. We currently employ about six hundred fifty people, with a little more than one hundred fifty people working at Love A Child Village. The rest work outside the Village on various projects. We have over two hundred fifty schoolteachers at our schools in various villages and cities throughout Haiti. We also have about seventy people who work at our office and warehouse in Fort Myers. We couldn't do all that we do without everyone's dedication to serving the people and children of Haiti. As the Haitian Creole proverb says, "With many hands, the load is not heavy."

The children at our orphanage, which was one of our very first ministries, are very special to us. Many of these children have been with us since they were babies. We have an ambitious goal of seeing all eighty children graduate from high school and, for those who want further education and are qualified, attend college. We consider this a great responsibility. When they finish their education, these young people can go out and make a significant difference in helping to change their country for the better.

Another of our goals is to greatly expand our feeding programs for Haitian families, especially in the mountainous regions. During the year 2015 alone, we will have distributed a little over twenty million meals through our Food Distribution Center, with the help of all our dedicated partners.

"Lord, Give Us Hispaniola!"

Recently, the Lord opened another unexpected door for us—in the Dominican Republic. Bobby explains, "One year after the earthquake, we went to the Dominican Republic with a huge gospel tent crusade, and thousands attended. When we started ministering there, we prayed, 'Lord, give us the whole island of Hispaniola!'—the island that the Dominican Republic shares with Haiti. Today, Love A Child ministers in the Dominican Republic through youth crusades; school scholarships; playground installations, sponsored by Pastor Randy Landis and Life Church; food distributions; gospel tent crusades; mobile clinics, which Joyce Meyer/Hand of Hope helps to sponsor; prison ministry; and much more. Our Field Director, Carlos Sylvester, has led many missions teams there. On July 12, 2015, we dedicated our first Love A Child church in the Dominican Republic! We want to thank David and Angie George for sponsoring this church in the Dominican Republic, along with so many other churches and schools in Haiti.

One of our main areas of ministry in this nation is to Haitians who emigrated there to find work in the sugarcane fields, or *bateys*. Some of these Haitians have been there for generations, and the workers in the sugarcane fields are treated inhumanely—worse than slaves. Pastor Randy Landis, our Senior Director, and Carlos have a very deep burden for these people. We've been trying to help them by distributing food and clothing, hosting gospel crusades, showing Christian movies, building playgrounds, and much more.

Also, because baseball is a hugely popular sport in the Dominican Republic (some of the best baseball players in the Major Leagues come from there), we've started a baseball ministry. Every year, Mark Ostrander's son, Jesse, who runs Sports Missions International, brings a father/son (sometimes mother/son!) baseball team there, and for five days, they play Dominican youth at different ball parks. They play the games in the mornings, and they distribute food in the sugarcane camps in the evenings. At the end of the week, they give away baseball gloves, bats, and other sports equipment. Many people are coming to Christ through this ministry.

Love A Child now has a headquarters in the Dominican Republic, which is registered with the government, and we're going great guns! It's possible that one day, the ministry in the Dominican Republic may even outgrow the one in Haiti.

Love Is Something You Do

Every day, we look at all the ongoing programs and projects at Love A Child, and we think, *How did the Lord do all this?* We give Him all the glory and honor for making miracle after miracle happen through the years to accomplish all His purposes, especially on behalf of the beloved Haitian people.

It is the children of Haiti who first drew us here, and it is for them and for their future, as well as for all Haitian families, that we continue to serve in this remarkable land. There is a Haitian Creole proverb that says, "The child who cries in the house and the one who cries at the door are the same." The Lord wants us to care for all His children.

Remembering so many children over the years who have suffered, we thank God today for every plate of food that we see a hungry child eat. We watch them as they take their fingers and run them across their plates, picking up every last grain of rice. Bobby and I know that we can't feed all the children, and we know we can't save all the children, but through Love A Child, we and all our partners are trying to save as many as we can—one child at a time. Love is something you do. It's what makes life worth living.

Sherry in front of
the Caribbean Market.

Dr. Hilarie (right) and colleague.

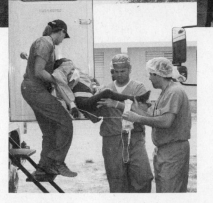

WHAT YOU CAN DO...

There are many ways that the Lord can use you to help those in need. Here are some suggestions of what you can do through Love A Child, Inc.

- Learn: Go to www.loveachild.com for more information.
- Pray: We need prayer partners to pray for us daily. Our load is very heavy. Haiti is a difficult country to work in, and every decision we make must count.
- Go: Join us on a mission team! Help feed a hungry child, work in a mobile clinic in the remote mountains, get dirty and sweaty on a construction team, or share God's Word on an evangelistic team.
- Give: Become a Love A Child Partner. Please prayerfully consider helping with any of our projects in Haiti. You can go to our website and click on "What We Do" or "Sponsor a Child" to learn about our current projects in Haiti. You may want to give a monthly gift or a one-time gift. Whether you donate toward sponsoring food, sponsoring a child, or "where most needed," it all helps more than you could ever know.

Contact Us:

To talk to someone at Love A Child, please call 239-210-6107.

Please send letters or contributions to: Love A Child, Inc., P.O. Box 60063, Fort Myers, FL 33906.

Please send donated items to: Love A Child, Inc., 12411 Commerce Lakes Drive, Fort Myers, FL 33913.

E-mail: info@LAChaiti.org

Website: www.loveachild.com

Follow us on Facebook and Twitter

ABOUT THE AUTHORS

Bobby and Sherry Burnette are the founders and directors of Love A Child, Inc. (LAC), a 501(c)(3) Christian nonprofit humanitarian organization serving the needs of children in Haiti. They began their ministry together in the late 1960s by preaching on street corners, under gospel tents, and in auditoriums and churches throughout the United States. In 1971, Bobby and Sherry made their first missions trip to Haiti, and the overwhelming poverty they witnessed there broke their hearts. They also ministered in many other countries, but they always found themselves drawn back to Haiti. Following their calling from God, Bobby and Sherry founded Love A Child in 1985 and focused on working to reduce poverty in Haiti's remote areas.

From their beginnings as visiting missionaries to Haiti, Bobby and Sherry have worked to spread the Word of God and show the love of Jesus by example through feeding programs, mobile medical clinics, and the building of Christian schools and churches. They moved to Haiti in 1991 and have never looked back, living year-round at the Love A Child Orphanage in Fond Parisien, Haiti.

Love A Child's outreach programs include a 21,500-square-foot orphanage, now home to seventy-eight children; many primary schools, which educate and feed over seven thousand children each day; mobile medical clinics; a regional medical clinic; and a feeding distribution program that serves more than twenty million meals per year. After the devastating 2010 earthquake in Haiti, Love A Child built several hundred houses for earthquake victims and developed eight sustainability projects, including *GWO Maché Mirak*, a large marketplace providing jobs for the poor; *Poul Mirak*, a project to train Haitians how to raise and sell chickens; a Tilapia fish farm; and an agricultural training center that teaches the farming of crops and trees. Bobby and Sherry believe that feeding the poor is essential, but that the ultimate goal is for Haitians to become self-sustaining.

Under the Burnettes' leadership, Love A Child has grown to become one of the largest Christian nonprofits in Haiti. Thanks to LAC's excellence in financial accountability, the organization consistently receives the highest industry ratings available through the Evangelical Council for Financial Accountability (ECFA), Charity Navigator, and the Independent Charities of America.

Bobby and Sherry want people to know what faith and love can do to change a nation. It is their deepest desire that their lives inspire others to reach out in response to the cry of the poor in some way, large or small—rescuing one child at a time.

Welcome to Our House!

We Have a Special Gift for You

It is our privilege and pleasure to share in your love of Christian books. We are committed to bringing you authors and books that feed, challenge, and enrich your faith.

To show our appreciation, we invite you to sign up to receive a specially selected **Reader Appreciation Gift**, with our compliments. Just go to the Web address at the bottom of this page.

God bless you as you seek a deeper walk with Him!

WE HAVE A GIFT FOR YOU. VISIT:

whpub.me/nonfictionthx

WHITAKER
HOUSE